BEST
YOU
EVER

BEST YOU EVER

365 WAYS TO BE

Richer, Happier, Thinner, Smarter, Younger, Sexier, and More Relaxed—Each and Every Day

Rebecca Swanner; Eve Adamson; Carolyn Dean, MD;
Rachel Laferriere, MS, RD; and Meera Lester

Avon, Massachusetts

Published by
Adams Media, a division of F+W Media, Inc.
57 Littlefield Street, Avon, MA 02322. U.S.A.
www.adamsmedia.com

ISBN 10: 1-4405-0657-4
ISBN 13: 978-1-4405-0657-4
eISBN 10: 1-4405-1071-7
eISBN 13: 978-1-4405-1071-7

Printed in the United States of America.

10 9 8 7 6 5 4 3 2 1

Library of Congress Cataloging-in-Publication Data
Best you ever / Rebecca Swanner ... [et al.].
p. cm.
ISBN 978-1-4405-0657-4
1. Self-actualization (Psychology) 2. Conduct of life. 3. Health. 4.
Finance, Personal. I. Swanner, Rebecca.
BF637.S4B49 2011
158.1—dc22
2010038483

The information in this book should not be used for diagnosing or treating any health problem. Not all diet and exercise plans suit everyone. You should always consult a trained medical professional before starting a diet, taking any form of medication, or embarking on any fitness or weight-training program. The author and publisher disclaim any liability arising directly or indirectly from the use of this book.

Many of the designations used by manufacturers and sellers to distinguish their product are claimed as trademarks. Where those designations appear in this book and Adams Media was aware of a trademark claim, the designations have been printed with initial capital letters.

This book is available at quantity discounts for bulk purchases.
For information, please call 1-800-289-0963.

INTRODUCTION

You've taken stock of your life and realized you want to be a better you. Welcome to the club! We all have areas we could improve in, and this book is here to help you do just that. Whether you want to eat better, improve your memory, boost your wealth, have better sex, look younger, feel happier, or just be able to relax, this book has you covered. The tips in this book will inspire you and provide jumping-off points for your own life.

Each tip in the book is basic enough for you to integrate into your life right now, but how much you want to get involved is up to you. For instance, in this book, I recommend that you volunteer. You can volunteer once a month, once a year, or even a few times a week. Use these tips to enhance your life, not as a chore. Some of these ideas you've probably heard before, while others will be new to you. Don't overwhelm yourself by feeling like you have to start doing them all at once. Instead, pick a few of your favorites and work on those. Add new tips gradually. Each one will require you to alter your life at least a little, so it's best if you start slow.

Within this book you'll also find 365 quotes on everything from making money to making love. These are here to inspire you and for you to keep in mind as you start to make changes that transform your life. I hope you discover within these pages a few quotes that move you. Some may even become your personal mantras.

When it comes down to it the rules of having a happy life are simple: Surround yourself with great friends. Be good to others. Eat well, be active, and wear sunscreen. Take chances and take time for yourself. Enjoy every moment. Oh, and here's one more tip for leap years: get your nose out of your phone, look up, and engage with the world around you.

Best of luck on your journey.

"If you owe too much on American Express, and your Diner's Club notes are too hard, take a loan on your Visa, and pay it off with your MasterCard!"

—Nipsey Russell, "Ode to Credit Cards,"
from *Your Number's Up*

Switch to Using Only Cash or Checks for a Year

If you're the type to whip out the plastic whenever you see something you like, try switching over to using only cash or checks for an entire year. When you make this change, you'll probably not only find it mentally harder to choose to purchase a nonnecessity item but also find that the amount your spending will feel more real. For online purchases and bills that you pay automatically each month, replace your credit card number with a debit card number so the money comes directly out of your checking.

But what are you going to do with your credit cards? Lend your cards to your spouse or put them in a safety deposit box or somewhere secure within your home. But if you're going out of town, make sure to take one credit card with you in case of emergency. In making this routine change to your daily life, your credit cards will be easily accessible in case of an emergency, but you can't reach for them whenever you see something you might want to buy, making it that much easier to stick to your budget and to put the leftover funds into savings.

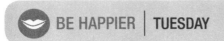

"Kindness is a language which the deaf can hear
and the blind can see."

—Mark Twain

Practice Random Acts of Kindness

When you're kind to others, you become happier. It doesn't take much to be nice, and even giving a sweet smile to a stranger as you pass by or holding the door open for the next person can brighten someone's day. Committing these simple acts of kindness sets in motion a positive domino effect, as you've improved another's life in a small but not insignificant way, and that person is now more likely to reach out and do the same.

By acting selflessly and paying kindness forward, you'll engage in positive social contact, feel less isolated, and might even feel a rush of those feel-good chemicals, endorphins, known as a "helper's high."

Here are some ideas to get you started:

- Pay for the coffee, toll, or other small purchase of the person in line behind you.
- Allow someone with only a few groceries to go in front of you.
- Share your umbrella with someone who is without one.
- Help an older person up the stairs.
- Walk your friend's dog if he or she is busy or ill.
- Tip well.
- Find a senior to connect with in your community.
- Send a friend an unexpected card to show you're thinking of her or him.

"Our food should be our medicine and our medicine should be our food."

—Hippocrates

Make Nutrition a Priority

Admit it, you want to look better naked. Your first step to reaching that personal goal is adapting the way you eat to fit a healthy lifestyle.

Some people like to call adapting the way you eat a diet. I don't. That's because this is the way you *should* be eating whether you're overweight, underweight, or a healthy weight. A diet is a fad, and it's not sustainable for the rest of your life. On a "diet" you'll likely still want to indulge in comfort foods that don't add fuel to your body but do add inches to your waistline. And as you work to cut out those foods, you'll probably be pretty miserable.

So stop the cycle. Instead of focusing on what you can and can't eat, focus on what provides your body with nutrition. Challenge yourself to include lean proteins, complex carbohydrates, and healthy fats to*gethe*r in every meal. Making this adjustment in the way you eat doesn't mean you have to go without your favorite junk food forever. It just means that most of your meals and snacks will both taste good and be good for you. Eating well can bolster your immune system; help your body to repair damaged cells; lower your risk of heart disease, cancer, and osteoporosis; and even improve your longevity.

"There is no more difficult art to acquire than the art of observation."

—William Osler

Pay Attention

It's easy to feel overwhelmed and look to tunnel vision as your relief when you're being bombarded with images, ads, and information on a daily basis. But by opening up your eyes to the world around you, actively listening, and striving to be more observant in the "real world," you'll train your brain to become better at absorbing and processing important information instead of allowing everything to pass by in a blur. If you have a hard time focusing on one object at a time, explore the various types of meditation outlined in this book. During meditation you learn to clear your mind, but you can also use it as a tool to teach yourself to negate distractions and be in the moment.

WHERE TO START

If you're eager to get going, here are a few ideas to move you along the right track and help you to become more engaged with the world around you.

- *Be mindful.* For five minutes, stop and notice all the sounds, smells, and images within the world around you.
- *Stop rushing.* Life is about the journey, not the destination we'll all eventually reach. Practice staying in the moment and appreciate it for what it is, not what it will become.
- *Cease multitasking.* When we do many things at once, we can't fully commit to any one thing well.

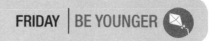
*"Grilling is like sunbathing. Everyone knows it is bad for you,
but no one ever stops doing it."*

—Laurie Colwin

Slather on Sunscreen Daily with SPF15 or Higher

After spending a long winter wrapped in layers, the first thing you might want to do when you see the summer sun is strip off your clothes and head for the closest sunbathing spot. That's all well and good, but before you do, make sure to apply sunscreen on all exposed parts of your body, including your face, thirty minutes before heading out the door. While you might think looking like a tanned beach hottie is sexy now, you probably won't like the premature wrinkles and skin cancer that exposure to the sun's harmful UVA and UVB rays can cause.

On days when you're spending many hours outdoors, make sure to bring the sunscreen with you, as you'll need to reapply it every two to three hours, especially if you've been sweating a lot or have been in the water. Yes, even if the sunscreen says it's waterproof or offers all-day protection.

Sunscreen isn't only for those sunny days of summer, either. Indeed, sunscreen should be applied daily, because even on winter or cloudy days, the sun's harmful rays penetrate the clouds and can damage your skin.

That said, if you're the type to slather on sunscreen every morning before you leave the house and reapply it throughout the day, you might want to ease up a bit on your routine. Recent studies have shown that sunscreen not only blocks the sun's harmful rays but it also prevents your body from producing vitamin D when it's exposed to the sun. However, you only need twenty minutes of sun exposure a day, so consider skipping that early morning application if you're going to walk around for that length of time.

 **BE SEXIER** | **SATURDAY**

"To love oneself is the beginning of a lifelong romance."

—Oscar Wilde

First, Love Yourself

You are amazing. Whether you feel it yet or not, it's true. You are sexy, you are intriguing, and you are interesting to talk with. You just have to believe it. As the saying goes, you cannot love another until you love yourself. Once you have worked through your insecurities, doubts, and worries about what love will or will not bring and once you have learned how to be comfortable with yourself, you can be ready for true love.

When you're secure and happy with who you are, you will project inner confidence and attract potential mates who are right for you. When you know who you are, you'll know what you're looking for and not looking for in a romantic partner. Going into the dating scene armed with this knowledge will help you to not be distracted by the pretty people who are superficially attractive but won't offer you what you want in the long term and to keep your dance card open for someone who will. Ironically, the moment you no longer need someone to rely on for our own happiness and to prop you up when you're down is when Mr. or Miss Right usually comes along.

"If people were meant to pop out of bed, we'd all sleep in toasters."

—Author unknown, attributed to Jim Davis

Quiet Your Mind Before Starting Your Day

Before you get out of bed and especially before groggily reaching for your phone to check your e-mail and messages, take a few minutes to breathe and enjoy the morning. Focus on the sounds, smells, and golden morning light. Can you hear any birds singing? Is a loved one lying peacefully next to you? Take some time to relax, breathe deeply, and let the beautiful morning envelop you. Release the tension that any bad dreams caused or any anxiety about the day ahead. Even if it's going to be a big day full of many tasks, starting off in a peaceful, meditative state will make it easier to stay calm and happy throughout the entire day.

IMPROVE YOUR WAKING MOMENTS

Make waking up a pleasant experience so that you feel alive—not stressed—when you open your eyes. Here are suggestions that could help you be able to breathe easy before you rise:

- Keep your bedroom free from clutter and shut the closet door before retiring.
- Open east-facing drapes before you go to bed so that you can enjoy the morning sun.
- Keep fresh flowers or a diffuser with a scent that you find relaxing on your nightstand.
- If you need an alarm to wake up, get one with a ring you like (such as a singing bird) or find a ringtone on your phone that doesn't irritate you (only use "Reveille" if it is a happy reminder of being at summer camp!).

"Every day I get up and look through the Forbes list of the richest people in America. If I'm not there, I go to work."

—Robert Orben

Calculate How Much You Really Make

Another good way to stop spending needlessly is to determine how much you *really* make per hour. To figure this out, start with the net amount you receive every month after taxes, 401(k), and medical and other withholdings have been removed. Then, make a list of all your work-related expenses. These can include money spent entertaining coworkers or clients, the cost of commuting (you can use the standard mileage rate to give you this number, which you can find at *www.irs.gov/formspubs/article/0,,id=178004,00.html*), the amount you spend on work clothes to look your best, supplies you purchase that are not provided or reimbursed by your employer, or any other money you spend that is job related.

Next, estimate how many hours you spend working, including all of the hours you spend commuting, working at home on projects, networking afterhours with colleagues, and shopping for work supplies. Now, take the net amount you make, subtract the expenses, and divide that number by the total number of hours you've spent doing work-related activities.

That number might seem depressing. But it can help keep your spending in check and make you richer in the process. Say you make $20 an hour after all is said and done and an item you want to purchase costs $160. Is it worth working eight hours to have it? By using this logic, you'll probably end up spending money only on the items you really want and are willing to work hard to have.

"Sing like no one's listening, love like you've never been hurt, dance like nobody's watching, and live like it's heaven on earth."

—Mark Twain

Let the Love Flow from You

When you've been hurt, it's hard to let down your guard and allow the love to flow from you unfettered. Fact is, we've all been hurt by love. It's how you choose to react and move forward that matters. When you permit feelings of fear, jealousy, angst, the need to control, or resentment to take charge, it's easy to become bitter and defensive. By doing so, you erect barriers that prevent you from finding true love. In fact, we often attract what we put out, which means that if you're approaching love in this negative way, you're more likely to find someone who is bitter, defensive, resentful, jealous, and so on.

Try instead to let go of your hurt and to take steps to heal yourself in healthy ways. Do all of those things for yourself that your last partner didn't. Write about the experience in a journal to allow yourself to process all of your feelings. Look within yourself to see where you can improve and be a better partner. Be a force of love, support, joy, and peace. Believe in the power of love and that you, too, will find someone who treats you as you deserve. You'll be impressed at how thinking positively and taking positive actions to support those thoughts will bring you what you want.

"I never drink water. I'm afraid it will be habit-forming."

—W. C. Fields

Reach for Water

As you'll learn later in this book, when you think you're hungry, you're often just dehydrated. That's because 70 percent of your body is composed of water and it's very easy for that number to drop below the optimum level. By drinking water, you can push that percentage back up, and in so doing you can feel fuller and be less inclined to reach for food or sugary drinks.

You also look better when you're hydrated. Water pushes the toxins out of your bloodstream, helps move things along in your colon, and improves your complexion and appearance. It also improves your endurance and lubricates your joints, making exercising easier.

If you want to kick up your metabolism a notch, drink cold water. For your body to use water, it has to expend energy to heat the water to the same temperature as your body. Heating sixty-four ounces of ice water requires your body to burn an extra seventy calories a day. It might not sound like much, but all of those small numbers can add up to a big weight loss!

To determine how much water your body needs, take your weight and divide it in half. That number is the minimum number of ounces of water you should consume in a day. If you're working out, add an additional eight ounces for each twenty minutes. But don't chug it all at once. Spacing out your water intake is healthier for you, because consuming an excess amount at one time can disturb your body's electrolyte balance and send your body into shock.

*"Logic will get you from A to B. Imagination
will take you everywhere."*

—Albert Einstein

Use Your Imagination

As we move further and further away from childhood, we can forget how to reactivate those childlike centers in our minds. Harnessing your imagination and your skills of observation can help you to reclaim this lost way of seeing.

Challenge yourself to look at an object and draw it without thinking about what that object "is." Start by drawing the negative space (the space around the object), if necessary. Allow your mind to daydream, to wander.

Imagination not only helps to increase your happiness, it also help you to achieve what you want out of life. According to Dr. Frank Lawlis, in his book *The IQ Answer*, "We only know our world through our senses and our interpretations of those sensations. If we hold on to the idea of those sensations, our bodies [and brains] do not know the difference. The imagery stimulates the same neurological network as the actual experience."

Use this to your advantage. Tell yourself things are going well—even when they aren't—and you'll start to believe it. Tell yourself you're successful, and you'll start to act in a way that supports that. Your brain can trick you when you don't want it to, but you can play that game right back.

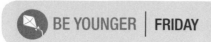

"Four be the things I'd have been better without:
love, curiosity, freckles, and doubt."

—Dorothy Parker

Pay Close Attention to Your Body

In between your annual "wellness" physicals, it's important to keep an eye on your own body. A few monthly tasks you need to add to your calendar are a breast self-exam or a testicular self-exam and a mole check. You may have had some of your moles since you were born. Others might be new. A new mole isn't a cause for panic, as most of us develop new moles throughout our lives. But it's important to know where your moles are and to keep an eye on them to see whether they change. An easy way to do this is to draw a crude sketch of the human body and mark down where your moles are, how large they are, and if they're round or an irregular shape.

Using the Cancer Research Institute's ABCD of identifying melanomas (skin cancers) will help you to identify the difference between a harmless (benign) mole and a potentially cancerous one:

A is for asymmetry. Melanoma lesions are not symmetrical; rather, they are irregular in shape.

B is for border. Melanoma lesions often have irregular borders in contrast with benign moles, which typically have smooth, even borders.

C is for color. Look for brown and black color in melanoma lesions in contrast to benign moles, which often are one shade of brown.

D is for diameter. Melanoma lesions routinely are about the size of a pencil eraser, roughly one-quarter inch or six millimeters across; non-cancerous moles are smaller.

If you find anything that might be suspect, call your doctor right away.

"Trust men and they will be true to you. Treat them gently and they will show themselves great."

—Ralph Waldo Emerson

Be the Kind of Partner You Want

What do you look for in your partner? Someone who greets you each evening with a loving embrace and is genuinely interested in hearing about your day? Someone who remembers to do the little things for you so your life is easier? Someone who reaches out to you just to tell you they're thinking about you?

If you're in a relationship and you're disappointed that your partner isn't living up to your expectations, consider that he or she might not know, or understand, what you need or want. Start acting toward your partner in ways that you find loving or that you know they find loving. As you build, or rebuild, the intimacy between each other, you'll likely find that your partner will start to do things that make you feel appreciated. If, however, after being the kind of partner you want for some time, you aren't feeling the love back, don't be shy in saying to your partner, "Honey, I love when you do X, but it would make me feel that much closer to you if you could do Y for me." Then your partner will understand he or she is making you feel good, and because you've been making your partner feel good, your partner is more likely to understand you and want to give you what you need.

*"We do not talk—we bludgeon one another with facts
and theories gleaned from cursory readings of newspapers,
magazines, and digests."*

—Henry Miller

Quell Your Need for Noise

In a world filled with the seemingly constant buzz of information, it's hard to disconnect. Do you spend most of your waking hours hooked to the Internet, texting, watching television, or listening to the radio? If that's the case, your mind will benefit from some silent time.

Focus on taking more time for yourself that is alone and as quiet as possible. If you live in a noisy city, at the very least don't fill this time with extra noise. Go for a walk by yourself and contemplate your own thoughts in silence. Though it might be painful getting back to your own mind, distracting yourself instead of facing your issues isn't helping you solve them. When you allow yourself to contemplate your life, you can start to work through things and rediscover the wonderful self you've been neglecting.

If you find your life so busy with work and/or with family, take advantage of those few minutes of your own that you might have while commuting or make it a priority to schedule quiet time for your whole family once a day, perhaps after dinner, so that all of you can benefit from this exercise.

"I'd like to live as a poor man with lots of money."

—Pablo Picasso

Record Every Penny You Spend for a Month

In order to improve your finances, it is important to have a monthly budget that you can stick to. The first step to starting that budget is to determine how much you make. Then, figure out your expected monthly payments as well as how much you spend on everything from groceries to entertainment. Without this information, it's impossible to determine how much you have to spend and save.

To figure out the total amount you spend, write down every penny you spend for one month, even if it's only to buy a latte or feed the parking meter. Or if you're not the paper-and-pen type, utilize an online program, such as Mint, that will record and categorize your bank-account transactions for you. You'll still need to look at your receipts and write down how much you spent in cash—Mint can't tell whether you've spent your $40 withdrawal on groceries or lattes. If you're not following step #1 (Switch to Using Cash and Checks for a Year), you'll be able to see your credit-card transactions as well.

From here, you'll be able to assess where you can cut back on frivolous spending and start to put that money into saving for things you really want to spend money on—such as a down payment for a house or a big vacation—instead of whittling away your funds on things you don't really need.

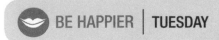

"I think the thing to do is to enjoy the ride when you're on it."

—Johnny Depp

Think Positively

Some scientists believe that each thought we have can create a positive or negative cycle. When you think positive, optimistic, and joyous thoughts, you convince your brain that things are going well and that leads to more happy, positive thoughts. When you think negatively, get down on yourself, or let anxiety take over, you can end up convincing yourself that the world is a sad, lonely place and then you focus on the bad things that happen and miss the good ones.

If a negative thought comes into your mind, don't be harsh on yourself. Instead, just move forward and replace that negative thought with a happy one. As long as you strive to think positively most of the time, you'll see the happiness in your life increase. If you find that you have a hard time dispelling negative thoughts or behaviors, consider speaking with a therapist who can help you learn some coping mechanisms and/or work through issues from your past that might be holding you back in moving forward.

"Lack of activity destroys the good condition of every human being, while movement and methodical physical exercise saves and protects it."

—Plato

Exercise Six to Eight Hours a Week

If you want to lose it (and look good), you've got to move it. To lose one pound, you have to burn off 3,500 calories. Since your body automatically burns some calories at rest, this means that you have to either eat less and let your body do the work on its own or move more—or some combination of both. For example, to lose a pound a week, you have to burn 500 calories a day or eat 500 calories less a day or some combination of the two.

If you were to only eat less, you would lose weight, but you wouldn't end up toned. So in order to improve your cardiovascular health and build muscle, you should work out at least six to eight hours a week. If the president of the United States can exercise six times a week, then you can find an hour a day to get to the yoga studio, make it to the gym, or jog in your neighborhood. If you don't want to miss your favorite TV show, DVR it and watch it when you return as your reward.

As you push yourself to achieve fitness, your metabolism will respond in kind and you'll start to lose weight and tone up at the same time. It might not seem like fun at first, but stick with it a month and you'll be happy with the results you've achieved.

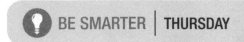

"Alcohol is a good preservative for everything but brains."

—Mary Pettibone Poole

Cut Back on Brain Drains

To give your brain the chance to operate at its best, cut back on alcohol and sugar and cut out aspartame and MSG. Each of these edible products affects the brain in a different negative way

Alcohol. While the occasional drink will affect your brain only in the short term, such as in temporarily slowing down your ability to process events, chronic over-consumption of alcohol can lead to brain damage, heart disease, dementia, strokes, major depression, and even death.

Sugar. Studies are slim on sugar's effect on the brain, but there are signs it can prevent the development of new brain cells, impair short-term memory, and increase your chance of feeling depressed or anxious.

Aspartame. Though the battle still wages as to whether this sweetener is dangerous to human health, its critics believe that this ingredient—which breaks down into the excitotoxin (a chemical that overexcites and kills cells) asparate—can cause insulin resistance, depression, and if you're allergic, migraines.

MSG. This food additive is used to "enhance" the flavor of certain foods, but no matter how good it tastes, what it does to your brain is unforgivable. Not only can it cause headaches, chest tightness, and other symptoms in those who are susceptible to it, but MSG is an excitotoxin that can also worsen autism, attention deficit hyperactivity disorder (ADHD), and can rewire the brain in ways that impair learning.

"All truly great thoughts are conceived through walking."

—Friedrich Nietzsche

Walk at Least 10,000 Steps a Day

Though we don't want to admit it, most of us live a sedentary lifestyle. The most exercise we may get during the day is going from our house to work and back again. This isn't good for your heart, your mood, or your waistline. Exercise is important if you want to look good and be healthy. But what if your current health only allows you to walk? That's okay!

Recent scientific studies have shown that all of us should be walking at least 10,000 steps a day for our heart and bone health and that walking 10,000 steps a day can cut the risk of heart disease up to 40 percent! To measure your steps, you can buy a pedometer at any local fitness store or at almost any big-box retailer. The device will measure all the steps you take throughout the day, and you might find you'll need to be a lot more active to reach your goal. If you're not ready to invest in a pedometer, keep this in mind: based on the average stride length, 10,000 steps is equivalent to walking five miles or to walking or running thirty minutes to an hour (depending on how fast you walk).

Note: *If you are planning to walk for weight loss, physicians and researchers recommend taking between 12,000 and 15,000 steps daily.*

"Life has taught us that love does not consist in gazing at each other, but in looking outward together in the same direction."

—Antoine de Saint-Exupéry

Contemplate the Qualities You Most Desire

Can you imagine your ideal partner? Make a list of the qualities you find most attractive. Start with writing down everything that might be important to you: kindness, confidence, empathy, good manners, fidelity, charisma, appearance, etc.

Then whittle down your "A" list to only the most crucial qualities, without which that person wouldn't make a good fit for you. As you decide which characteristics are mandatory, move the qualities you wouldn't mind them having—but that aren't absolutely necessary—to a "B" list.

Next, for each of those "A"-list qualities, write down precisely what you mean. If, say, a sense of humor is important to you, what kind of humor—sarcasm or slapstick; clean jokes or blue ones? Though the partner you eventually choose everything on the list, having a clear idea of what you're looking for can help you make a good selection.

IF YOU KEEP FALLING FOR MR. OR MS. WRONG

In addition to your "A" list, make a list of qualities that you tend to be attracted to and where they lead. Do you tend to confuse charismatic with cocky, confidence with dramatic, or flirtatious with a cheating heart? By identifying your missteps, you can help prevent them in the future and stop repeating your mistakes.

"Silence is a voice of great strength."

—Lao Tzu

Go Silent for a Day

Do you talk to fill space or because silence makes you anxious? Try not speaking for an entire day and refrain from emailing or posting any updates on your social network(s). At first, it's bound to feel weird and you'll have to fight the urge to say what you're thinking and feeling. But permitting yourself to remain silent for a day will allow you to observe your world more deeply and to get in touch with your inner thoughts.

Through this exercise, you'll become more at ease with what you used to feel were awkward silences and you'll be less likely to jump at the chance to fill the space with chatter. By allowing these moments to pass without anxiety about who is going to say what next, you'll ultimately feel more at ease.

If done with a partner, this can be a very intimate exercise, because sometimes words can get in the way. On this day of silence, instead of telling each other how you feel, you'll have to show it. Moments of tender eye-gazing might be followed by gentle kisses and more, and after a day together of silence, you'll probably feel that much more connected to each other and understand one another on another level.

"A big part of financial freedom is having your heart and mind free from worry about the what-ifs of life."

—Suze Orman

Make Specific Financial Goals

Before you sit down to sketch out your monthly budget, it is helpful to give yourself some goals. When you have a reason for why you're cutting back on your spending and why and what you're saving for, it's easier to do. Otherwise, what would be the point?

Start by imagining all of the things you want to save for. These can be long-term goals or shorter-term ones. They can be as small as wanting to buy a new computer or a television you don't have to squint at or as large as buying a house, putting your children through college, and making sure you can live comfortably when you're retired. Some of these goals, especially the bigger ones, are best worked out with a financial planner. But even before meeting with a financial planner, you can start to get an idea of what you want to save for.

For smaller goals, consider setting up a "fun account" in which you sock away money to use for things like a TV, vacation, or new clothes. As you see this money grow every month, it will probably make you want to save more and might even inspire you to cut back your monthly spending even further.

"When you are grateful, fear disappears
and abundance appears."

—Tony Robbins

Stop Focusing on What You Lack

If you want to start improving your outlook on your life, turn your focus away from what you don't have and toward what you do have. When you put a magnifying glass on what you think is wrong with your life—you can't afford what you want, you weigh too much, you don't have a significant other, you don't have a fulfilling job—that attitude succeeds in doing one thing and one thing only: making you miserable.

Start putting attention on what is right in your life. What are you grateful for? Who and what bring you joy? How can you build on this joy by giving back to others?

When you direct your attention away from yourself and what you don't have and focus on enriching the lives of others and on the positive aspects in your life, you can boost your own happiness.

That said, if there are things in your life you'd like to improve—your debt, your weight, your love life, your career—start making an action plan. What changes do you need to make to get moving in the direction you want? Do you need to go back to school? Join a gym? Sit down with a financial manager? Use the tips in this book to help put you on the right path, but don't forget about the great things in your life now.

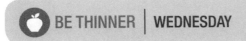

"I love to ride my bike, which is great aerobics, but also just a great time for me to think, so it's like this terrific double bill."

—Robin Williams

Understand the Benefits of Aerobic Exercise

Aerobic exercise is the fastest track to losing weight and keeping healthy. Each week, aim for at least 150 minutes of moderate-intensity exercise (this means you can talk but can't sing, or if you're using a heart-rate monitor, it is 55–69 percent of your maximum heart rate) for at least 20 minutes at a time. This will get your heart rate/circulation up and improve the oxygen flow to your body, which, in turn, will help boost your metabolism. If you're looking for other reasons to inspire you to exercise, here are just a few:

- Exercising regularly reduces your risk of heart disease, type II diabetes, stroke, certain types of cancer, and osteoporosis.
- Exercising regularly and burning at least 800 calories per week could have a beneficial impact on your cholesterol by raising your HDL (the "good cholesterol") and lowering your LDL (the "bad cholesterol") and triglycerides.
- Aerobic exercise reduces muscle tension and the amount of stress hormones in your body.
- Aerobic exercise boosts endorphins and releases additional serotonin in your brain, which helps to balance your mood or relieve depression.
- Exercising improves circulation, which flushes away harmful toxins and protects against fine lines and wrinkles.

IDEAS FOR MODERATE-INTENSITY EXERCISE

Brisk walking	Mowing the lawn
Active video games, like the Wii	Tennis
Biking on level ground	Canoeing

"I find television very educating. Every time someone turns on the set, I go into the other room and read a book."

—Groucho Marx

Limit the Time You Spend Watching TV

Television makes you dumb. Okay, perhaps it's not that bad, but television definitely doesn't improve your intelligence, even if you only watch the Discovery Channel. This is because you're taking in information passively, instead of actively acquiring it.

When we center our lives around television, we're also missing out on moments when we could connect with our family and friends. Though they might be in the same room with us, our focus is on the show on the screen and not on building deeper relationships.

While you're at it, remove that television from the bedroom. It's killing your intimacy and love life, because I'll guess that the moments you spend watching a late-night show are the same moments you'd otherwise spend talking or making love.

Fill the time you usually spend watching television doing something that enhances your life. Read a book. Go on a walk and enjoy the outdoors. Visit a museum. Take photographs. Call a friend. Anything in which you're required to use your brain is better for your happiness and your intelligence than sitting on the couch blinking mindlessly at the television.

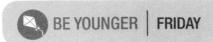

"Walking is man's best medicine."

—Hippocrates

Thwart the Onset of Osteoporosis

For the first thirty to forty years of your life, your body builds and stores bone very effectively. But at around age thirty-five for women and forty-five for men, bones can start to lose their density and become more likely to fracture. But this loss of bone can be prevented. While you can't stop aging, you can reduce your risk factors.

Osteoporosis (bone loss) can be caused by a vitamin D deficiency, smoking, lack of physical activity, drinking too much alcohol, drinking soda, and/or low body weight. To help guard against bone disease, quit smoking, increase your ingestion of calcium to 1500 mg, and take a vitamin D supplement, which helps your body absorb calcium. Engage in weight-*bearing* exercises (ones in which you can add weight to your body to enhance your workout such as walking, running, yoga, or aerobic dance) and consider lifting weights or another form of strength training. Making these changes will enable you to be more active throughout your life.

GREAT NON-DAIRY SOURCES OF CALCIUM

Getting enough calcium, D3, and protein will help prevent this bone disease, but if you don't eat dairy, here are some other sources you can look to for your calcium.

- Firm Tofu prepared with calcium sulfate (1721 mg)
- Sardines (569 mg)
- Sesame Butter (64 mg per tablespoon)
- Cooked Spinach (245 mg)
- Figs (241 mg)

Note: These amounts are based on one-cup servings unless specified otherwise

"Whatever our souls are made of, his and mine are the same."

—Emily Brontë

Create a Healthy Cycle

Some of us continually fall for people who are wrong for us. It's not that you mean to do it; it just happens, right? Well, it's time to break that unhealthy cycle before you end up in another dead-end relationship. In a future chapter, we'll take a look at what qualities you want to attract, but it's also important to look at what unhealthy qualities you're attracted to.

Do you find yourself interested in people who are unavailable, perhaps because you like the thrill of the chase, but then once you're with them, you find out they're unable to provide you with what you need emotionally or otherwise? Do you find yourself dating people who have a hard time working out difficult issues within the relationship because of their own baggage? Do you date "bad boys" or "bad girls" because they're exciting, but then find out they're immature or worse?

Once you've identified how your Cupid's arrow has misfired, you can start to work on changing its trajectory. For instance, if you crave excitement, try finding someone who loves to travel to exotic locations or who participates in high-adrenaline sports. By finding other, healthier ways to fulfill what you need, you're more likely to have a long-lasting and fulfilling relationship with less drama. With this knowledge in hand, put your best self out there— the confident, loyal, trusting one—and make sure to accept only partners who will respect and treat you like you deserve.

"Breathe. Let go. And remind yourself that this very moment is the only one you know you have for sure."

—Oprah Winfrey

Be Aware of Your Breathing

The way you breathe affects your mental state. When you hyper-ventilate—breathing rapidly in reaction to a stressful or frightening moment—you put yourself into a hard-to-break cycle, because the quick breathing doesn't allow enough oxygen to reach your brain, which can make you feel even more anxious. However, if you become aware of your everyday breathing and slow its pace so that with each breath you fill your lungs fully when you inhale, but not to the point of being uncomfortable, and then exhale completely, you'll find that you go through the day with less tension. When you breathe properly, your brain receives more oxygen and can function more effectively. The result is a positive feedback cycle of relaxation. You might even notice that as you work on your breathing, you are better able to remain present in the moment instead of thinking anxiously about what is coming next.

IMPROVE YOUR LUNG EFFICIENCY

When you start becoming aware of your breath, you might notice that you aren't able to breathe very deeply. If this is the result of an anxious or tense lifestyle, keep practicing. You will get there. Here are some ways to improve the efficiency of your lungs and perhaps even your longevity.

- Engage in regular aerobic exercise
- Play an instrument that requires you to use your breath
- Practice deep breathing
- Exercise at higher altitudes where there is less oxygen

"My problem lies in reconciling my gross habits with my net income."

—Errol Flynn

Make a Household Budget and Stick to It for at Least a Month

Congratulations! You've reached the step where you can create your monthly budget. You've already done a lot of the hard work of figuring out how much you make in a month, what your monthly expenses are, and what you spend (on average) on nonessential items. You will use all of this information to create a workable budget by following these steps:

1. **Categorize your spending**. For example, take all of the car-related expenses, such as gas, insurance, payments, maintenance, parking, and tolls, and put them into a category titled "Car." Do the same with your entertainment expenses, your home expenses, etc.

2. **Compare how much you spent to how much you made last month**. Were you under budget? If you were under, did you put this money away into a separate savings account? Or did you go over?

3. **Trim down your expenses**. This is especially important if you spent more than you made. Examine each category for places where you can cut costs so you can stay within budget.

4. **Don't forget to save**. Look at what is left over. You'll want to give yourself a small cushion if you can—whether, depending on where you are financially, it's $20 or $200— but take the difference between the amount you make and the amount you have budgeted to spend and put it into your savings.

WEEK FIVE

"If we think happy thoughts, we will be happy. If we think miserable thoughts, we will be miserable."

—Dale Carnegie

Use the Right Language

It may surprise you, but the language you use can have a profound impact on whether you will manifest a positive or negative outcome for yourself. If you're skeptical about the power of manifestation (a topic we discuss in greater depth later in this book), just think of it as "setting your intentions."

For example, pretend you're about to go onstage and give a speech in front of hundreds of people. If you're like most people, that would probably give you a few butterflies! If you were to think before going onstage, "I'm so nervous, I'm going to forget what I'm saying and they're all going to laugh at me," you're likely to make yourself even more anxious and you might even forget your speech! But if you were to tell yourself, "Hey, this is pretty exciting. I get to go up there and share my views with all of these people," then you're going to psych yourself up and stand a better chance of delivering a powerful presentation.

It's important to be mindful of the language you use in all areas of your life. By empowering yourself with uplifting language and setting your intentions to get a new job, move to a new place, or even find a great partner, you'll subconsciously start to make choices that put you on the path to deeper happiness.

"In general, mankind, since the improvement in cookery, eats twice as much as nature requires."

—Benjamin Franklin

Keep a Food Diary

If you've had a hard time losing weight, consider what you've been eating. While it's important to eat healthily, a calorie is still a calorie, whether it's from an apple or a chocolate bar. And while it's unlikely you'll eat so many apples that you'll go over your caloric needs for the day, try to be cognizant of how much you are eating. To do that, try keeping a food diary.

A food diary can be as basic or as complicated as you want it to be. But let's begin with the basics. Take a journal or a notebook (something portable and easily accessible) and write down the dates for the next five days on the top of the first five pages. Then, for the next five days, write down everything you eat and drink. You can separate this into meals if you want. Everything goes into the diary—adding cream to your coffee, having a beer out with friends, spreading butter on your bread—because it all adds up.

After you've completed the five days, take the time to look up the calorie content of each item of food and write down the total for each day at the bottom of the page. Were you over or under your calorie budget for the day? Even with your exercise, did you end up netting more calories than you burned? If so, you'll need to cut back your calories or increase your exercising—or both—to lose weight.

"A hobby is hard work you wouldn't do for a living."

—Anonymous

Turn on Your Mind

Start using your brain. But, you might protest, I use my brain every day! Do you really, though? Do you consciously think about the choices you make in your daily life, or do you spend more time going through the motions? Do you follow a routine that involves challenging your mind, or do you let it off the hook and spend many of your evenings vegging out in front of the television? Throughout this book, you'll learn ways in which you can turn on your brain so that you can get the most out of it at work, at home, and at play, when socializing with family, friends, and colleagues.

In the meantime, here are a few ideas to get those mental juices flowing again:

- Travel a new way to a familiar destination.
- Brainstorm new uses for common objects.
- Find a new hobby or get more involved in one you have.
- Learn to play a musical instrument.
- Stop multitasking—you'll be more efficient and less stressed!
- Travel to a new place and do things you wouldn't normally do.
- Read books you enjoy but add in some books that challenge you with their vocabulary, their philosophy, or their writing style.

"Be true to your teeth and they won't be false to you."

—Soupy Sales

Take Care of Your Teeth and Gums

Your dentist will thank me for this one. If you want to live a long, healthy life, you've got to brush your teeth with a soft bristle brush and floss at least twice a day. As you get older, although your chance of getting cavities goes down, the likelihood you'll be struck with gingivitis goes up. Gingivitis isn't just bad for your breath; it can also lead to serious illnesses, because the bacteria in your mouth makes its way into your bloodstream. Another gum disease to watch out for is periodontitis, a condition that causes bone loss below the gum, which causes receding of the gum line, making it harder to prevent nasty bacteria from entering your blood stream. These two gum diseases have also been linked to osteoporosis, cancer, and even type 2 diabetes.

If it's been longer than six months since you've gone to the dentist, make an appointment so that you can try to nip these diseases in the bud with a deep cleaning. Though it's not uncommon to fear sitting in the dentist's chair, these days there are numbing creams and other tools your dentist can use to make your experience much more pleasant than in days past.

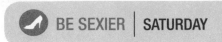

"Never get involved with someone who wants to change you."

—Quentin Crisp

Accept Your Sexual Self

We all differ in our sexual desires and appetites. What one person loves may be a complete turnoff for another. While one person might want to have sex every day, another might be content having sex once a week or less. Knowing what feels good for you and accepting that part of yourself not only is important for your own happiness but it also helps you find a compatible mate.

Allow yourself to pursue your own sexual self-interests and explore what turns you on. You may surprise yourself as you do so and open new pathways to explore. As long as your desires can be fulfilled by yourself or with a consenting adult (or adults), then they're a-okay. Once you open yourself up to the pleasure of touch in its many forms, you'll be more comfortable in the bedroom and you'll find it that much easier to have powerful orgasms more often.

"The affairs of the world will go on forever. Do not delay the practice of meditation."

—Milarepa

Take Five Deep Breaths at Regular Intervals During the Day

There are many types of yoga practices, but all pay special attention to breathing, because as one moves between difficult poses, bringing the focus back to the breath allows the yogi to remain present and work through the pain. But you can also use this practice outside the yoga studio to increase the oxygen flowing to your brain and, in turn, to encourage the relaxation response and help you be more present in your daily life.

To breathe deeply, start by slowly and fully exhaling through your nose or mouth, allowing your stomach to push outward for a count of five, then breathe in slowly through your nose for a count of five and hold this breath for two counts before slowly releasing it. Try to put the focus on your diaphragm or your stomach instead of your lungs to fully engage with your body as your breathe.

At regular intervals throughout your day and at any time you're feeling overwhelmed, take five deep breaths to help you relax and think clearer.

*"At the beginning of the cask and the end take thy fill,
but be saving in the middle; for at the bottom
the savings comes too late."*

—Hesiod

Automate Your Savings

Now that you've made your budget and figured out your financial goals, make it easier for yourself to work toward those goals each month by automating your savings. Allow your brick-and-mortar or online bank to automatically transfer a set amount out of your checking account into a savings account each week.

Before you start panicking, please understand that I'm not suggesting you start by transferring all of your extra cash—at least, not at first. Begin small, whether it's $25 a week or 3 percent of a week's pay. If you see that you can do that without struggling, raise the amount slowly and keep doing so as you get better at not spending frivolously. As you start to see that amount in your savings increase, it should help keep you on track and decrease the temptation to spend unwisely. Plus, having that cash on hand for later will help you when you have an emergency or when you're ready to make a large purchase.

WEEK SIX

"Start wide, expand further, and never look back."

—Arnold Schwarzenegger

Fix Visualization Problems

You already know just how important it is to use positive language. This week you'll learn how important it is to create positive images in your mind. When you think about the future, even in the short term, what do you imagine? Do you see yourself struggling with a partner who doesn't support you in the ways you need to be supported? Sometimes, when we feel down about where our life is heading, it's easy to take the low road and imagine our future as bleak, lonely, and downright depressing! Sadly, this just creates a negative cycle, as it's hard to feel inspired to make important, positive changes when all you can see is a lackluster future ahead.

Let's revisit that public-speaking engagement you were thinking about in week five. If, coupled with telling yourself negative language, you imagined the audience laughing at you, it wouldn't help your nervousness at all. But if, instead, you imagined them giving you a standing ovation, then that would help fuel your excitement. It's all about using language and imagery together to create a satisfying self-fulfilled prophecy.

This week, start to imagine your future as full of success and happiness, with loving, supportive people surrounding you. After resetting your mind on this more positive track, you'll start to move toward this vision and make the changes necessary to achieve it—whether it's finding a new job, a new home, or a new partner. You can do it!

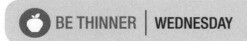

"To say that obesity is caused by merely consuming too many calories is like saying that the only cause of the American Revolution was the Boston Tea Party."

—Adelle Davis, nutritionist

Avoid High-Fructose Corn Syrup

With a proliferation of products on the market now boasting they contain "real sugar," you might be wondering if there's a difference between "real" sugar (sucrose, or table sugar) and the ingredient known as "HFCS," or high-fructose corn syrup. Turns out, there is. While natural sugar isn't "healthy," the chemical compound HFCS, which was created in 1957 and has become an extremely popular and inexpensive alternative to sugar, is worse for you. In 2010, researchers at Princeton University revealed that rats fed a diet of HFCS gained 48 percent more weight (especially around their abdomen) and saw a marked increase in the fat in their blood than those fed table sugar.

But that's not all. Other researchers claim that, in addition to causing rapid weight gain, HFCS can cause insulin resistance, leading to type 2 diabetes and fatty liver disease. Studies have also shown that HFCS can affect your body's ability to recognize when it's full, so you keep eating. Unfortunately, HFCS has wormed its way into many processed food products, so you have to be vigilant about looking at labels, even if you're not reaching for something sweet.

WHERE TO WATCH FOR HFCS

Bread and cereal products	Soups
Chocolate and other candy	Salad dressings
Soda	Dairy products
Tomato products, such as ketchup and pasta sauce	

"It is the mind that builds up the body strong and shiny or wastes it to skin and bone."

—Sri Sathya Sai Baba, Indian spiritual leader

Give Your Brain the Vitamins It Needs

To function at its best, your brain requires certain vitamins. Though it's best to get these through the food you eat, you can also take them as supplements if you're not getting enough of these vitamins from your diet. The following are the most essential vitamins for long-term brain health.

Vitamin A. Helps protect brain cells from harmful free radicals and improves circulation within the bloodstream and, thus, to the brain.

Vitamin B12. Helps DNA production and fatty acid synthesis.

Vitamin B6. Helps convert sugar into glucose, which the brain uses for fuel. It can also improve memory, help prevent heart disease, and ease the symptoms of PMS.

Vitamin B1. Helps the brain by acting as a building block for serotonin, a chemical that regulates mood, digestion, learning, and memory.

Vitamin B9. Aids cerebral circulation by inhibiting narrowing of the arteries in the neck. Studies also suggest that daily supplements of B9—also known as folic acid—can reduce the likelihood of certain age-related psychiatric problems, including dementia.

Vitamin C. A key ingredient in the creation of other neurotransmitters and may help prevent Alzheimer's disease.

Vitamin E. Restores damaged neurotransmitter receptor sites and in doing so helps prevent age-related brain deterioration. When taken in combination with selenium, it can improve the overall mood and cognitive function of the elderly, and may prevent or slow the progression of Alzheimer's disease.

"A custom loathsome to the eye, hateful to the nose, harmful to the brain, dangerous to the lungs, and in the black, stinking fume thereof nearest resembling the horrible Stygian smoke of the pit that is bottomless."

—King James I

Quit Smoking

I shouldn't need to tell you that smoking is unhealthy for you. Hopefully, you already know that. It's bad for your lungs, bones, mouth, and reproductive organs. It's bad for your budget, for the environment due to the pollution and trash you're creating, and for those around you.

If those reasons aren't good enough, smoking will also prematurely age you. Because, while those old-school Hollywood types might have looked cool smoking a cigarette, you are unlikely to look like the Marlborough Man by age fifty if you smoke.

Smoking constricts the blood vessels and damages facial collagen, causing your skin to dry out and become more wrinkled and giving it less of a chance to bounce back after you quit. So, before you do any more damage to your beautiful (or handsome) face, put down the cigarette and find a way to quit.

With so many options available to help you stop smoking— from gum and prescription medications to hypnotherapy and acupuncture—something is bound to work for you if going cold turkey hasn't. Learn more at *www.surgeongeneral.gov/tobacco*.

"I don't really trust men who claim they are not interested in porn."

—Moby

Banish Shame

Shame is the biggest mood killer in the bedroom. Shame about your performance, your body, or your participation in a sexual act is pretty much guaranteed to turn your partner off and prevent you from fully enjoying the sexual experience. Before getting into a sexual relationship with someone, it's important for you to work through these feelings of shame, if possible, so that they won't have a negative impact on your sex life.

If you're feeling shame about your sexuality, start by trying to determine where these feelings are coming from. Were you teased when you were younger about something related to sex or your body? Did your upbringing or religion have an impact on how you see sex today? Do you have low self-esteem or a poor body image? Did some sexual trauma happen in your past that you're ashamed of? Whatever the cause of the shame, work to identify it, and if you cannot process the feelings on your own, consider seeing a counselor or therapist. After you have purged these negative thoughts and feelings from your life, you'll not only be happier, you'll also be more in tune and comfortable with your own sexual needs and those of your partner.

"You are never alone or helpless. The force that guides the stars guides you too."

—Shrii Shrii Anandamurti, guru

Choose a Personal Spiritual Symbol

For centuries, humans have been using images to symbolize larger ideas that inspire their lives. If you would like to tap into a spiritual center or are looking for an image or idea to focus on while meditating as something you would like to achieve or as a mantra for your life, pick up a guide to symbols. These books offer hundreds of symbols to choose from. Some symbols have different meanings in different cultures or religions, so you may find that while an icon doesn't work for you in one setting, it is fitting in another. Here are a few symbols to consider:

Infinity. Represents not only the infinite but also perfection, equilibrium, and the balance of male and female energies

Ankh. Used by the ancient Egyptians to represent everlasting life and also the joining of male and female

Lion. Represents bravery, power, and dominance

Om. A Buddhist mantra representing the four parts of consciousness: waking, sleeping, dreaming, and the transcendental state. It is believed to be the sound of the cosmic universe and can be used as a point of reflection.

Pentacle. A five-sided star representing the four elements: earth, air, fire, water, spirit

Phoenix. This mythical bird can symbolize a physical, spiritual, or emotional rebirth

Spiral. Often connected with female energies and fertility

Yin Yang. A Taoist symbol that represents two sides of the same coin: dark/light, male/female, good/evil

"I hate banks. They do nothing positive for anybody except take care of themselves. They're first in with their fees and first out when there's trouble."

—Harvey Goldsmith

Don't Tolerate Bank Fees

If it feels like every time you open your bank statement there's some strange new fee that's been added, it's time to give your bank a call. Four popular fees that your bank may charge are: monthly fees, check cashing fees, minimum balance fees, and overdraft fees. If you've seen these or any other mysterious fees on your statement, call your bank and ask if they can remove or permanently waive the fee. If they can't, push a little harder and ask them what they can do for you to keep you as a customer. They may have a type of account that's a better fit for your financial situation, or they may require you to do something like have one check directly deposited a month in order to have certain fees waived. There is usually a way around the fees, so if your bank isn't willing to work with you, look for one that will.

"Don't let the negativity given to you by the world disempower you. Instead, give to yourself that which empowers you."

—Les Brown

Kick That Negativity Habit

By now, you know it's important to think positively and think of the future in an uplifting way. But that's not always so easy. Do you melt down in times of crisis? Do you sometimes let a negative inner voice get the best of you? Do you allow those nasty little thoughts to take control of your day, week, month, or even life? Work on breaking that cycle.

First, take some quiet time by yourself to identify where that voice is coming from. Whose voice is it? The voice of a frenemy from your childhood? The voice of a teacher? The voice of a relative or parent? Most likely, that voice isn't your own, and recognizing whose it is will be the first step to stopping it. Once you've identified it as something outside yourself, it will be easier for you to tell it to shut up. And I recommend doing that, literally. The next time that voice starts telling you negative things, be as forceful as you need to be with it, saying something along the lines of, "You know what, [insert person's name here], I'm not listening to you." Then, remind yourself that you are awesome, lovable, successful, etc. and continue moving forward on your journey.

This process may take time, but it will lead to a much happier, calmer, more well-balanced you!

"When one has tasted watermelon he knows what the angels eat."

—Mark Twain

Eat a Variety of Fruits and Vegetables

When you dine on fruits and vegetables, you're providing your body with foods packed with the essential vitamins and minerals it needs to survive. Though you can get some of your nutrients from supplements, eating foods containing them is still the most efficient way for your body to receive the nutrition it needs. Most researchers believe that while supplements can be useful, the nutrients in whole vegetables work together so they're absorbed and processed in a way that enables your body to derive the most nutrients possible from them, which is something supplemental vitamins can't do.

In addition, by eating fresh fruits and vegetables, their fiber and water content will help you to feel fuller for longer and make you less likely to reach for that unhealthy snack or second helping.

To make sure you're getting all of your important nutrients, aim to have as colorful a plate as possible and at least five servings a day. Different vegetables, as you'll learn in later chapters, are packed with different nutrients, so fill your diet with a wide variety of these natural foods.

"Don't dig your grave with your own knife and fork."

—Proverb

Limit High-Fat Foods to Keep Your Brain Young and Healthy

High-fat foods aren't good for your body or your brain. One study revealed that fatty foods may be an addictive substance on a par with cocaine and heroin. When the rats in the study ate fattening foods, their dopamine receptors—the neuroreceptors in the brain that register pleasure and reinforce behavior—became overloaded, and the more fattening foods they consumed, the more the levels of these receptors dropped. This means they had to eat more fattening foods just to regain the same pleasurable feeling, just as a drug addict has to do more of the drug to reach the same high.

Another study showed that the higher the amount of fat in a woman's diet, the more likely she is to have a stroke. The study used a pool of 88,000 women and found that those who ate ninety-five grams of fat a day versus twenty-five grams of fat were 44 percent more likely to have a stroke. Considering some of those burgers at fast-food chains have sixty grams of fat or more, if you're female and you want to avoid a stroke, you're going to want to start reading those nutrition menus and cut out, or at least cut back on, those fast-food burgers.

In addition to this research, a 2008 Canadian study linked a high-fat diet to brain changes similar to Alzheimer's. So, if you want your brain, and your body, to be healthy, keep your fat intake on the lower side and make sure you eat only healthy fats like those found in avocados, salmon, and olive oil.

"Eat little, sleep sound."

—Proverb

Restrict Your Calories to Reduce the Effects of Aging

Cutting down the amount of fat in your diet will keep your brain functioning at its best, but did you know that just cutting back on your overall calorie intake may have an impact on the aging process? The idea, first proposed by UCLA scientist Roy Walford, has been supported by many scientific studies. In recent studies, participants who ate less than 1,000 calories a day of nutrient-dense food experienced such results as a decrease in blood insulin levels and in body temperature, two traits often found in those who have led long lives. The leaders of these studies believe that the low-calorie diets may work to increase longevity because you are metabolizing less food and producing less free radicals and because severe calorie restriction is capable of affecting certain genes.

If you are considering embarking on a low-calorie diet, consult with your doctor beforehand to see if he or she believes doing so might cause any health complications. Keep in mind, too, that this type of eating plan can be very hard to stick with. While you will likely lose weight, you're bound to be irritable and have headaches for the first few days or weeks. Eating much less food will also slow down your metabolism.

"In real life I'm bone dry and when I play I'm a mango and in sex I'm starving to be a dripping mango."

—Tori Amos

Stimulate the Erogenous Zones

All over your body lie erogenous zones just aching to be turned on. These areas are packed with nerve endings, and when stimulated they can signal arousal. There are two types of erogenous zones: specific and nonspecific. Specific erogenous zones are those that come into contact with a mucous membrane, such as the lips, vagina, and penis. The nonspecific erogenous zones are those that are sensitive but don't come into contact with a mucous membrane. Here's a rundown of the most common erogenous zones and how to stimulate them:

Scalp. Run your fingers all over your partner's head and through her or his hair.

Ears. Nibble on them, breathe into them, or just trace them with your finger to elicit a positive response.

Lips and tongue. Tease your partner by running your tongue over her or his lips, kiss deeply, and don't be afraid to use your tongue to explore your partner's mouth seductively.

Neck and shoulders. Kiss the back of your partner's neck and down her or his shoulders. Use your fingers to trace the sexy curve of her or his neck following it down to the shoulder blades.

Hands and feet. Massaging the hands and feet can help your partner relax after a long day, but licking and sucking on them may get things moving in a whole new direction.

Butt. Playfully running your hands over your partner's shapely behind can get him or her going!

Genitals. There are plenty of ways to turn on your partner by touching him or her in these areas even before you have intercourse.

"Art can only truly be art by presenting an adequate outward symbol of some fact of the interior life."

—Margaret Fuller

Enhance a Symbol's Esoteric Meaning

Focusing on a symbol can help you in your image-guided meditations and by anchoring you to something larger. However, it's not always easy to find a symbol that fits your needs if you're just examining their primary meanings. Many symbols used today have had many different meanings over the course of their history. So, if you've found an image you feel a connection with but aren't sold on its meaning, dig a little bit deeper into its history to see if there is a second or third meaning that speaks more directly to you. For instance, the cross, the symbol we associate today with Christianity, is also the symbol representing earth for the Chinese and was previously used by the Babylonians to worship the fertility god Tammuz.

Whichever symbol you choose, make sure it is one with a positive meaning that can help bring you relief when you need to find your center.

"If saving money is wrong, then I don't want to be right!"

—William Shatner

Find a Savings Account with a High Interest Rate

Before you put your money into a savings account, look for one with the highest interest available. Even if you can't deposit your money in an account so that it grows faster than the rate of inflation, you can probably find a savings account online that offers a higher rate than your bank. Plus, with your money in an online account, it will be more difficult to access it on a daily basis, so you'll be that much less tempted to harvest funds from it.

THE LONG-TERM DIFFERENCE

The difference between a savings account that generates 0.10 percent interest per year and one that generates 1.10 percent might not seem like much, but in the long run, even that 1 percent difference adds up. Let's pretend you invest $100,000 dollars. In ten years, the account with 0.10 percent would have gained $1,005 while the 1.10 percent account would have gained $11,561. And, when the economy is healthier— like a few years ago when 3 percent savings accounts weren't uncommon, the returns are that much better.

"Those who are free of resentful thoughts surely find peace."

—Buddha

Don't Harbor a Grudge

Eventually, someone—be it a friend, a partner, or a stranger—will cause you grief. They might say something hurtful, forget something important, or just cut you off in traffic. Your natural reaction might be to explode or to bury the hurt inside and let it create anger or resentment toward this person, and you might let it ruin your whole day. Instead of giving this moment power, try to give the offending person the benefit of the doubt that they probably did not intend to hurt you. Sometimes, we all forget to think before we act or speak.

On the other hand, if the person was just being a downright jerk, realize that their action or outburst probably wasn't caused by you but rather by something going on in their own lives and you were just in the wrong place at the wrong time. But if that person was responding to something you did or said, think of how you could act differently in the future. When the injurious person is a friend or loved one, being able to sit down with the person and express that he or she hurt you can be an important step in the healing process. When this type of closure isn't possible, try your best to work through the pain on your own and release it so it doesn't continue to injure you or those around you.

"When you go to the grocery store, you find that the cheapest calories are the ones that are going to make you the fattest— the added sugars and fats in processed foods."

—Michael Pollan

Limit Refined Sugar and Watch Out for Hidden Sugar

To help lose weight, it's important to limit the amount of refined sugar you're consuming. That's because sugar adds calories but doesn't add anything to your body in terms of vitamins or minerals, so while it tastes good, it isn't doing anything good for you. In fact, some studies show it might be doing you some serious harm and increasing your chances of high blood pressure, type 2 diabetes, and high triglycerides, not to mention that eating a diet heavy in sugar will make your energy levels peak and then plummet.

Refined sugar differs from naturally occurring sugar that is found in fruits and dairy, because it is sugar that is added to a product to make it taste different. You don't have to watch out for natural sugars as much, but do be careful of how much refined sugar you're consuming.

The easiest way to avoid eating sugar is to avoid processed foods that are found in jars, boxes, cans, etc. But if you choose to eat these food products, do your best to limit your sugar intake to less than 10 percent of your daily caloric intake. It's important to know the many names under which sugar lurks because it isn't always listed as "sugar." For more hidden sugar types, go to *www.fitsugar.com/Other-Names-Sugar-Appear-Labels-810571*.

"No diet will remove all the fat from the body because the brain is entirely fat. Without a brain, you might look good, but all you could do is run for public office."

—George Bernard Shaw

Don't Surrender All Fats

As you cut back on the fats within your diet to achieve optimum brain health and also to possibly lose weight, don't be tempted to avoid all fats. Some fats, in moderation, are good for you. This is because nearly two-thirds of your brain is made of fat! And the myelin sheath—the protective membrane that covers the neurons in your brain—is composed of 70 percent fat, mostly fatty acids such as oleic acid (an acid found in avocados, olive oil, and nuts). These membranes are being constantly recycled throughout your lifetime, which means that the fats you ingest play a role in building these protective sheaths.

The omega-3 fatty acid DHA and the omega-6 fatty acid arachidonic acid (AA) are other important fats for the brain. DHA makes up 50 percent of a neuron's membrane and is necessary for healthy brain development. Alzheimer's, depression, and overall cognitive decline have been connected with DHA deficiency. Fish oil and grass-fed beef are two good sources of this fatty acid. AA is also found in the brain's protective membranes. It helps guard the brain against stress and assists with the repair and growth of neurons. You probably don't need to take a supplement of AA, as it's readily available in dairy products, eggs, and beef.

"We've discovered the secret of life."

—Francis Crick

Meet Your Amino Acid Needs

When you eat proteins, the digestive system breaks down the protein into amino acids, which help create important molecules, or they help to build another protein.

There are twenty standard amino acids. Twelve of these are produced by your body, while the other eight are known as essential amino acids and must be consumed. Animal sources of protein are known as complete proteins because they contain all eight essential amino acids, while, for the most part vegetarian sources do not. By combining certain vegetables together, such as brown rice and beans, you can supply your body with all essential amino acids. The other vegetarian sources that are complete proteins are quinoa, buckwheat, amaranth, soy, hemp, and spirulina.

THE EIGHT ESSENTIAL AMINO ACIDS	
Name	Function
Isoleucine	Required for hemoglobin formation; stabilizes blood sugar
Leucine	Heals muscle, bone, and skin tissue
Lysine	Assists with calcium absorption; aids in formation of collagen and antibodies
Methionine	Serves as antioxidant; protects against radiation; reduces histamine levels; helps with breakdown of fats
Phenylaline	Necessary for production of norepinephrine; improves mood, lessens pain; boosts memory and learning
Threonine	Key to the formation of collagen, elastin, and enamel; prevents buildup of fat in liver
Tryptophan	Building block for serotonin and niacin; regulates mood, sleep, and appetite
Valine	Used in tissue repair; acts as an energy source for muscle tissue

"I find it very difficult to draw a line between what's sex and what isn't. It can be very, very sexy to drive a car, and completely unsexy to flirt with someone at a bar.

—Björk

Create Your Arousal Map

Do you know what gets you hot and bothered? Before you step into bed again with your current partner or with a new one, take the time to figure out what gets you from zero to wanting to jump their bones. Is there an order of events that gets you particularly revved up? Think of this as your arousal map or your sexual blueprint. They're different for all of us, and when you're having a hard time getting in the mood, it will help to put yourself on that path.

To get those wheels turning, think of the times you felt most aroused. Was there a particular smell in the air or on your partner? Was the light a certain way? Were you or your partner wearing something you found sexy? In what way did your partner touch you? How much sexual tension had been built up between you and your partner before any actual touching occurred? If you have yet to feel turned on with a partner, think of what makes you turned on when you look at visual images or read sexy literature. Are there particular scenarios that you find hot?

As you develop your map, don't censor yourself. Something that may seem taboo to you at first—such as bondage—may be very normal to someone else and something that person is happy to try with you!

"At least for today, do not be angry. Do not worry. Be grateful."

—Mikao Usui

Experience the Healing Power of Energy

In the 1920s, Japanese Buddhist Mikao Usai started teaching a healing technique that we now call Reiki. Those who practice and partake in Reiki believe that energy flows through the palms of the person doing the healing into the person who is being healed. The Reiki, or energy, will flow to where it is needed in order to clear physical, spiritual, or emotional blockages that are preventing you from being able to heal or move forward in a positive direction within your life. It is also believed that very experienced Reiki practitioners are able to heal others even when they are far away.

During a typical Reiki session, you (as the person who has requested healing) lie down on a table, fully clothed. The practitioner places his or her palms on or just above your body and holds them in this position for a few minutes before moving them to another place on your body.

Scientists have begun to conduct studies to determine whether they can prove within a clinical setting that Reiki can reduce pain, depression, and have a healing effect on illness.

"Happiness: a good bank account, a good cook,
and a good digestion."

—Jean-Jacques Rousseau

Use a Checking Account That Offers High Interest

Like with your savings account, it's important that your money is earning as much as it can at all times, particularly if it's not invested in a CD, stock, or mutual fund. And while checking accounts have always had lower rates than savings accounts, you shouldn't settle for the one your bank offers just because it's convenient. Take the time to look around both offline and online, using sites such as Money-Rates.com, to find the bank or credit union that offers you the highest return on your money.

> **TRY AN ONLINE, HIGH-INTEREST CHECKING ACCOUNT**
>
> Traditionally, banks have offered very low rates for checking accounts. Even though it's not as crucial to have a high-interest checking account as it is to have a high-interest savings account because your money isn't in there as long, you should make your money work as hard as it can for you. Online checking accounts provide you with a debit card and allow you to use certain ATMs for free, so it's similar to using a brick-and-mortar bank but there are less overhead costs for them so they can often offer you better rates. Some even will mail your checks for you so you save on time and postage.

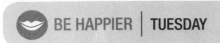

*"You may have a fresh start any moment you choose,
for this thing that we call Failure is not the falling down
but the staying down."*

—Mary Pickford

Put a Troubling Moment in Perspective

You're having a bad day. The worst of all days. Someone or something has died. There's been an awful natural disaster. Your partner split up with you. You got fired. Unfortunately, these things happen, and sometimes, to fully process them you need to go through the seven stages of grief: denial/shock, pain/guilt, anger/bargaining, depression/reflection, the lift of sadness, reconstruction, and acceptance/hope. But there is a light at the end of the tunnel, and the original moment of trauma has passed. You do not have to live through that precise moment again, and with the help of your support system, you can work through it.

In less serious matters, when there has been a fight or your car got a flat tire or you find out the one who got away just got married, try to put the moment in perspective. Ask yourself how important this moment is of all the moments you will experience. Remember that you should allow no one to take away your happiness, and force yourself to think of the good things that go on in your life. This moment will not last forever—you will not be stuck forever with a flat tire, a bad haircut, or the nasty words someone spewed at you in a fight. These things can be fixed. They may require the help of a professional or the strength to walk away, but when you're feeling thrown, just remember you will not endure these feelings forever and do not waste your energy or sacrifice your happiness by reliving them.

"We are what we imagine ourselves to be."

—Kurt Vonnegut, Jr.

Use Visualization

Earlier, you learned about the power of positive visualization. One of the ways you can use this technique is to achieve your weight-loss goals. This visualization has two parts. First, instead of looking at yourself and seeing your flaws, look at what you love about yourself. Whether it's your eyes, your nails, your skin, or your stomach, find at least a few things that you think are beautiful about yourself, and whenever you're looking in the mirror, turn your attention toward those. This way, as you work to reach your fitness goals, instead of feeling discouraged when you look in the mirror, you'll feel happy and that positive attitude will help you work through those tough workout weeks. As you transform your body, you'll also start to find even more things to love!

Second, start to imagine what your ideal body looks like. Is there a picture of you from years ago in which you're a size you want to get back to? Stick that on the fridge or on the bathroom mirror as inspiration. If you don't have a photo of yourself like that, look through magazines and find someone who has a body that you want to strive for. Just keep in mind that most images in magazines are enhanced, so even that person might not look that way in real life. Imagine yourself achieving this shape while you're working out or when you are getting ready for your day, and you'll start to find that you manifest this destiny by making changes in your life that guide you toward it.

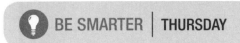

"I remember Gene always had to take cod's liver oil or drink yeast with orange juice. As a result, he's like six inches taller than me."

—Paul Elias, fisherman

Take Fish Oil

Be Smarter! Thinner! Healthier! Just by taking fish oil! Goodness, sounds like these health nuts are hocking snake oil and "magic" cures, doesn't it? But it's not. Fish oil refers to omega-3 fatty acids, eicosapentaenoic acid (EPA), and docosahexanoic acid (DHA), which together help protect the body and the brain. When these three acids are combined, they can help ward off the onset of Parkinson's, Alzheimer's, and schizophrenia and can reduce the effects of mild to moderate depression. Look for a supplement that contains at least 300 mg of EPA and 200 mg of DHA in each serving and take two of these every day. *Note: If you have a condition that puts you at an increased risk of bleeding, speak with your doctor before adding these to your daily regimen.*

WHICH FISH OIL IS BEST?

Head to your local pharmacy or health food store and you might find yourself overwhelmed with your choice in fish oils. Since PCBs (chemicals that can cause birth defects and cancer) were recently discovered in some popular brands of fish oil, it's important to look for the following:

- The bottle states the type of fish from which the oil was sourced and the fish's location (wild anchovies and sardines are the best)
- Companies that claim their oils are tested by third parties for mercury levels, PCBs, and toxic chemicals might be safer
- Supplements with much higher levels of EPA may be more effective in helping to treat depression and other cognitive issues

"Everybody has different perceptions, but olive oil and fish with its omega-3 oils are good for you. In my life, I have fish once a week."

—Linda Johnson, poker player

Love Those Omega-3s

Who thought something fatty could be so good for you? Not only are omega-3 fatty acids great for the brain, they're also great for your heart and your diet. They help reduce inflammation in the body, which aids in relieving joint pain, and they help your body maintain normal blood sugar and blood pressure levels, lower bad cholesterol levels, decrease the risk of stroke, and protect the heart. In addition, according to studies conducted by the University of Southern Australia, they can help you to lose weight faster because they help burn fat. Most fish, but especially wild salmon, are great sources of this fatty acid.

If you don't eat fish, opt for flaxseed. It contains the most omega-3 fatty acids of all plant sources and has three grams of fiber per tablespoon. Other good sources of omega-3s are walnuts, kidney beans, broccoli, spinach, fortified eggs, cabbage, and soybeans.

BREAKDOWN OF OMEGA 3 LEVELS

It's important to achieve your daily Omega-3 needs, but you probably don't want to eat salmon every day. To make wise choices, take a look at this list we've culled with help from *www.WHFoods.com*.

- Flaxseed (2 tablespoons, 146.3%)
- Walnuts (.25 cups, 95.6%)
- Soybeans (1 cup, 42.9 %)
- Sardines (one fish, 56.7%)
- Salmon (4 ounces, 87%)

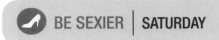

"Sex is a two-way treat."

—Franklin P. Jones, engineer

Change Your Definition of Treating Yourself

Want to be sexier and healthier? Stop treating food as a treat! If you've had a hard week or month at work or have been good about sticking to your workout schedule and you need a "treat" to reenergize you, I can empathize. But instead of reaching for something unhealthy that will likely cause your sugar levels to peak and then your mood to plummet, replace your food treat with something more lasting. Promise yourself you'll get that pair of shoes you've been wanting, take yourself out to a ball game, or splurge on a spa day. Think about what really makes you smile, what makes you feel confident, or what makes you feel sexy, and you'll be happier in the long run, because you'll be able to look at an item or remember a memorable experience and what you did to earn it. That sense of inner pride will surely make you shine and attract good people to you.

BUILD TREATS INTO YOUR LIFE

It's important that you treat yourself, just don't do it with junk food. If you're working toward a goal, write down a list of twenty-five things you would like and determine the effort you'd have to put in to "earn" that item. If you just want to find ways to take the edge off after a hard day or week, write down a list of twenty-five actions that make you feel rejuvenated. Keep these lists handy and when you reach a goal or have a stressful event, turn to them to pick yourself up or reward yourself for a job well done.

"Happiness is not a matter of intensity but of balance and order and rhythm and harmony."

—Thomas Merton

Tune Up Your Chakras

According to Hindu and Buddhist texts, chakras are the centers of energy that align along the spine from the top of the head to the tailbone. Some believe that they can be energized to spin at their proper frequency. When off-balance or they are producing too much or too little energy, poor health can result. If you've noticed that one part of your body or your life is consistently out of order, see if there are one or two chakras of the seven major ones below that correspond to your issue. Practices such as acupuncture, tai chi, Reiki, and certain types of massage can help tune up your chakras.

NUMBER	NAME	LOCATION	ELEMENT	COLOR
First	Muladhara	Perineum	Earth	Red
ASSOCIATION: Confidence, a realistic concept of our body and its needs, security in the physical comforts of life				
Second	Svadhishthana	Genitals	Water	Orange
ASSOCIATION: Pleasure, sexuality, stable emotions, gracefulness, self-acceptance, creativity				
Third	Manapura	Solar plexus/navel	Fire	Yellow
ASSOCIATION: Ego, self-esteem, energy, authority, longevity, reliability, independence				
Fourth	Anahata	Heart	Air	Green
ASSOCIATION: Sharing, love, service, compassion, devotion				
Five	Vishuddha	Throat	Space	Violet
ASSOCIATION: Truth, knowledge				
Six	Anja	Pineal gland/third eye	None	Bluish-white
ASSOCIATION: Enlightenment, self-realization, self-mastery, intuition, insight				
Seven	Sahasrara	Fontanel/top of head	Lotus flower	Golden-white light
ASSOCIATION: Supreme consciousness, compassion, self-awareness, mindfulness, awareness of the world				

"I don't like money, actually, but it calms my nerves."

—Joe Louis

Automatically Build an Emergency Fund

Back in week six, you learned the pros of automating your savings—one of which is so that when things go south (and, as Murphy's Law predicts, they inevitably will at some point or another), you'll be prepared. Whether you've been hit with a natural disaster, your car breaks down, you lose your job, or worse, you're likely to feel pretty stressed. And if you don't have any savings to fall back on to help you through this tough time, you'll be that much more stressed. It's not a good place to be.

But if you prepare yourself for such an event, you'll be that much more equipped to deal with the experience and able to move forward with greater ease. Since you've already set up an automated savings account (you have done that, right?), section off part of that savings account as an emergency fund so you know that cash isn't going to come out of college savings, fun money, or anything else. Think of this money as you would an umbrella. If you step outside on a rainy day and have an umbrella, you're still not going to be happy that it's raining and you'll probably get a little wet, but you won't get soaked. Same with the emergency fund. If disaster strikes, you're not going to like it but at least you'll be prepared.

"I find hope in the darkest of days, and focus in the brightest."

—Dalai Lama

See the Glass as Half Full

Feeling happy isn't as easy as just saying, "I'm happy! Things are great!" But that sort of attitude doesn't hurt. As you've learned, you can trick your brain into believing things are going well or poorly in your life. It's all in how you frame it. The happiest people out there aren't always the ones who had great childhoods, were successful early in life, or were born beautiful. They're the people who, when they create the story of their lives, create a story in which they're the hero, not the victim.

If you can work to see the glass as half full, see the silver lining in a cloudy day, and find a way to paint your memories in a positive light, you're on your way to a life filled with happiness.

Here are some mantras you can begin your day with to get yourself on the right path:

- "I am love. I am loved."
- "I will enjoy myself today."
- "No matter what happens, I won't judge myself."
- "Today will be a good day."

"Get people back into the kitchen and combat the trend toward processed food and fast food."

—Andrew Weil

Avoid Sugar Substitutes

You know to avoid added sugar, but does this mean you should stay away from food products with sugar-free substitutes, like diet soda? Surprisingly, yes. While added sugar isn't good for you, sugar substitutes (honey and molasses excluded) are worse. Ingredients like saccharine have been known to cause cancer in rats, and long-term studies have yet to be done on newer sugar replacements, such as Splenda.

But beyond the potential long-term health impact, sugar substitutes can make you fat. That's because they make it harder for our bodies to recognize when we're full, and some researchers suggest that the use of artificial sweeteners may convince the body that sugar-laden foods are actually low in calories. In fact, one study showed that for each can of diet soda the participants drank, their chance of becoming obese went up 41 percent.

If you crave drinks like soda, try making the switch to unsweetened sparkling water instead. It has the carbonation of soda but doesn't have the calories. And if you make your own sparkling water with the use of a soda siphon, you'll be helping the environment while you get healthy!

"A fat stomach never breeds fine thoughts."

—St. Jerome

Use Omegas to Stabilize Mood Swings

Omega-3s are great for preventing cognitive decline and for improving your overall health, but did you know they can also improve your stress levels and improve your overall mood? If you're prone to depression or mood swings, you might want to take note of recent research showing that adding omega-3s or fish oil to your diet can have a profound impact that might be equivalent to that of a prescription antidepressant. Researchers have found that the levels of omega-3s are lower in those who suffer from depression, and they theorize that adding it back into the diet either with food or with a supplement can help reverse this imbalance.

Other studies have shown that a concentrated form of E-EPA—a type of fish oil that has a much higher level of EPA and much lower level of DPA than other varieties—can have a profound impact on depression and other mental health problems and in reducing stress levels. However, E-EPA can be hard to find and the research is relatively new, so you might want to wait until more research has been done before trying this alternative to regular fish oil.

Note: If you are taking an antidepressant, do not stop taking it and replace it with an omega-3 supplement unless you have your doctor's approval.

*"If a queen bee were crossed with a Friesian bull,
would not the land flow with milk and honey?"*

—Oliver St. John

Create Homemade Beauty Products

You don't have to book an expensive facial at a spa to rejuvenate the look of your skin. External use of common household products can go a long way in making you look great. Apple cider vinegar adds shine to your hair. Lemon juice can be used to reduce oily skin. Cucumber slices alleviate puffiness around the eyes. Mashed, cold bananas can be used to make your face look fuller. By combining oatmeal and whole milk together, you'll create an excellent exfoliant. To make an all-natural facial scrub, combine one tablespoon of olive oil with three tablespoons of sea salt. The list goes on, and the great part about these homemade beauty products is that they're easy on your budget and they don't contain any chemicals that could harm you.

Here's a recipe for a facial mask to try if you want to soften your skin:

1. Mix one raw egg yolk with enough honey to create a spreadable mixture.
2. Wash your face with warm water, then apply the mixture.
3. Wait until the mask has dried completely, about a half hour, and then gently wipe it off with a warm, damp washcloth.
4. Rinse your face with cool water.

For a tighter feeling, use only an egg white and follow the same steps.

"Those Kegel muscle exercises are really paying off, huh?"

—From *American Pie Presents: Beta House*

Do Your Kegels

Want to feel a super intense orgasm? Then do your kegels. Kegel exercises are traditionally used to strengthen the vagina's PC muscle (short for *pubococcygeus*) in preparation for bearing down during childbirth and to help your bladder from leaking in your later years. But doing kegels also improves orgasms, because when you're aroused the PC muscle automatically sends signals to the brain, which causes the brain to send signals that you're aroused to the body. The more the PC muscle pulses, the more signals of arousal the brain sends back. When this muscle is toned, it can pulse more often—which, as you might imagine, heightens orgasm. It also can allow the potential for multiple orgasms and female ejaculation for women and for stronger erections and orgasm without ejaculation for men if men squeeze their own PC muscle just before ejaculation is achieved.

To find the PC muscle, put your fingers between your vagina and anus or between your testicles and anus. Now pretend you are urinating and need to hold it for a moment. Those muscles you feel tightening are the PC muscles. In order to exercise the PC muscle, or to do kegels, all you do is squeeze to lift the muscles and then release them. Start out with 10–15 repetitions a day, making sure to fully relax between each time you tighten the muscle to achieve maximum toning.

"Within you there is a stillness and a sanctuary to which you can retreat at any time and be yourself."

—Herman Hesse

Learn to Meditate

In the 1960s, tests conducted by Harvard cardiologist Herbert Benson revealed that when a person sits silently with her or his mind focused on a single thought, word, or idea, that person's heart rate slowed, stress levels decreased, muscle tension relaxed, and cortisol and adrenaline levels dropped. Benson coined the term the "relaxation response" to describe these physiological changes that meditation will elicit. Benson believes that any activity in which you feel you are "one" with what you are doing and in which you see the hours disappear as you're happily focused on something can have the same effect.

Meditation can also work to improve your self-esteem and help you avoid negative thought patterns. Other studies show it can improve cognitive function and memory.

To practice a basic meditation, find a quiet space where you will not be interrupted for at least thirty minutes. Take off your shoes, get into a comfortable sitting position, and close your eyes. Turn off the lights if you find them distracting. Now, begin to breathe deeply and try to clear your mind. As you do, allow your mind to flow where it wants but allow thoughts and images to pass without judgment or engagement. Don't get discouraged if this is harder than you thought it would be. Eventually, by practicing meditation regularly, you will be able to clear your mind and allow it to rest.

"I put my money in the bank: I have to think of life after modeling, when I'm not famous any more."

—Eva Herzigova

Open Up a 401(k) or 403(b) Now

Does your work offer a 401(k) or 403(b) plan? If so, sign up right now. Having a solid 401(k) or 403(b) is like having that emergency fund umbrella, except this one is for your retirement.

The great part about both of these plans is that the money is taken out of your paycheck pre-tax, just like your medical benefits. In doing so, you'll reduce the amount you're taxed on, and thus the net amount you receive won't go down as much as you think, even if you're contributing 10 percent. If, at any time, you want to contribute more or need to contribute less, you can make that adjustment.

One note of caution, though. Try your best not to raid your plan when you need money. The tax penalties for taking out cash from these plans is high if you haven't yet reached retirement age. If you happen to lose your job, also understand that your 401(k) will stay with that company until you find a new job, at which time you can roll it over without cost.

Bonus! Some employers offer to match contributions up to a certain amount. If you can make it fit your budget, and by all means try to, contribute the maximum they will match. Not only will this mean you're putting away money for your own future, but you'll be doubling that with practically free money!

"Sometimes your joy is the source of your smile, but sometimes your smile can be the source of your joy."

—Thich Nhat Hanh

Smile More Often

The more often you smile, the happier you'll be. And you might even live longer! A recent study that examined the smiles of retired baseball players found that those who smiled big lived longer than those who didn't. Perhaps that's because the mere act of smiling can make you feel happy and happier people tend to live longer than those wrought up with angst. If you're in a negative mood, you can improve it just by smiling. That's because when you activate the smile muscles, you're telling your brain that you're happy. And this creates a positive feedback loop within your body. Though it might not be easy at first and you might not *feel* like smiling, smiling for a count of ten and then deepening the smile and holding it can actually shift your mood in a positive direction, even if you're faking it.

Plus, when you smile, you attract other positive people to you. It's a great cycle: smile at someone and he or she might smile back, which will make you feel good and want to smile more!

"The first time I ate organic whole-grain bread,
I swear it tasted like roofing material."

—Robin Williams

Eat More Complex Carbs

Thankfully, things have improved since Robin Williams first tried organic whole-grain bread. Carbohydrates are important to helping your body and brain function. In addition to being absolutely necessary for survival, without enough of them you might become crabby and depressed. On the other hand, if you consume a lot of simple carbohydrates, like sugar, fruits, and milk (though the latter two are also great sources of nutrients), they will rapidly raise your blood sugar levels and your body will quickly burn through the fuel they provide.

To avoid crabbiness and provide your body with fuel that will last, opt for complex carbohydrates instead. These longer-chained molecules take more time for your body to digest and also won't spike your blood-sugar levels. They're also more likely to be packed with fiber and more nutrients than simple carbohydrates. So swap out your refined carbs (white bread, white rice, etc.) for whole-grain choices like brown rice, whole-wheat bread, and grains like quinoa. Add more vegetables, beans, and nuts to your meals and snacks, as well.

"Keep a quiet heart, sit like a tortoise, walk sprightly like a pigeon, and sleep like a dog."

—Li Ching-Yun

Try Kola for the Brain

Soda is horrible for you, but gotu kola (*Centella asiatica*) is awesome. Not to be confused with the caffeinated kola nut, this ancient herb that grows in Australia and in Southeastern Asia has become known as the "food for the brain" because of its ability to alleviate stress, improve concentration, prevent Alzheimer's disease, and strengthen memory. It can also enhance your reflexes and improve circulation, reduce varicose veins, and lower blood pressure because it's believed to strengthen the walls of the veins and capillaries.

Though it's most popularly used in the West in the form of a supplement, people in Southeast Asia use the leaves for the base of some of their salads. You can also use it to make a pesto or steep the leaves to make tea. Follow in the footsteps of Li Ching Yun, a Chinese man who, according to the *New York Times*, *Time Magazine*, and Chinese records, died in 1933 at the age of 256. It is said that this longevity master ate gotu kola, *goji* berries, *he shou wu*, and ginseng on a daily basis and practiced inner calm.

However, do keep in mind that this herb should not be used by pregnant women or anyone with a thyroid condition.

"The wise ones fashioned speech with their thought, sifting it as grain is sifted through a sieve."

—Buddha

Eat Quinoa

Known as the mother grain to the Incas, this nutty, grain-like plant contains all nine essential amino acids, and each 3.5–ounce portion is packed with fourteen grams of protein and just sixty-four calories. No wonder it's also known as the "gold of the Incas," especially by vegans and vegetarians who can use it as an effective substitute to the protein they would receive from eating animals.

Not only can this psuedocereal help you combat diabetes, hardening of the arteries, migraines, and heart disease, it also contains high levels of potassium and magnesium, which are good for lowering blood pressure. In addition to feeling younger, this nutritious protein will also help you to look younger because of its extra-high lysine levels, an amino acid that aids in tissue growth and repair. To dine on quinoa, make sure to rinse it first to remove the bitter coating of saponins. Then, feel free to eat it as a breakfast food or as a side dish in place of rice.

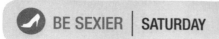
"The eyes are the mirror of the soul."

—Yiddish proverb

What Lovely Eyes You Have

Over the course of a relationship, partners can start to drift apart. The distance can affect their love life and their sex life, but as long as there was originally a strong foundation, the two can come back together by working to heal their lack of intimacy. Small events like laughing together, sharing new experiences, and taking pleasure in the other's interests can help rebuild what has been lost. This more in-depth exercise can also help build or restore intimacy to your relationship:

Eye gazing: They say the eyes are the windows into the soul. That is very romantic, but for some people it can be frightening. Looking and holding another's gaze can make you feel very vulnerable, especially in a new relationship or in one that has caused a lot of hurt. But it can also be a way to reconnect.

To engage in this exercise, sit across from your partner and look into each other's eyes for five to ten minutes (set a timer, if necessary). Try to resist the need to be silly and instead notice the look in your lover's eyes and the emotions you feel. When the physical part of the exercise is complete, share what thoughts arose for you. You can use the "hand-on-heart/soul sharing exercise" in Week Twenty-Five if that helps.

"You can make it with meditation if you're a Christian, a Mohammedan, or a Jew. You just add meditation to whatever religion you've got."

—John Lennon

Practice Mantra Meditation

There are many types of meditations, all of them relaxing, but mantra meditation is one of the easiest for beginners to practice. It's the type we associate most readily in our minds with traditional meditation, as it's what we've seen in film and on television. Mantra meditation is the type of meditation that requires you to repeat a sound and concentrate on it as the focus of your meditation. This word, or group of words, can be anything, from a simple noise, to a single word such as "om," to a full prayer that you repeat. You can even create your own mantra, such as "I am loved," to focus on during your meditation. Anything that brings you comfort will do.

To prepare for practice, find a tranquil place in which you can sit, take a few deep breaths, and start to slowly repeat the mantra with every exhale. Begin slowly and do not get discouraged if you have interrupting thoughts. Just allow them to fade away. Eventually, as you put your energy into this, the rest of the world will drop away and your thoughts will become clear.

"Like almost everyone who uses e-mail, I receive a ton of spam every day. Much of it offers to help me get out of debt or get rich quick. It would be funny if it weren't so irritating."

—Bill Gates

Contribute Regularly to That Investment Account

Congratulations on signing up for an investment account so that you can save for your retirement. Whether your account is an IRA, a 401(k), or a 403(b), it's important to keep contributing. With 401(k)s and 403(b)s, it's pretty easy. When you signed up, you put down a percentage that would be deducted from each paycheck and go into this account. Unless you absolutely must lower this percentage, don't.

On the other hand, with an IRA, the burden is usually on you to make regular contributions. Consider setting up an automatic withdrawal on your checking account so the funds for these retirement accounts are removed at regular intervals without you having to think about them. Considering you can't invest more than $5,000 per year into a traditional IRA and up to $6,000 into a Roth IRA, if you space those contributions apart during the year, it won't be too painful on your wallet, and after even just ten years, you'll be impressed by how much it's grown.

"I don't like myself, I'm crazy about myself"

—Mae West

Write Yourself a Love List

It's so easy to criticize yourself. Perhaps you too aren't happy with how much money you're making, or what you look like, or that you're taller/shorter/thinner/fatter, etc. than the person who just stole the heart of the one you were interested in or the person who got a job instead of you. Stop.

Instead of hitching a ride on the negative train again, write down at least three things you admire about yourself. (A list of three is long enough to spark your brain to think of other things and short enough to easily remember.) Anything from inner to outer beauty is acceptable, but stay true to yourself as you're writing. Are you good with animals? Compassionate? Have great legs? Know how to whip up a mean homemade dish? Whatever it is, write it down and then put it up somewhere you know you'll look at it every day, be it the fridge, next to your computer keyboard, tucked it into your wallet, or pasted on the bathroom mirror so you can be reminded of just how awesome you are each and every day.

"Life expectancy would grow by leaps and bounds if green vegetables smelled as good as bacon."

—Doug Larson

Choose Lean Protein

To lose weight and for your body to function at its best, you need to eat carbohydrates, proteins, and fats. The food choices you make in each of those categories plays a big role in how effective your weight-loss strategy will be and how easy or difficult the process will be for you. Some foods will make you feel more full, while others will leave you hungry for more.

When it comes to carbohydrates, you know that complex carbohydrates, like brown rice and quinoa, are better than simple carbs, like white rice and pasta. For fats, you know that unsaturated fats are best and you should choose olive oil and avocados over coconut butter and whole-fat dairy products.

When you are selecting the proteins for your meal, reach for lean proteins. The healthiest proteins you can eat are poultry; deep-water fish, such as tuna, mackerel, and salmon; shrimp; and legumes. These proteins are low in calories and overall fat, and some provide other important nutrients. For example, a three-ounce serving of lean, broiled turkey contains eleven grams of fat versus seventeen for beef and eighteen for pork. If you do decide to dine on proteins that contain saturated fat, such as beef, make sure to trim as much fat off the protein as possible in order to cut down on the harmful fats and the total calories. The best lean proteins are:

- Skinless chicken breast
- Skinless turkey breast
- Egg whites
- Shellfish
- Fat-free dairy products
- Beans
- Fish

"Sage helps the nerves and by its powerful might palsy
is cured and fever put to flight"

—Unknown (French)

Try Sage and Lemon Balm to Improve Your Memory

Though the herb may have little to do with wise gurus of the same name, dining on sage may improve your memory and your overall cognitive function. A British team of scientists conducted a trial to see if sage lived up to its hype. When given a memory test before and after taking sage oil, those who took the sage oil scored much higher the second time around than those who were given a placebo. Another study found that sage can have a measurable impact on those suffering from mild to moderate Alzheimer's disease. Sage can be used in cooking or taken as an essential oil.

Another brain-friendly herb is lemon balm. Otherwise known as Melissa (Melissa officinalis), lemon balm is actually a member of the mint family and unrelated to the lemon, though the leaves taste like the citric fruit. Native to Europe and the Mediterranean, it has been known to reduce stress, and despite its ability to act as a mild sedative, it was revealed by scientists in 2003 that it can also improve learning and memory. Lemon balm also has powerful antioxidant properties, so not only can it help your brain learn, it can also help keep it young. Lemon balm is most commonly found in supplement form.

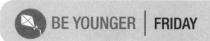

"Have a mouth as sharp as a dagger, but a heart as soft as tofu."

—Chinese proverb

Try Tofu

Some people shy away from tofu because they're unsure about the taste or the consistency, but they shouldn't—because tofu takes on the flavors you use with it and can be found in a variety of consistencies. There's soft tofu, which is great in soup, and firmer tofu, which can be used in stir-fry and other dishes in place of animal protein.

Tofu, which is made from soybean milk, is extremely high in protein, and unlike animal products, it doesn't contain cholesterol. Though a long-term study has revealed it also is unlikely to lower cholesterol levels, it can help maintain consistent blood sugar levels, which makes it an excellent choice for diabetics. In addition, tofu also has no saturated fat and is an excellent source of fiber and nutrients, such as calcium, vitamin E, and a variety of B vitamins.

"There are two kinds of light—the glow that illumines, and the glare that obscures."

—James Thurber

Choose Mood Lighting

That overhead spotlight has got to go. It's important to have soft, romantic lighting in your bedroom that can create sexy shadows on your body. The lights that are most often installed in apartments, dorm rooms, and houses by the builders or former owners usually are of the utilitarian variety. They are very effective at lighting a room. And, that's great . . . until you want to have sex. Or be romantic. Or do anything except read or work on a model car. So take down the interrogation light and replace it with lights you can dim or a light that creates a pleasant glow across the room on its own.

If you're not permitted to replace the light fixtures, then purchase some lamps that will create the same effect and don't turn on the other light. If all else fails, buy candles and light these when you're setting the mood, and you could even use them during sex. Candles come in many sizes, shapes, colors, and scents and are also available unscented if you or your partner are sensitive. Just remember to extinguish these before going to bed or leaving the house, as burning down the house is not a turn-on.

"As soon as you trust yourself, you will know how to live."

—Johann Wolfgang von Goethe

Trust Yourself

When you're immersed in a complicated emotional situation, it can be easier for you to let your brain take over and use logic to reason your way out of it. But in these tricky moments, rationalizing is not the way to go. You have to let your gut and your heart lead you instead of convincing yourself of reasons to make one choice or another. Your body knows what is best and will point you in the right direction, like the needle on a compass. To reconnect with your emotional guidance system, sit quietly with yourself and breathe. Unlike with meditation, sit with the thoughts and feelings and allow yourself to feel them instead of brushing them away and turning to your rational mind for help.

Even in less emotionally complicated situations, such as trying to decide whether to take a job offer, it's important that you are able to trust yourself and rely on yourself to make difficult decisions. Consult with friends and loved ones if you need or choose to do so, but ultimately, if a decision is yours to make, have faith in yourself to choose the right path.

"Successful investing is anticipating the anticipations of others."

—John Maynard Keynes

Consult with an Investment Expert

If the words "diversified portfolio" make your eyes glaze over, it might be wise to meet with an investment expert who can be your guide as you create a financial strategy that fits your long-term and short-term goals. A financial planner already knows the ins and outs of the tax code and how to balance complicated needs. A solid financial planner will help you build a nest egg, move out of debt, plan for your future, choose stocks wisely, and deal with the paperwork.

When you're ready to hire someone to help you with your fiscal matters, look for someone who has passed the Certified Financial Planner Board of Statistics exam and has earned a CFP. Make sure that the person listens to your goals and that you have a good gut feeling about the planner. After all, you are taking advice about what to do with your money. If you meet with a planner who pushes you to be riskier with your money than you think is wise (sometimes those who make their money from commissions instead of a flat fee do this) or boasts he or she can make your portfolio do better than the market, go with someone else. You can find fee-based planners by looking for leads through the National Associate of Personal Financial Advisers (NAPFA) or the Garrett Planning Network.

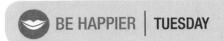

> *"If you don't like the road you're walking,*
> *start paving another one."*
>
> —Dolly Parton

Write Your Vision of a Purposeful Life

Are you following the path you've always wanted to be on? If not and you're displeased about it or don't even know what path you should be on, start contemplating your life's purpose. What do you believe you're meant to do? In what areas of your life do you succeed easily? What activities make you feel the most refreshed and exhilarated? What places have you visited that have given you the feeling of home? How do you see your family life evolving?

As you start to think about where you fit in, start to think about what actions you need to take to put yourself on this path. It might be necessary to make some major life changes in order for you to refocus your life so you're following the path that will lead to your utmost happiness. Should that be the case, don't make these decisions rashly. While without risk there is often no reward, sometimes risk is not required. But as some doors close, you'll see others open.

Once you've set yourself on this new path, continue to revisit your vision and update it, but always stay true to yourself. If you start to reach your goal, make a bigger one. As the saying goes, If you reach for the moon, you might not make it, but you'll land in the stars.

"Not eating meat is a decision. Eating meat is an instinct."

—Denis Leary

Trim the Fat from Your Meat

Here's an easy way to shed calories: trim the fat off of your meat. Although you'll need some fat to enhance flavor, if there is excess fat on the edges of your protein, trim it off before cooking it. In doing so, you'll not only reduce the overall amount of fat in your diet, you'll also reduce the most harmful type of fat: saturated fat.

When trimming fat, always use a sharp knife, and if you can, arrange the protein so that the fat is closest to you. Hold onto a small piece of this fat and insert your knife in between the fat and the meat. As you cut, keep the fat taut and don't try to cut it all off at once. If you've tried this method and are still having trouble, consider putting the meat in the freezer for twenty minutes so that the fat can solidify before allowing it to reach room temperature for cooking. Never thaw meat and put it back in the freezer, as this is a great way to trap harmful bacteria.

*"Their smiles / wan as primroses gathered at midnight
/ by chilly-fingered spring."*

—John Keats

Take Primrose Capsules

When your heart is healthy, your brain is healthier. Evening primrose, a wildflower native to North America, Europe, and parts of Asia, is good for your heart because it is very high in the omega-6 linolenic acid. It lowers blood cholesterol, can help prevent cancer, and reduces the risk of adult-onset diabetes. The flower also contains a small amount of gamma-linolenic acid, a fatty acid that is converted into dihomo-gamma-linolenic acid, which produces prostaglandins for the body. Prostaglandins can reduce inflammation, and currently, the flower is being tested for use in reducing inflammation for those who suffer from auto-immune diseases, eczema, and arthritis. Some believe primrose is also capable of helping to protect the brain against Alzheimer's disease, though studies have not yet been conducted to prove this theory.

The typical dose is one 250 mg capsule three times a day. If you are pregnant or have an epileptic condition, consult your doctor before using primrose.

"It is a scientific fact that your body will not absorb cholesterol if you take it from another person's plate."

—Dave Barry

Work to Lower Your LDL and Raise Your HDL

You might think all cholesterol is bad, but cholesterol helps the body build hormones, bile, and vitamin D and helps maintain the fluidity and integrity of all cell membranes. It's important to keep your cholesterol levels in check.

HDL is commonly known as "good cholesterol" because it removes the cholesterol that has built up in the arteries and delivers it to the liver for excretion, thus lowering your risk of heart disease. It may even protect against dementia.

LDL is best known as "bad cholesterol." It transports cholesterol and triglycerides from the liver to the tissues, but in doing so, some cholesterol molecules may get stuck on the arterial walls. Because of this, levels of LDL elevate your risk of having a heart attack or stroke.

Triglycerides transport dietary fat, and their breakdown provides cells with energy. However, high levels of triglycerides have been linked with atherosclerosis.

For a healthy heart, you want your HDL numbers to be high and your LDL and triglyceride numbers to be low. Your total cholesterol should be below 200, with your LDL lower than 100, HDL around 60, and triglycerides lower than 150. Your cholesterol values are determined by your genetics, by your diet, and by your lifestyle.

- Stop smoking.
- Exercise 30 to 60 minutes a day.
- Avoid foods high in saturated fat
- Take fish oil.
- Eat fish, oatmeal, nuts, and olive oil.

"Let me lie / let me die on thy snow-covered bosom, I would eat of thy flesh as a delicate fruit, I am drunk of its smell, and the scent of thy tresses / Is a flame that devours."

—George Moore

Sample Scent-uous Surroundings

Just as you want to create a sexy atmosphere through the use of romantic lighting, having a great-smelling bedroom will help make the average bedroom feel more like a love nest. All of us have certain scents that turn us off and those that turn us on, but when you're first with someone, you won't know what aromas fall into which category.

Until you learn that your partner goes wild at the scent of leather, fresh cut grass, or honeysuckle, hedge your bets and try some aromas that have been given the green light for most men and women. Cinnamon buns, strawberries, and pumpkin pie are said to send more blood flow to the penis, whereas a woman can be turned on subconsciously by the scent of licorice. For both sexes, vanilla, lavender, peppermint, banana bread, cucumber, jasmine, orange, and musk can get the juices flowing.

To bring these scents into your home, choose scented candles, diffusers, or fragrance oils, or put a few drops of one of these essential oils onto your pillow or cotton sheets. Just start small so your bedroom doesn't end up smelling like the perfume section of a department store.

"Peace comes from within. Do not seek it without."

—Buddha

Retreat within to Nourish Your Inner Being

It's important to take care of your body through exercise and a healthy way of eating, but it's also necessary to take care of your mind and inner self. Find time each day to sit quietly and retreat within your mind to calm yourself and find your center. When you are centered, it is easier to make good choices that support the path you want to follow in life and to be proactive instead of reacting reflexively.

Meditation is an excellent way to achieve this tranquility, even for skeptics. Scientists have proven that meditating reduces stress levels and can even promote healing to happen within the body. Talk about mind over matter!

If you're having a hard time retreating within your home because you find yourself distracted by your partner, your children, or just the things that need to be done, travel to someplace where you can clear your mind, like a nearby park, a body of water, the woods, or even the ocean and sit quietly with nature as you breathe deeply and collect your thoughts. Should you find that your mind is full of to-do lists and thoughts that keep circling and prevent you from moving on to others, bring a journal and write them down so that you can clear these distracting thoughts away and make room for you to get deep within yourself.

"Money is like manure. You have to spread it around or it smells."

—J. Paul Getty

Use a Simple Method to Choose Investment Options

If you know you need to get your financial planning in order but don't want to or can't afford to hire a professional planner, consider using a simple method for now to get started. In addition to starting an IRA and saving using an automatic savings plan, open a retirement account. There are a multitude of options, but at the moment, the easiest way to choose an account is to select a plan based around the year you plan to retire. If the year you have in mind for retirement isn't available, pick the plan that is closest to that year. How close you are to this number will determine how risky or reserved your plan will be. If decades span between now and the time you plan to retire—and good for you if you're getting started this early—then the plan is likely to be riskier because you have more time to make the money back. If there aren't that many years left, the plan will be more conservative.

Should a plan of this type not be available through the firm with which you're investing, here is a formula you can use: Subtract your age from 100 and invest that percent in stocks. Place the rest in a bond fund that has the best returns. For example, if you're thirty, put 70 percent into stocks and 30 into bonds. Depending on how conservative or risky you want to be, you can always adjust these numbers, though you'll want to reconfigure the split about every five years.

"Man is fond of counting his troubles, but he does not count his joys. If he counted them up as he ought to, he would see every lot has enough happiness provided for it."

—Fyodor Dostoevsky

Create a Happiness Blog

To improve the happiness of others and your own in return, consider beginning a blog (or devoting part of the blog you already have) that focuses on happiness. By looking for and writing about positive events in your community, your own life, and the world, you'll start to spend more time focusing on the happy events in your life. Sharing these moments with others will allow them to also feel the glow, and suddenly you will have created a domino effect and could be spreading positive energy throughout the globe.

If you're not the technical type, that's okay too. Find a journal you like, and at the end of each day write down three good things that happened—from hearing a bird sing to your loved one proposing. Recognizing how wonderful your everyday life is can boost your happiness and make you more grateful for what comes your way.

This is an especially useful exercise if you've felt down lately. If you feel like nothing is happy in your life, start to focus on the little positive things, and soon you'll notice more small things that can put a smile on your face.

"Life goes faster on protein."

—Martin Fisher

Eat Your Recommended Daily Protein

As you age, your protein needs change. They also change depending on your exercise routine. If your regimen consists of strength training or serious endurance workouts, you'll want to add some protein to your diet if you're eating within the guidelines for your age and gender group and eat 1.2–1.4 grams of protein per kilogram of body weight. This is because the added protein can help rebuild sore or torn muscles and help you recover faster. Keep in mind, however, that while protein is important, anything you eat but don't burn off will be stored as fat.

Here are the recommended daily protein amounts, according to information provided by the Institute of Medicine's Food and Nutrition Board:

CATEGORY	AGE OR CONDITION	PROTEIN GRAMS
Males	14–18 years	52 grams
Males	19–plus years	56 grams
Females	14–plus years	46 grams
Females	Pregnant or lactating	71 grams

Familiarize yourself with how much protein is available in some lean sources like meat (25–35 grams per serving), low-fat cottage cheese (28 grams per cup), beans (18 grams per cup), and peanut butter (7 grams in 2 tablespoons).

*"I not only use all the brains that I have,
but all that I can borrow."*

—Woodrow Wilson

Take Gingko Biloba for Your Brain

Extract from the leaves of the gingko biloba tree, the national tree of China, has been used medicinally for years in North America, and the seeds have been used for centuries in China. Though it's been used as an antioxidant and to help improve blood circulation, macular degeneration, and sexual dysfunction, it has received the most attention as an herb that helps the brain.

It's been touted as a supplement that can improve dementia and prevent Alzheimer's, but there are now conflicting reports on whether this is true. One recent study of 3,000 participants over 75 who took 240 mg of gingko daily for six years reported no proof of its ability to prevent or improve either dementia or Alzheimer's. Another study, however, showed that the leaf extract did improve certain cognitive functions and memory in otherwise mentally healthy patients over sixty.

Should you choose to take gingko, opt for the leaf extract over the seeds, as the seeds, depending on how they've been treated, can be potentially dangerous. A standard dose of gingko is between 120 and 240 mg for the day, taken in three separate doses. If you take antidepressants, have an epileptic disorder, or are on immune-suppressing medications, diabetes medication, or a diuretic or blood thinner, consult your doctor first, as the interaction of these medications and gingko can cause serious side effects.

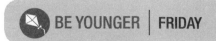

"My dream is to become a farmer. Just a bohemian guy pulling up his own sweet potatoes for dinner."

—Lenny Kravitz

Be Pro-Antioxidants

One key to living a longer, healthier life and having a younger-looking appearance is to get enough antioxidants in your diet. Antioxidants are molecules that protect your cells against the damaging effects of molecules known as free radicals. Free radicals can come from the breakdown of the food you eat, the pollutants in your environment, or through your lifestyle, if you smoke or expose yourself to the damaging effects of the sun or a tanning bed. Free radicals do serve a purpose, as they aid white blood cells in eating harmful bacteria, but they're unstable and can bounce around the body, causing damage to tissues.

To eliminate the effect of free radicals on your body, it's important to make changes within your lifestyle (like stopping tanning and smoking) so you're not helping your body generate free radicals. But you can also eat foods high in antioxidants (including red beans, wild blueberries, kidney beans, pinto beans, cultivated blueberries, cranberries, artichokes, russet potatoes, gala apples, and more) and take supplements, such as beta-carotene, lutein, lycopene, selenium, vitamin A, vitamin C, and vitamin E, to protect yourself.

"Music melts all the separate parts of our bodies together."

—Anaïs Nin

Make a Playlist

Making a sensual playlist can be a lot of fun. You could even make it into a date! If your lover is musically inclined, the two of you could spend time going through each other's music collections and finding songs that get you in a romantic or sexual mood or ones that you think it would be fun to make out or have sex to. You'll learn a lot about each other and what gets each of you in the mood as you share your songs, and you might even find a favorite new band or two!

Whether you choose to take on this project as a couple or compile songs on your own, it makes sense to make more than one playlist. Your sexual mood can change, so while one night you're going to want to have slow and intimate sex, on another night you might just want to tear your lover's clothes off. And if you like listening to music while you're making love, you're not going to want to have the same soundtrack for both of those nights. So put a few different collections together for each type of sex you like to have.

"Have nothing in your house that you do not know to be useful, or believe to be beautiful"

—William Morris

Build a Personal Sanctuary

When you step into your home, you want to feel it is reaching out and comforting you after a long day of work. But perhaps you live with a messy roommate, or your kids leave their toys strewn about, or you're just not the most organized individual. So you open the door to find the sink full of dishes, laundry to be done, your roommate lounging on the couch with her feet on your nice coffee table . . . you get the point.

Before you lose your mind, take control of what you can. If it's just your bedroom you have domain over, transform it into a sanctuary. Of course, if you can work your magic on the whole house, even better. But no matter what, you'll need a room to which you can escape for relaxation.

To take a room from four walls to sanctuary, first clean out the clutter using my favorite William Morris quote, above, to guide you. Paint the rooms in colors that are pleasing to you. Put lights on dimmers so they're not so intense. Add candles to be lit at night to add an even softer glow to the atmosphere. Replace unsightly, uncomfortable furniture with pieces that fit your style, getting inspiration from design blogs like Apartment Therapy, if necessary. As you start to remove items that don't make you feel happy or at peace and you add ones that do, it won't take long until your space becomes somewhere you feel truly at ease.

"If only God would give me some clear sign! Like making a large deposit in my name at a Swiss bank."

—Woody Allen

If You Have an Unexpected Windfall, Put It into a CD

In the game of life, sometimes a little extra cash comes our way that we didn't expect. Perhaps you were playing the tables in Vegas, or won your legal settlement, or received an unexpected bonus at your job. No matter what the cause, I recommend taking that extra cash and putting most of it, if not all, into a certificate of deposit. Since this wasn't money that you had worked into your budget, if you put it into your savings, you'll reach your goals faster. And while savings accounts are good, a CD earns interest at a faster rate, because you're not permitted to touch it. After the CD has reached the end of its term, allocate the funds into the different items you're saving up for within your savings account.

"Too much work, too much vacation, too much of any one thing is unsound."

—Walter Annenberg

Find Balance in Your Life

To lead a happy life, you must find a balance between your leisure time and your work. Those who play too much are rarely successful in their careers, and those who work too much can miss out on time with friends, family, and seeing the world.

Breaks allow us the time to recharge and help us think of creative ways to solve problems. They also give us the time to enjoy outings with the ones we love and experience our world. After a break, you'll come back better equipped to work. Even in these lean times, remember to strive for a healthy work/life balance. Having trouble getting away? Here are some ideas on how to unchain yourself:

- Join an after-work exercise group or league.
- Sign up for a mid-week class. You'll meet people, and after paying the money, you'll probably be motivated to leave anything you didn't finish until the morning.
- Restrain yourself from checking your work e-mail over the weekend if your projects are complete. The same goes for vacations.
- Turn off your work phone when you're not at work. If your work and personal phone are the same, tell your family and friends when you'll be reachable and keep the phone off otherwise.

If some of these feel unreasonable, don't think of them as permanent changes. Just select a set amount of time for trying them. Once you learn to let go, you'll create your own solutions for designing boundaries.

"Red meat is not bad for you. Now, blue-green meat? That's bad for you!"

—Tommy Smothers

Know Your Fats

Fat can be good for you—that is, of course, if you choose the right fats. There are two main types of fats: saturated fats and unsaturated fats.

Unsaturated fats are the healthiest types of fats. They can help your brain function more effectively, lower blood cholesterol, and even help with weight loss. They are liquid at room temperature and can help to lower blood cholesterol levels.

Unsaturated fat comes in four varieties:

Monounsaturated. Can reduce your LDL cholesterol levels. Can be found in olive oil, nuts, and avocados.

Polyunsaturated. Can reduce the chance of getting Lou Gehrig's disease and can help protect against certain kinds of cancers. Can be found in fish, peanuts, whole grains, canola oil, safflower oil, and soybean oil.

Omega-3 fatty acids. Can help with weight loss, to lower cholesterol, and to improve heart health. Can be found in fish and eggs.

Trans fat: This fat is not good for you. Can raise your cholesterol levels and your risk of heart disease.

On the other hand, saturated fats do more harm than good. These are solid at room temperature, raise LDL cholesterol and triglyceride levels, and put you at greater risk for heart disease, stroke, and certain types of cancer. These fats are most commonly found in animal meats, cheeses, and other dairy products not made from skim or one-percent milk, coconut oil, palm kernel oil, and cocoa butter.

"Try not thinking of peeling an orange. Try not imagining the juice running down your fingers, the soft inner part of the peel. The smell. Try and you can't. The brain doesn't process negatives."

—Douglas Coupland

Take Coenzyme Q10

Each day, our bodies are bombarded with environmental toxins. By maintaining a healthy diet and a consistent exercise schedule, we can work to reduce the impact of these dangers on our bodies. And we can also help our bodies by adding this antioxidant to our routine. As we age, our bodies produce less coenzyme Q10, a substance that produces energy for the body in all tissues but especially in the hard-working ones of the liver, heart, brain, and skeleton. By supplementing your diet with foods that contain this enzyme, such as fish, nuts, organ meats, beef, broccoli, chicken, and oranges, you can work against time to decrease your chance of getting a blood clot that could lead to a heart attack or stroke, reduce your bad cholesterol, and improve heart conditions that have been caused by mitochondrial diseases and oxidative injury. Plus, coenzyme Q10 has also been shown to protect against or delay the onset of cognitive diseases, such as Alzheimer's and Parkinson's.

However, if you suffer from heart disease, talk to your doctor before investing in a supplement of coenzyme Q10. It's been shown that some people who have heart disease, exercise regularly, and take the supplement suffer from organ damage. Whether the enzyme is the cause is not yet clear.

"I'm allergic to chemicals so I eat only organic foods."

—Carol Channing

Add Superfoods to Your Diet

Food is like money. The choices we make in our diet and with our budget can have a profound long-term impact. If you're looking for a great return on your investment, superfoods are the way to go. Superfoods are foods loaded with vitamins, minerals, and other great nutrients that help fight disease, boost metabolism, and make you feel great. All of these foods are unprocessed and reasonably easy to find, so unless you're allergic, there's no excuse for why you can't add them into your diet.

We'll go over many of these in later chapters, but in preparation, some superfoods include:

- Avocado
- Beans
- Blueberries
- Broccoli
- Dark greens
- Flax
- Oats
- Olive oil
- Oranges
- Pomegranate
- Pumpkin
- Salmon
- Soy
- Spinach
- Tea (green or black)
- Tomatoes
- Turkey
- Walnuts
- Yogurt

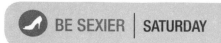

"I'm just missing some condoms—I didn't find my size."

—Gael Garcia Bernal, in *Amores Perros*

Get Tested

Before you hook up with your next partner, get tested for sexually transmitted diseases (STDs). And if you've never gotten tested but you're with someone, get tested now. Getting tested can be scary, but it's the responsible thing to do, and you can get tested at anonymous free clinics or at your doctor's office. In some cities, testing is also offered by outreach centers.

Though the pressure of waiting for your test results can be intense, it also might cause you to rethink some of your risky behaviors and consider not repeating those mistakes in the future. If it turns out you're negative for all STDs, that's great, but make sure you continue to use protection and still get tested every so often, even if you're in a monogamous relationship. We're not saying your partner is unfaithful, but no one thought Tiger Woods was a cheater, so it's better to be safe than sorry.

If it turns out you do have an STD, it's better to know so that you can take the steps to treat it or reduce its impact on your life. Make sure to tell all prospective partners that you have this STD before you engage in any behavior that might put them at risk. Condoms, dental dams, and finger cots (these are condoms for your finger), can protect you against most STDs, but your partner deserves to know *before* the act. If you're under the age of twenty-six, I strongly urge you to also get the HPV vaccine. According to the CDC, 50 percent of all sexually active people will get genital HPV at some point during their lives. Like other STDs, HPV can be passed through vaginal or anal sex, oral sex, or genital-to-genital contact. Certain strains of HPV are known to be the leading cause of cervical cancer and genital warts, and it can also cause penile cancer, anal cancer, and head and neck cancer.

"I always tried to turn every disaster into an opportunity."

—John D. Rockefeller

Shift Your Perspective

Hindsight might be 20/20, but that gift of perspective doesn't usually apply to the present or the future. When you find yourself caught up in a difficult scenario, you can envision it as the worst thing that's ever happened to you or as something that will go on forever. Essentially, you take that event and magnify it until it's so large and important within your life's story that it grows completely out of proportion and you lose your perspective.

It's critical in these moments to get a grip of your visual picture. You are not going to actually be stuck in that meeting forever. You will not spend the rest of your life not being able to find the right partner, or job, or place to live. You are not a complete screw-up if you make a mistake. These problems are temporary, unless you choose for them not to be. By taking a step back and allowing yourself to see the reality of the situation versus relying only on how you *feel*, you'll be more equipped to resolve it in a way that is healthier for you, and you'll be less likely to bring yourself additional stress.

"Many things grow in the garden that were never sown there."

—Thomas Fuller

Plant a Vegetable or Herb Garden

One great way to cut your food costs and know you are eating produce that hasn't been treated with any dangerous chemicals is to grow your own fruits and vegetables. Though you might have to put up with fending off birds and squirrels, you can rest assured that no food manufacturer is spraying your plants with pesticides, and you won't need to pay the higher cost for buying organic produce. You can purchase organic starter plants for a relatively low cost at your local nursery or farmer's market—the local one I frequent sells all plants for one dollar. Though you'll also need to invest in a few gardening tools and pots (if you're using containers rather than a patch of ground), perhaps some soil, and compost, you'll recoup your costs after just one season.

In case you live in an apartment building or a location where you are unable to grow vegetables outdoors or in a greenhouse, consider an indoor herb garden kit like AeroGarden. These compact kits come complete with seeds, lights, and an area in which to plant and can fit in small spaces like on top of your fridge. Though you won't see large vegetables sprout, you will save on the cost of herbs and be able to snip fresh herbs like parsley, thyme, and basil to use in your dishes.

If you have kids, growing vegetables is a great way for you to teach them where their food comes from. If they have a role in the planting and growing, they'll be excited and proud when they see the first vegetables start to come up. And, even better, they might even eat them!

"All things carry the yin/while embrace the yang.
Neutralizing energy brings them into harmony."

—Lao Tzu

Find a Balance of Yin and Yang

Within Taoist philosophy, the symbol of the yin yang, also called the *tajii*, has three parts. The circle connecting the two sides represents Tao—the Law of the Universe—while the black half within represents the yin energy, and the white half represents the yang energy. Without the two sides, the larger circle could not exist. The smaller circles within each half represent how everything is in constant flux as well as the connections between seemingly opposite constructs.

Taoists believe that within each of us there is yin energy and yang energy. Yin energy is quiet, thoughtful, and passive. This energy relaxes and nourishes us when we are spent. It represents the female. Yang energy is just the opposite. It is active, focused, and aggressive. This is the male energy. To live happily, we need a balance of both. Without yang energy, we would be slothful and unmotivated. Without yin energy, we would never rest or retreat within our minds to center ourselves.

Feng shui practitioners suggest that yin be the predominant energy in the bedroom while the communal areas should be filled with a yang energy. Setting up your life in the same way can be effective. Be energetic and engaging when out with friends or at work but retreat inside to your quiet inner sanctuary when you are on your own.

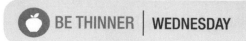

"The best way to detoxify is to stop putting toxic things into the body and depend upon its own mechanisms."

—Andrew Weil

Avoid Artificial Trans Fats

Trans fats have gotten a bad rap, and the artificial ones have earned it. But naturally occurring trans fats, such as those found in dairy products, beef, and lamb, are transformed into conjugated linoleic acid (CLA) within the body. This substance can help prevent heart disease and cancer and will even help you shed fat and maintain lean body mass. CLA is also available as a supplement in both vegetarian and non-vegetarian forms.

Artificial trans fats do just the opposite to your body. This type of fat is produced when vegetable oil is treated with heat, chemicals, and hydrogen to produce a product that is semi-solid (instead of liquid) at room temperature. Things were going well until scientists discovered that these artificial fats were terrible for the human body. Instead of eliminating them during the digestion process, the body treats them as they would a normal fatty acid and incorporates these artificial fats into the lining of arteries and veins, into cell membranes, and into the brain, liver, and kidneys. The result can be catastrophic. Hormone levels are disrupted. Good cholesterol is lowered, and bad cholesterol is raised. Cell membranes are damaged and no longer absorb nutrients as effectively. Blood vessels become less flexible. Insulin levels rise. Weight is packed on around the midsection. Free radicals thrive in the bloodstream, increasing the risk of cancer.

To avoid eating trans fats, stay away from margarine and shortening and anything with the word "hydrogenated" in the ingredient list. To be extra careful, you can also avoid corn oil, canola oil, and soybean oils, which also contain artificial trans fat but at levels much lower than those of shortening and margarine.

"Before the seed there comes the thought of bloom."

—E. B. White

Take Magnesium

To make sure your neurons are firing at their maximum potential, take a 350 mg supplement of magnesium each day—or eat foods high in magnesium, such as legumes, avocados, whole grains, wheat germ, seafood, fruits, spinach, and pumpkin seeds.

This macro mineral creates the strong, lattice-like structure within our bones and metabolizes fats, carbohydrates, and proteins. Magnesium not only prevents the onset of neurobiological disorders, including Alzheimer's disease, it also builds a protective layer around your neurons and activates a chemical that converts waste ammonia in the brain into urea, without which we wouldn't be able to concentrate.

Stress and alcohol lower the levels of magnesium within our bodies, so if you've been feeling on edge or have been partying a lot on the weekends, definitely consider this supplement. However, if you have kidney disease, consult your doctor first.

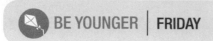

"The avocado is a food without rival among the fruits, the veritable fruit of Paradise."

—David Fairchild

Enjoy an Avocado

Whether they hail from California, Mexico, or Florida, these "alligator pears" will help you maintain a youthful appearance. That's because they are packed with omega-3s, which guard against heart and vascular diseases, and oleic acid, a monounsaturated fat that can reduce the risk of breast cancer and boost memory. These delicious fruits are also chock full of vitamin K, which protects against osteoporosis, and folate, which helps the heart.

Avocados also make a great facial mask that will rehydrate your skin with its oils and nourish it with omega-3s. Crush half an avocado into a bowl, add honey, and mix until it is a smooth consistency. Apply this to your face and leave it on for ten minutes before rinsing.

To get all of the benefits of avocados, try making a homemade guacamole, use them as a healthy alternative to mayonnaise, or just enjoy these yummy fruits raw.

"I love lingerie and feminine things. It makes me feel nice to look good and turn somebody on by doing so. It's an incredible rush. And when it turns a man on—fantastic. But no matter what, I'm getting off."

—Lorri Bagley, actress

Buy Some Sexy Lingerie

If you want to turn your man or woman on, go buy some sexy lingerie. For men, this could be a hot new pair of boxer briefs or something more speedo-like. It depends on what turns your partner on. Women, you know the options are vast. There's the corset and garter-belt route. Or the teddy. Or a tempting push-up bra and matching panties. Or just a sexy thong and a pair of heart-shaped pasties.

As your partner is doing the dishes or relaxing on the couch or in the bedroom, go into another room and slip on your sexy outfit. Do up your hair and your makeup. Then come out in just your sexy outfit and watch his jaw drop. If the moment feels right, start doing a little striptease for your partner with or without music. The key to a sexy striptease is confidence and going slow enough to tease your partner. So, even if you're feeling nervous, don't rush.

"The harder I work, the luckier I get."

—Samuel Goldwyn

Notice Synchronicity

At certain times in our lives, it feels like things just line up for us. Call it coincidence, fate, or something in between. It's important to notice those moments when it feels like everything is going just right, because often these are also the times when we're operating at our best. Take note of your mood, your actions, and what you're putting into the world. You might want to then record all of this into a journal so you can look back on it when things aren't going so well and figure out how to put yourself back on this path where everything feels like it's just flowing.

If you've requested something of the universe or have set the intention for something to happen in your life, take heed of events that happen that could lead you in a direction in which these requests are fulfilled. Getting to your goal often involves a lot of little steps, so be sure to keep an eye out so you can recognize them as they happen.

On the other side of things, if you're continually getting blocked at trying to achieve something, ask yourself if you're requesting something you're not meant to do. Sometimes these hurdles are in place so you can prove to yourself that you can overcome them; at other times, these blockades appear because you're heading in the wrong direction.

"Credit is like a looking-glass, which when once sullied by a breath, may be wiped clear again; but if once cracked can never be repaired."

—Sir Walter Scott

Find a Credit Card That Offers Rewards

What are you getting out of your credit card? If all you are receiving each month is a bill and you're the type to pay off your balance each month, it's time to consider switching cards. Find a card that rewards you for the money you spend with airplane miles, money off your grocery or gas bill, or points that you can use toward merchandise or a trip. Most rewards cards only allow you to recoup the rewards once the bill has been paid in full, but the advantages are great, especially if the card doesn't come with a yearly fee. With this type of credit card, instead of paying for a trip or item out of your own pocket, you can cash in your rewards without spending a dime.

WEEK SEVENTEEN

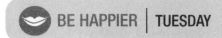

"Dream as if you'll live forever. Live as if you'll die today."

—James Dean

Live More Spontaneously

When you look back on your life, will you be happier knowing you did the things you wanted to do or the things you were *supposed* to do? It's important to be responsible, of course, but I'll bet you that your best memories aren't of the times you worked late at the office to finish a project for your boss. They were probably the times when your girlfriend or boyfriend picked you up in the morning, you called in sick, and the two of you headed out of town for an unexpected adventure.

In other words, time-manage as much as you need to have a productive life, but also don't be afraid to throw your plans to the wind if life calls. If you've been feeling like you're in a rut, make a change. Cut your hair (it'll grow back), drive to a new city you've always wanted to visit, grab a bottle of wine and walk with your significant other to a local park at night so you two can enjoy the stars. Go sing karaoke. Remind yourself that happiness and beauty are all around and you just have to allow yourself to see it.

Just because you're an adult doesn't mean you *always* have to act like one. Where would be the fun in that?

"Middle age is when you choose cereal for the fiber, not the toy."

—Unknown

Clean Up with Fiber

You don't have to love bran muffins to get the benefits of fiber. Fiber, the indigestible part of the plants you eat, is available in many healthy foods, from blueberries to, yes, bran—and it's an important part of your diet. Fiber pushes foods through your system, and in so doing, it shuffles cancer-causing compounds through the body quicker, giving them less time to do their toxic damage, It helps to regulate blood sugar and prevent diabetes; assists with the lowering of cholesterol, which helps your heart stay healthy; and can reduce your chances of developing colon cancer.

Fiber will also help you lose weight. When you eat a high-fiber meal, you will feel fuller and more satiated for longer, and because fiber moves things along in the digestive tract, your body will have less time to absorb calories from the food you eat, which means those calories won't be stored as fat. Aim for twenty-five to thirty grams of fiber a day, but if you've been lax on your fiber intake, add this in slowly so you don't suffer from gas or diarrhea.

High-Fiber Foods:
- 1 cup of beans: 14–16 grams
- 1 cup of split peas: 16 grams
- 1 cup of bran cereal: 19 grams
- 1 medium avocado: 11 grams
- 1 half medium grapefruit: 6 grams
- 1 cup soybeans: 8 grams

"A vitamin is a substance that makes you ill if you don't eat it."

—Albert Szent-Gyrogyi, biochemist

Get Plenty of B Vitamins

The eight B vitamins can help guard your body against age-related diseases and improve mood disorders, especially depression. The eight B vitamins are: thiamine, riboflavin, niacin, pantothenic acid, pyridoxine, biotin, folic acid, and cyanocobalamin (and other cobalamins).

Depression can occur if your diet is low in B-vitamins or if your body is not processing B vitamins as it should and allowing them to also work in the brain. B vitamins are destroyed by nicotine, refined sugar, alcohol, and caffeine, so if you're feeling down but you think you're getting enough B vitamins, look to see if you can connect a B-vitamin killer with your lifestyle habits. If you are depressed, your condition may be linked to another cause, but changing your lifestyle and upping your intake of B vitamins isn't a bad place to start.

Certain B vitamins can also help treat Alzheimer's disease, dementia, sleep disorders, and diabetic neuropathy, reduce stress, and improve the metabolism of fats, carbohydrates, and proteins. They also reduce levels of the amino acid homocysteine, which in high levels can cause heart disease.

"I try and take lots of vitamins and I don't drink."

—Kate Beckinsale

Eat Thiamine

When you eat carbohydrates, it's thiamine, also known as B1, that helps break them down so your body can take energy from them. Thiamin is also essential for the normal functioning of the heart, muscles, and nervous system. Without enough of this water-soluble vitamin, you can experience fatigue, mental confusion, nerve damage, muscle weakness, and even psychosis. Though you can take it in over-the-counter supplement form, it is also found in all fortified grain products, whole grains, lean meats, peas, and soybeans.

EASY WAYS TO INCORPORATE B1 INTO YOUR DIET

B1 isn't hard to get enough of, but here are some well-balanced dishes that will help you get nearly all of your daily needs in one meal.

- Mix in mushrooms, sunflower seeds, peas, and tomatoes into a romaine salad
- Combine corn, black beans, and tomatoes for a healthy side dish
- Enjoy yellowfin tuna seared or as sushi (and get your Omega-3s too!)
- Make a hearty bean soup from pinto beans, navy beans, and lima beans

---

"Poor is the man whose pleasures depend on the permission of another."

—Madonna

Get In the Mood

When we're stressed, it's hard to be in the mood. Instead of forcing yourself to feel sexual right when you come home from work, allow yourself time to unwind. If you live with your significant other, give him a kiss and a hug to let him feel loved and appreciated, but then take some time for yourself. Meditate. Take a hot bath. Read a relaxing book. Sit down with your partner and share a glass of wine as you tell him about your day. Whatever you need to decompress after the day, do it.

By giving yourself the space to allow your sexual feelings to come into being naturally, you're more likely to get in the mood. When you come home, consider slipping into something more comfortable—sexy underwear, pajamas, a hot nightgown—or asking your partner to go do something active with you that will take your mind off of looming deadlines or projects. At night, the two of you could go on a walk, play tennis, or enjoy an evening bike ride. These bonding activities will help you move from work mode to play mode, and they'll help you be more interested in what could happen in the bedroom.

Consider using play to get yourself in the mood or to just reconnect with your partner after a long day. Start a pillow fight, a wrestling match, or a tickle war. Once the two of you start laughing, you might start kissing, and then who knows where things will go!

"It is not the strongest of species that survive, nor the most intelligent, but the one most responsive to change."

—Charles Darwin

Learn to Adapt to Change

Change is inevitable. Without it, there would be no progress or growth both in a larger sense and within yourself. But change can also be hard to weather. It requires a shift in perspective for things to start to fall into place to fit the new direction, and some things might need to be discarded. Think about moving from one house to another. You like your first house, but you are looking forward to the benefits of your new place. In your old house, you know where everything goes, what floorboards creak, and what memories you experienced there. The new house may be better, but you don't know much about it. But as you spend time there, you start to learn that house's quirks and you build memories within its walls.

Spiritual, physical, and emotional changes are similar. When you get used to a path, it's hard to get off of it, even when you know it would be better for you. Exercising more, eating a healthier diet, or doing most of the things in this book require change. But if these are changes that you want to make, then you can find the willpower to stick with them. That leap of faith and the time it takes to make an important life choice will often pay off, just like that move to the new house.

"A man who pays his bill on time is soon forgotten."

—Oscar Wilde

Pay Off Your Credit Card Balance Every Month

The best way to avoid credit card debt is to spend within your means and to pay off your balance in full every month. It might seem easier at the time to use the money you spent on your credit card toward something else, but unless you want to avoid getting buried in debt, pony up the cash. Credit cards aren't free money; they're essentially a short-term loan with no interest (at first). Paying only the minimum balance every month allows the credit card company to start charging interest to those previous purchases, and by next month, you'll see a much larger bill than you had probably anticipated and you'll already start to feel behind the eight ball.

If you've spent beyond your means and have the extra cash in your savings, use your savings to pay off the credit card balance. Hopefully, the pain of taking money from your savings account will make you careful not to overspend the next month.

"I am part of everything that I have read."

—John Kieran

Spend Your Afternoon at a Local Bookstore or Coffeehouse

Break your routine. Instead of spending your after-work or week-end hours going where you usually do, head somewhere unexpected. Sometimes, especially if you're single, it can be hard to get out and do things on your own. For instance, it's easy to curl up in your favorite chair and read undisturbed for a few hours on the weekend, but if you take yourself and your book to a local coffee shop, the kind full of comfy couches, you'll get a change of scenery and you might make a new connection with someone. At the least, you'll treat yourself to some fun people watching.

If coffee shops aren't your thing, consider other places where people mingle freely. Consider buying tickets to a sporting event, going shopping at your local farmer's market, or checking out a local craft fair. Unlike spending time at a bar, where ultimately you're part of the "meat market," these locales (and others like them) offer you the chance to have a good time on your own without the added pressure that you must talk to someone else. That said, the more you expand your social connections and build new friendships, the happier you can become.

"Chlorine is a deadly poison gas employed on European battlefields in World War I. Sodium is a corrosive metal which burns upon contact with water. Together they make a placid and unpoisonous material, table salt. Why each of these substances has the properties it does is a subject called science."

—Carl Sagan

Stop Shaking the Salt Shaker

Without a doubt, salt can enhance the flavor of food, but too much can be very harmful to our health. And here, in the United States, we're practically drowning in it. Your body requires only 200 mg of sodium a day to function properly, but the average American consumes between 3,000 and 3,600 mg a day. Aim for no more than 2,300 mg (this is equivalent to one teaspoon) if you are under forty and do not have a health condition adversely affected by salt. If you suffer from hypertension or are over forty, aim for 1,500 mg or less a day.

Excess sodium consumption can lead to muscle cramps, heartburn, osteoporosis, high blood pressure, edema, ulcers, and stomach cancer. On a day-to-day basis, salt can cause bloating and fluid retention. Not only will this make you look heavier, it also will make you weigh more on the scale. So if you want to look lean and lose weight, cut back on the salty snacks.

"A man paints with his brains and not with his hands."

—Michelangelo

Load Up on B6

B6 is great for the brain. This water-soluble vitamin improves the brain's ability to handle stress and also serves as a building block for four important neurotransmitters, including serotonin. With the help of B9 and B12, B6 lowers homocysteine, an amino acid, which in high levels can lead to heart disease and bone weakness. In addition, B6 bolsters the immune system, helps the body to maintain the proper chemical balance, and supplies muscles with energy. Because this vitamin is toxic in high levels (above 100 mg), for your body's daily B6 needs, look to food sources high in B6, such as chicken, fish, beef, bananas, carrots, lentils, rice, whole grains, soybeans, or avocados, instead of supplements.

THE B6 BREAKDOWN

To get your B6 fix, look below at how much of each food you'd need to consume. Mix and match!

- 3 bananas
- 4 cups of spinach
- 5 cups of baked potatoes
- 8 ounces of yellowfin tuna
- 12 ounces of chicken breast
- 12 ounces of snapper or cod

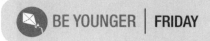

"All sorrows are less with bread."

—Miguel de Cervantes, in *Don Quixote*

Try Niacin

Scientists are beginning to believe that niacin might hold the key to longevity. Niacin bonds with and activates sirtuin receptors, enabling the body to more effectively use sirtuin enzymes. Sirtuin enzymes can reduce the risk of type 2 diabetes and obesity. Studies indicate they may also extend longevity.

Niacin is also helpful on its own, as it releases energy from food so the body can use it for fuel. It also aids in the synthesis of DNA; prevents macular degeneration; lowers blood cholesterol levels; prevents and slows the progression of atherosclerosis; and maintains the health of the skin, nerves, and the digestive system. The best way to get niacin is through food sources, such as whole-grain carbohydrates, lean meats, fish, poultry, peanuts, yogurt, and sunflower seeds.

A HEALTHY NIACIN DINNER

Though you can take niacin in supplement form, it can cause an uncomfortable rash in high doses or if you don't take the timed-release type. For an easier, hassle-free way to meet your daily requirements, enjoy four ounces of chicken breast (75 percent) or tuna (67 percent) with a side of peas (16 percent) or mushrooms (27 percent).

"Absence sharpens love, presence strengthens it."

—Thomas Fuller

Don't Give Up Activities That Give You Pleasure

When some people get a new boyfriend or girlfriend, they stop doing the things they used to enjoy in their single life, or, worse, they neglect to spend time with their family and friends because they're too preoccupied with their new relationship. Next time you get involved with someone, try not to do this. If you're already involved with someone and you've been guilty of this, start reaching out to your friends and family again, make plans with them, and make time to do the activities you love.

The person you're dating fell for you because of who you are, so make sure to strive to keep your individual identity even as the pair of you merge together as a couple. Time apart from each other doing your own things and spending time with your own friends can stoke the flames of interest and make the two of you eager to make plans to see each other again soon.

"A quiet mind cureth all."

—Robert Burton

Wander Around a Labyrinth

Within Western society, the labyrinth has most often served as a puzzle to *keep* someone within—such as with the labyrinth constructed by King Minos to hold the Minotaur—rather than to help one *see* within. But you can use these interesting structures to do just that—to look deep within yourself. To calm yourself and help yourself to look within, start at the beginning of one of these mazelike paths and take slow, deliberate steps until you have reached the middle. Stay there and meditate for as long as you like. Then, slowly and deliberately make your way back out. Repeat this pattern until you feel centered, using deep breathing while you walk to and from the center and while you meditate at the center.

Hand-built labyrinths made of stones or carved into the earth can be found in cities across the world. To find a labyrinth near you, visit LabyrinthLocator.com.

Some Labyrinths to Visit:
- Grace Cathedral, in San Francisco
- Hampton Court Hedge Maze, near London, England
- Dole Plantation Maze, in Oahu, Hawaii
- The maze in Reignac-sur-Indre, France
- Chartes Cathedral, near Paris, France

"Some debts are fun when you are acquiring them, but none are fun when you set about retiring them."

—Ogden Nash

Use a Snowball to Move Down Debt Mountain

You can move beyond your mountain of debt. You just need a plan. If your debt situation is particularly complicated, consider meeting with a professional who can help you get a handle on it. But if your situation is centered around a few maxed-out credit cards, the "debt snowball" method might help. Popularized by personal finance consultant Dave Ramsey, the debt snowball concept is simple. Each month, you pay the minimum amount of all of your debts and make a larger payment on the one with the lowest balance (or, if you can, the one with the highest interest rate). Once you've eventually paid off that debt, add the amount you were paying each month to that debt to the minimum payment of the next-lowest debt, and continue that payment pattern until that debt is paid off each month—and so forth with each of your other credit accounts, until you've eliminated your debt.

One important note: as you're doing this, try your best not to rack up any extra debt.

WEEK NINETEEN

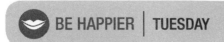
"Non-cooks think it's silly to invest two hours' work in two minutes' enjoyment; but if cooking is evanescent, so is the ballet."

—Julia Child

Cook Yourself Your Favorite Dish

It can be hard to cook for yourself. All the preparation and planning may feel like a lot to do for just one person. But just because you're dining alone doesn't mean you shouldn't eat well. In your life, no one is more important than you, so make sure you treat yourself to delicious meals. Even if you don't eat alone, sometimes your meals are determined by what the people with whom you share your table will or won't eat. Does your partner or your child hate something you love? Don't lose out on eating your favorite dish because not everyone enjoys it.

From time to time, treat yourself and make those dishes you love from scratch. Or plan a week with your partner where you'll make his favorite dish and he'll make yours. You can even cook these special meals together, guiding your partner along the way if he's not as skilled in the kitchen as you are (or vice versa) or if you know a few little tricks here and there to make the dish taste *magnifique*. This not only will make you both feel more appreciated, it can also serve as a great bonding time for you and your family as you come together to make the meals each person enjoys.

"The resistance that you fight physically in the gym and the resistance that you fight in life can only build a strong character."

—Arnold Schwarzenegger

Join a Gym

By now, you know the importance of exercise. If you're having a hard time getting motivated, join a gym. For the cost of a monthly membership fee, you'll be granted access to aerobic machines, weight machines, free weights, and group exercise and/or aquatic classes. Some luxury gyms even offer saunas, juice bars, and massage treatments to enjoy post-workout. Once you're in there, you'll likely stay long enough to get in a solid workout.

If you're still having a hard time getting motivated, take a look at your gym's class schedule and find a few classes you'd like to try. Depending on the facility, the options can range from kickboxing and boot camp classes to pole dancing, acrobatics, and just plain old step aerobics. By setting these classes into your schedule, you'll not only ensure a good workout, you also might be more motivated to work out on the days you aren't taking classes.

Another benefit of joining a gym is that they have personal trainers you can hire to get your butt and other body parts into shape. Personal trainers will work with you to develop a lean physique through aerobics and strength training or weight lifting, and they can also help you work on your diet.

*"Knowledge is that which, next to virtue, truly
raises one person above another."*

—Joseph Addison, English essayist

Increase Your Brain Power with Vitamin B12

It may still surprise you, but the foods you eat and the supplements you take can have a powerful effect on your brain as you get older. As we age, our brain eventually starts to shrink and the neurons don't fire as well. This can result in memory lapses, a decrease in cognitive ability, and even dementia. Though your brain health is partially determined by genetics, it's important to do what you can to improve your odds for the future.

One of the things you can do is supplement your diet with B12, also known as cyanocobalamin. Researchers at Oxford University in England revealed that older adults with higher levels of B12 in their blood were six times less likely to experience brain shrinkage than those whose levels were lower. Brain atrophy/shrinkage is known to be associated with lower levels of cognitive functioning and Alzheimer's. It's also worth noting that when B12 levels are even slightly below normal, memory problems and mood disorders, such as depression, can crop up.

If you choose not to take B12 as a supplement, make sure to keep your levels high by eating dairy, poultry, tuna, oysters, crab, and beef.

"Me, sexy? I'm just plain ol' rice and beans."

—Pam Grier

Ingest Inositol

Inositol, a vitamin once known as B8, is contained in many fruits, vegetables, nuts, and legumes—which is good, because it's a crucial nutrient for your muscular and nervous systems. It also helps keep fat from building up in the liver, reduces blood cholesterol levels, metabolizes fat, and helps guard against arthritis. Without sufficient ingestion of this vitamin, you could suffer from heart disease, memory loss, hair loss, constipation, and other unpleasant maladies. Eating a high-fiber diet that includes bran and beans will ensure that you receive enough inositol.

BEST INOSITOL FOODS

Though it's not as popular as some of the other B vitamins, to see benefits you'll want to have at least one gram daily. Here are some foods packed with it:

½ cup bran—54 mg
½ cup Brussels sprouts—80 mg
¼ cup cantaloupe—355 mg
½ cup grapefruit—199 mg
½ cup green beans—193 mg
1 lime—194 mg
½ cup navy beans—283 mg
1 orange—307 mg
2 tablespoons peanut butter—121 mg
1 slice stone-ground wheat bread—287 mg

"To succeed with the opposite sex, tell her you're impotent.
She can't wait to disprove it."

—Cary Grant

Think Outside the Dating Box

When you want to start dating again or more, it's important to open all possible doors. The traditional methods of meeting people by chance, through friends, or at a bar are all still excellent ways to meet your potential mate. But your dating opportunities stand only to improve by trying new ways to meet potential partners. Such as these alternative methods.

Online Dating. Though it might feel unusual to first meet someone over the Internet instead of in person, online dating is a great way to meet people whom you might not otherwise have come across. There are a variety of dating sites out there, and you can choose the one that's right for you—whether you're looking for Mr. or Ms. Right or just for someone to have fun and/or sex with. Sites range in cost and in the type of members they attract, so do your research to see if the service fits your needs.

Speed Dating. In this round-robin affair, you'll have three to ten minutes to meet a person, take in his or her personality, and decide whether you want to see the person again before moving on to the next. It's a great way to work on overcoming shyness, as you'll have to talk to many different people and you'll learn quickly how to describe yourself in a nutshell, which is a tool you can use in various situations.

Matchmakers. This ancient practice of bringing two people together so that they may marry has been repopularized in modern culture. Matchmakers are available for hire, and people use them with the hope that these professionals will have better luck at connecting them with a good partner than they have had on their own.

"That's the best thing about walking, the journey itself. It doesn't matter much whether you get to where you're going or not. You'll get there anyway. Every good hike brings you eventually back home."

—Edward Abbey

Try Walking Meditation

Walking meditation can be very calming. If you have a difficult time finding a quiet place to sit and meditate or if you are better at clearing your thoughts while moving, give this a try. Walking meditation can be done indoors or outdoors, but if you choose outdoors, try to have a path in mind so that you don't have to think about it while you're moving forward.

When you walk to meditate, don't walk as if you are exercising. Walk slowly and deliberately as you focus on your breathing and on how your body feels. Let the thoughts flow through you and dismiss the need to hold onto them. Drink the world in as you pass through it, but try not to allow anything specific to engage you. Should you become distracted, bring your focus back to your breathing.

*"If you think nobody cares if you're alive, try missing
a couple of car payments."*

—Earl Wilson

Consolidate or Refinance Any Debts

When you have debts, it's usually not the principle but the inter-est that is the killer. Each month your principle accrues interest, leaving you with more to pay off. If you're having a hard time pay-ing more than just the interest rate, it's important to see if any of your debts could be refinanced under a lower interest rate so that you'll owe less every month and can start to pay off the principle. Even if you're not having a hard time paying your bills, it's worth it to see if refinancing a large purchase—such as a home or auto loan—is possible, because if interest rates have fallen since you took out the loan, it isn't financially wise to continue paying the higher interest rate of yesteryear.

An alternative to refinancing is consolidation. When you con-solidate, you combine multiple loans into one larger loan. and because it extends the payment calendar, you may end up with lower monthly payments and, depending on the current rates, lower interest. If you have outstanding student loans, this is a great way to reduce your payments without being penalized.

WEEK TWENTY

*"Joy is the holy fire that keeps our purpose warm
and our intelligence aglow."*

—Helen Keller

Book Your Own Birthday

Putting your trust in your friends, family, or lover to surprise you with or treat you to an incredible birthday isn't unreasonable, but sometimes it's important to take matters into your own hands. Those close to you might not know exactly how you want to celebrate your birthday—especially if it's a big one—and they might plan a big bash when you wanted something small and intimate, but you might not want to tell them because you want it to be a surprise.

If there is something you'd really like to do for your big day, drop clear hints, or take it a step further and plan the event yourself. Have you always wanted to take a canoe down the Amazon or go shopping in Tokyo? Start booking those flights and making an itinerary. Invite whomever you want to be there to come along. When your birthday arrives, you'll be having too much fun to regret that it isn't a surprise, and you won't be sitting at home wishing you were somewhere else.

"If you spend too much time warming up, you'll miss the race. If you don't warm up at all, you may not finish the race."

—Grand Heidrich

Warm Up Your Muscles

To avoid injury when you're working out, always warm up your muscles before starting any strenuous exercise. When your muscles aren't properly warmed up, it's easy to sprain or even tear ligaments and tendons. When you warm up, you increase the blood flow to the muscles, which, in turn, improves the muscle's ability to stretch and move without injury. During the warm-up, more oxygen is delivered to the muscles, which can help reduce the chance of muscle fatigue as you're working out. Warming up also stimulates the production of hormones that are broken down into fatty acids and glucose for fuel as you're working out.

A warm-up doesn't have to take long. You can accomplish it within five to ten minutes, by either doing the same motion you'll be doing for your regular exercise, such as walking for five minutes before you start to jog or run, or by doing a motion that gets the limbs warmed up that you'll use during your exercise, such as dribbling before playing basketball.

After your exercise, make sure you do a five-minute cool-down and then stretch to alleviate muscle soreness and increase flexibility.

"An ounce of prevention is worth a pound of cure."

—Proverb

Eat Folic Acid

Take folic acid, and you might be able to slow down the aging effects on your brain. According to a study published in 2007, researchers in the Netherlands found that subjects aged fifty to seventy who took an 800 mg supplement of folic acid each day improved on tests that measured "information processing speed and memory, domains that are known to decline with age."

Folic acid, which is also responsible for the proper development of the brain, spinal cord, and spine during fetal development, helps to maintain DNA, reduce depression, improve fertility, and protect the body from heart disease, stroke, and cancer. It also helps the body by preventing obesity, the creation of allergies, and bone loss, among other benefits.

To get plenty of folic acid, you can take a supplement or you can eat leafy vegetables, oranges, avocados, dried beans, peas, or nuts. Most fortified bread products also contain folic acid. Women who are pregnant should make sure to get an additional 400 mg of folic acid daily. The chance of toxicity is very low with this vitamin, because it is water soluble and any excess will be excreted in the urine.

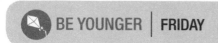
"He that but looketh on a plate of ham and eggs to lust after it hath already committed breakfast with it in his heart."

—C. S. Lewis

Eat Biotin

For fresh-looking skin and healthy-looking nails and hair, make sure you're getting this water-soluble vitamin in your diet. Though deficiency is rare, it can lead to fatigue, depression, and heart problems. Biotin, also known as B7, works with other B vitamins to build fatty acids for cell membranes as well as glucose, which can later be broken down into energy. It also assists with the metabolizing of carbohydrates, fats, and proteins and turns these into fuel when you're exercising. Healthy foods that contain biotin include oatmeal, fortified breads, Swiss chard, and eggs.

BIOTIN BREAKDOWN

To reach your daily goal of 30 micrograms of B7, include these foods in your diet:

- Swiss Chard: 1 cup has 10.5 mcg
- Whole Wheat Bread: 1 slice has 6 mcg
- Salmon: 3 ounces has 4 mcg
- Eggs: 1 has 25 mcg
- Bran: 1 ounce has 14 mcg

"Pursuit and seduction are the essence of sexuality.
It's part of the sizzle."

—Camille Paglia

Practice the Art of Flirting

Get out there and flirt with someone today. If you're in a relationship, flirt with your partner; if you're single, flirt with someone cute you see. If you start innocently, most people will flirt back, and that can be a big confidence booster. Flirting, which is usually done with the intention of sparking a romantic or sexual interest in the other person, can take many forms.

You can flirt just by starting a conversation with someone. As you continue to talk, keep eye contact (but don't stare), smile, and laugh when the person says something funny or cute. If you feel a connection, you can brush the person's shoulder or touch him or her in a playful way. If you keep it going and the flirting is mutual, it might even lead to something more.

Top Signs Someone Is Flirting with You
The object of your attention:

- Mimics your body movements
- Smiles and makes eye contact with you
- Keeps walking by you
- Plays with her hair
- Acts intentionally coy
- Touches you when you're talking

"Pressure and stress is the common cold of the psyche."

—Andrew Denton

Avoid the Mental Stress Cycle

Sometimes, stress just seems to take over. Whether you've been piling too much on your plate at home or at work (or possibly both) or it's just been one of those days where it feels like the universe is out to get you, it's important to find ways to escape the cycle before it fills you with anxiety and stress.

It's easy to get caught up in the cycle when one aspect of your life is suffering. Then, instead of tackling that problem head-on, you throw yourself into something else and try your best to race as far away from that issue as you can. Problem is, that only traps you in the cycle. The problem remains, and as the anxiety and stress of it drain your emotional energy, your ability to continue to push forward runs out, leaving you burnt out and depressed. Even positive stress—such as an upcoming marriage or the birth of a child—can be detrimental if you don't carve out enough time to prepare for the event.

When you start feeling yourself becoming overwhelmed by stress, break the cycle. Confront the issue head-on or use a calendar to plan out time for a big event so you feel like you're preparing adequately. Remember to also take some quiet time for yourself to release the stress through exercise, meditation, or thoughtful contemplation.

"Creditors have better memories than debtors."

—Benjamin Franklin

Confront the Credit Card Companies

It may sound scary, but one of the tools you can use to lower your debt and increase your wealth is to call the credit card company. If, after consolidating your debts, you still have some high-interest credit cards remaining, call the number on the back of your card and ask to speak with a supervisor. Explain calmly to this person that you have a debt-repayment plan and are working to pay off your card, but the high interest is making it difficult for you to do so and, as a result, you are requesting they lower your rate. Also explain that if they choose not to lower your rate, you'll have no other choice but to transfer the balance to another card with a lower rate. Because credit card companies make their money from outstanding debts, it is likely they'll offer you a lower interest rate in order to keep receiving payments from you.

"You will not be punished for your anger.
You will be punished by your anger."

—Buddha

Do No Harm the Buddhist Way

The ethic of reciprocity, better known as "the golden rule" in Christianity, states to do unto others as you would wish they do unto you. The golden rule of Buddhism is not so different. It states that "putting oneself in place of another, one should not kill nor cause another to kill." The Buddhist philosophy is built upon four noble truths and an eightfold path. Some of these focus on doing no harm through thought, words, or action.

Even if you are not and have no interest in becoming a Buddhist, you can incorporate these important tenets into your life. By making sure that the words you speak are honest but not harmful, that the thoughts you think about yourself and others are honest and without judgment, and that the actions you take are not intended to have a negative impact on another, you can add to others' happiness and your own. This type of belief helps to improve your tolerance of others, enabling you to be kind to others when you disagree with them and kind to yourself when you do not live up to your own expectations.

"Sports do not build character. They reveal it."

—John Wooden

Increase Your Workout Intensity

So you've been exercising. That's great. Now it's time to step up the intensity. As you exercise, your body becomes used to performing at a certain intensity, and as you become stronger, you also become more efficient at preserving energy/calories. To jolt your system so that it continues to be a fat-burning machine, you need to periodically switch up your exercises so you aren't going through the same routine each week and to push yourself further by adding in more intense exercises.

One of the most effective types of training for weight loss is interval training. Interval training alternates moderate-intensity exercise with high-intensity exercise so that your body has a chance to recover before the next big push. If you're healthy enough for the challenges of interval training and looking for faster results, interval training combined with a healthy diet is the way to go.

If you are not quite ready for interval training, try to push yourself a little bit each week. If you're walking briskly for forty minutes, try to add in ten minutes of jogging to each session every week until you can eventually jog for the entire time.

"Fresh fruits are so untainted. We don't process them, cook them, or package them. There are some fruits out there that are packed with natural energy that kids like, like kiwi fruit . . . . One kiwi has all the vitamin C you need for the day."

—Robert Stanley

Take Vitamin C

When you're sick, the first thing you may think of is to take vitamin C. But you should also work to include this vitamin in your diet when you're healthy. It's great for brain health and has been shown to greatly reduce the chance of developing vascular dementia and can even boost your memory—which means you might actually remember where you put the keys next time instead of taking the house apart to find them.

Vitamin C is also great for the body. It lowers blood pressure, aids in the breakdown of fats by synthesizing the amino acid carnitine, and mops up the free radicals that build up on artery walls and that float in the bloodstream.

To indulge in vitamin C naturally, enjoy mangos, citrus fruits, parsley, dark leafy green vegetables, tomatoes, and peppers. However, moderation is important. Too much vitamin C—more than 2,000 mg a day—can cause nausea, diarrhea, kidney stones, and stomach inflammation.

"Parsley—the jewel of herbs, both in the pot and on the plate."

—Albert Stockli

Eat Parsley

Parsley is an excellent source of vitamin C. In fact, it has more vitamin C than citrus fruit does, and it's also packed with vitamin A, vitamin K, iodine, and iron. All that vitamin C will keep your skin looking young by helping your body to create the right atmosphere so it can produce collagen and prevent your skin from drying out. In addition, the flavonoids contained in parsley protect against free radical damage that can harm skin and other organs, while parsley's chlorophyll acts as an antioxidant within your bloodstream.

For a great way to eat parsley, try making fresh tabbouleh from bulgur wheat, tomatoes, lemon juice, olive oil, mint, spring onion, and parsley. It's a super-healthy dish packed with ingredients that are great for your body.

A BRIEF HISTORY OF PARSLEY

This popular, flavorful herb has a history that dates back at least as far as the Greeks. In Ancient Greece, the plant was dedicated to Persephone, goddess of underworld and of spring. It was used in funerals and laid in tombs, and was also used to crown the victors of athletic contests. However, while the Greeks didn't eat parsley, the Romans used it as a garnish and as a way to flavor their dishes.

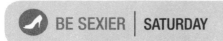
"Dancing is a perpendicular expression of a horizontal desire."

—George Bernard Shaw

Get Dirty on the Dance Floor

It's said those who are great dancers are also great in the bedroom. Though there hasn't been an official study to prove whether that's true, we think it holds water. Confidence is key to dancing well, and to be a good dance partner, you have to be able to take your partner's skills and movements into consideration.

If you find someone out on the dance floor that spikes your interest, don't wait for him to approach you; go over to him or give him a clear signal that you want him to come to you by making eye contact and smiling. Depending on the type of dance venue you're at, the two of you could end up dancing dirty. As the two of you get closer and closer, the fires of desire and anticipation might start burning hotter and hotter, until the pair of you can't take it anymore, and suddenly, you're kissing and making plans for things to go further.

SEX UP YOUR APPEAL

When you're heading out for a night on the town, here's a few things you can do to make yourself more approachable:

- Groom before you go. Shower, brush your teeth again, apply perfume, cologne or just deodorant.
- Pump up the Jams. Get ready to songs that get you in the mood to go out and that give you a boost of confidence.
- Skin is in. Whether you're a man or a woman, you want to come off as sexy, not slutty. So, show some skin with a sexy, slightly opened button-down or with a dress that shows off some cleavage or your legs. And always wear great shoes.

"All pressure is self-inflicted. It's what you make of it or how you let it rub off on you."

—Sebastian Coe

Identify the Cause of Your Stress

Stress can be a good thing. It can help us stay on track when we have a big deadline looming, or it can act as a force that pushes us to persevere in the face of adversity, such as when we're running a physical race. But it can be very detrimental to our health if it is a constant in our lives.

At first, the fight-or-flight feeling of stress boosts our adrenaline and cortisol levels to propel us forward toward our goals. But when we start to feel chronically stressed, these hormones can start to wreak havoc on the body, leaving us with depression, obesity, heart disease, sexual dysfunction, ulcers, and more.

If you suffer from chronic stress that is causing you to feel emotionally and physically burnt out, try to identify the primary cause. Start to think about what changes you can make that will help reduce your stress level. Can you go to therapy with your partner? Can you redecorate your living quarters so they're more pleasing to you? If small changes aren't going to do the trick, don't be afraid of making big ones. Though getting a new job, breaking up with a partner, or moving homes will be stressful at first, in the long run, you'll probably be glad you did.

If you are unable to eliminate the cause of your chronic stress—for instance, the loss of a loved one—find ways to relieve your stress in your daily life by discovering ways you can relax and by developing a strong support system of family and friends. You might also want to consider going to therapy to address how to handle these new emotions in a healthy way.

"Some people use one half their ingenuity to get into debt, and the other half to avoid paying it."

—George Dennison Prentice

Pay Off Your Debt with the Highest Interest Rate First

A quick way to reduce your debt is to use the snowball method of paying off your debts with the lowest balance in succession, as discussed in Week Nineteen. Another debt-reduction method is to focus on paying off the credit card, or other debt, with the highest interest rate first. By doing so, you'll avoid sinking exponentially faster into debt, because this is the card that is sending you to the poorhouse the fastest. Though either method works—paying off the lowest debt and working your way to the highest, or paying the one with the highest interest rate and working your way to the lowest—if you focus on paying off the debt with the highest rate first, you'll have a bit more cash left over when you're done.

*"Never give up. Keep your thoughts and your
mind always on the goal."*

—Tom Bradley

Exercise Mind over Matter

When you're practicing yoga and you're working on holding a particularly difficult pose, using mind over matter is what helps you stay there. It's also how you can make it through fasts, run a marathon, and push yourself beyond what your thought were your limits. Sometimes, your body just wants to give up, and that's when you have to use the strength of your mind to convince your body to operate as you wish for it to. When you feel like you're doing something just enough to get a B rating, push yourself harder. You *can* run longer and faster. You *can* write a book. You *can* learn how to play the piano or surf or whatever it is you want to do. But you will likely encounter hurdles along the way that you will have to overcome. When you reach a point at which all you want to do is to stop, you will need to tell yourself that you can keep going so that you can overcome the pain, exhaustion, stress, fear, or whatever else is holding you back from achieving your dream.

MENTAL TOUGHNESS

Have you ever started on a journey, possibly even seen progress, and then given up? Then begin working on your mental toughness today. Perhaps it takes bargaining with yourself and telling yourself you'll give yourself a healthy treat or mentally pushing yourself to do what you need to do, whether it's go for your workout or get through the last section of a project, but don't let yourself give up. If you give up on yourself, you'll be perpetuating the same cycle that disappointed you last time, but if you don't, you'll find yourself full of pride that you reached your goal.

"Manufacturers are always trying to show their machines burn the most calories. The bottom line is that if you push yourself to a moderate level you're going to burn about the same amount of calories."

—Richard Cotton

Choose High-Octane Activities

You want to lose weight? Stop using speed knitting as a workout activity. One obstacle to losing weight is that it's easy to assume you're burning more calories than you actually are during a day. One way to get around this is to use a calorie tracker, such as a bodybugg or GoFit device, but if that isn't in your price range, you need to do the work to determine how many calories you're burning when you work out. There are many online calorie calculators that can help you with this.

High-octane activities, such as running, playing football, swimming, rock climbing, snowboarding, kayaking, parkour, jumping rope, handball, and skiing will get your heart rate up and burn more calories than low-intensity activities, like gardening, walking, and golf. This doesn't mean you should give up your low-intensity exercises; just make sure that you add enough high-intensity ones to burn more calories than you eat during a day. If you work out in a gym, do not rely on the numbers the machines show you to estimate your caloric burn. Even if you put in your weight, those numbers can vary widely in accuracy and might show you're burning as much as 50 percent more calories than you actually are.

*"Why, then the world's mine oyster, which
I with sword will open."*

—William Shakespeare

Get Plenty of Zinc

Zinc is a mineral that provides many health benefits. It regulates blood sugar and carbohydrate levels, preventing your insulin levels from spiking and then plummeting, which slows your metabolism. It assists with cell growth and division, protects your sense of taste and smell, and cleans up antioxidants in the blood. It also helps your central nervous system by scrubbing your brain free of lead that enters your body—for example, by inhaling the fumes of lead gasoline when you're filling your car's tank, by breathing in particles of windblown soil containing traces of lead, or by drinking water that flowed through lead pipes. In doing so, it helps prevent brain damage.

The mineral is also necessary for healthy brain development and may even help with memory and learning throughout our lives. Zinc can be found in oysters, beef, herring, seafood, pork, poultry, milk, soybeans, and whole grains, or you can take a supplement as long as you don't exceed 40 mg a day.

OTHER USES FOR ZINC

Zinc isn't just great for the internal working of the body and helping your immune system repel viruses that can cause a cold. It can be used in other ways as well. It can help cure dandruff, act as a sunblock or a deodorant when oxidized, coat steel to protect against rust, and repel insects, and it is the base of pennies.

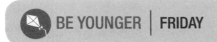
"All those vitamins aren't to keep death at bay.
They're to keep deterioration at bay."

—Jeanne Moreau, actress

Try Alpha-Lipoic Acid

You've already learned about one fatty acid that can help you lose weight and look younger: omega-3. Another powerful but less well-known fatty acid is alpha-lipoic acid (LA). This fatty acid is found in foods rich in lipollysine, such as spinach, broccoli, Brussels sprouts, and rice bran. Within the body, it functions to convert glucose into energy that can be used as fuel. It is also an antioxidant that can operate in both water and fat. By protecting against the damage done by free radicals, it can help prevent premature aging and the onset of a chronic illness.

Alpha-lipoic acid has been approved as safe by the FDA, but if you suffer from a thyroid condition or take medications that alter your blood sugar levels, consult with your doctor before adding a supplement of it to your diet.

SOME SIDE EFFECTS

Your body makes this acid, but it can also be found in supplement form or in various foods. However, higher doses may come with some possible side effects including headache, skin rash, and a feeling of pins and needles, insomnia, fatigue, and—at very high doses—hypoglycemia.

"Every woman wants to feel sexy and be made to feel sexy, no matter what she may say that is what we all want and feel good about."

—Mariska Hargitay

Send Your Partner a Sexy E-mail or Text

When you're in the mood for getting busy later, send your partner a sexy e-mail or text (also known as a "sext") in the middle of the day to their phone or e-mail account. Make it as tame or as risqué as you want, but don't be surprised if you start a sexting episode right then and there that might even lead to a lunchtime rendezvous. However, if you send out a suggestive message and your partner doesn't send anything back, don't worry. Some people just aren't fans of texting, or sometimes they're too shy to know what to say back.

This is also a great thing to do when you're traveling and away from your significant other, so you can let him know you're thinking of him. Send a few texts or e-mails while you're away that are just sweet, but sprinkle in some naughty ones as well so you can get him all hot and bothered and ready to pounce on you when you return home.

"Where we have strong emotions, we're liable to fool ourselves."

—Carl Sagan

Tame Your Emotions

Tapping into what your heart feels is important to living happily, but you cannot let your emotions take control of your life. If your rational mind didn't have some control over your actions, you'd be more likely to give in to hedonistic, risky behaviors or to let your anger get out of hand and regret your actions later or fall into a deep well of depression. If you're the type who has "cynical hostility," you'll definitely want to work on that, because not only can it hurt your personal relationships, it can also lead to the development of high cholesterol and heart disease.

Tempering your emotions, especially in emotionally intense situations, can help you to get the upper hand. When you're fighting with your partner, initially it might feel good to lash out and say all the negative things that are going through your mind, because at that point in time you feel hostile toward her or him. But consider the long-term consequences of your actions. You will likely regret your statements, and your partner might hold them against you in the future or feel alienated from you. Instead, next time you're feeling heated, ask for a time-out and let your partner know when you're ready to begin discussions again, because you don't want to say anything that might hurt him just because you're upset. Research has shown that when you fight, adrenaline pumps into your system and your heart rate can go up by as much as 20 percent. It then takes at least twenty minutes for this "emotional flooding" to recede, so you can speak rationally with your partner.

If you feel that you are quickly overwhelmed by emotions and have a hard time regulating them even when you know you should, you might want to meet with a therapist who can help you develop coping mechanisms and tools that will help you gain more control.

"Call on God, but row away from the rocks"

—Hunter S. Thompson

Practice the Law of Attraction

The basic concept of the law of attraction is that you can manifest into reality the things that you want in your life by asking for them from the universe and that you can also inadvertently manifest things you don't want in your life by focusing on them. This idea has been kicking around for more than a century, but it wasn't until 2006, when Rhonda Byrne's film *The Secret*—and the book that followed—took the world by storm. According to Byrne, there are three steps to getting what you want:

1. Ask for what you want very clearly. Have you ever heard the term "be careful what you ask for?" This is a good time to think your idea through fully to avoid asking for something you might regret.
2. Believe that you will receive what you ask for.
3. Be ready to receive the gift. It may come in an odd form at first, but it won't be long before you realize it's what you requested.

The verdict is still out, at least in terms of hard scientific data, as to whether you can manifest your own reality using the Law of Attraction. But anecdotal evidence reported by people who practice the Law of Attraction suggests that it can help you be more happy and successful. After all, working hard to achieve your goals will probably only help your cause, so it is wise to combine positive thought with positive action.

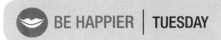

"Gratitude is the open door to abundance."

—Yogi Bhajan

Praise Behavior You Want Repeated

When you train a dog, the easiest way to get it to repeat a behavior is for you to praise the dog or give attention to that behavior. When a dog is barking and you yell at it, you're encouraging the dog to continue barking because it's getting attention. The dog doesn't know that it's getting negative attention; it just knows it's getting attention. If you are capable of only praising the behaviors you prefer—such as the dog sitting on command—and ignoring its other behaviors, then you'll be on the way to a happy and calm home.

This training tool doesn't begin and end with dogs. You can use it in parenting your children and in your relationships with other people as well. If your child or your partner is acting in a way you don't like—such as throwing a temper tantrum in a store or leaving dirty socks on the floor—the quickest way to make sure that behavior is repeated is for you to give them what they want. But that creates a negative stressful cycle. If, instead, you ignore your child's outburst or explain to her that you understand what she needs but you can't give her what she wants at the moment and crying isn't going to change that and then praise her when she is being thankful or polite or kind, the dynamic will start to become one of mutual understanding instead of a challenging push-pull conflict.

"You've got to be in top physical condition.
Fatigue makes cowards of us all."

—Vince Lombardi

Lift Weights

Starting at age thirty, you begin to lose 1 percent of your muscle mass each year. Losing muscle mass means that you'll look less toned, and because muscle burns more calories than fat, you'll have a harder time losing weight. The great news is that you can replace your lost muscle. You just have to work at it.

By doing exercises that build muscle, you'll also decrease your chances of getting osteoporosis. To build muscle, you'll need to do either strength training or weight lifting, or ideally, a combination of both. Unlike aerobic exercise, you don't have to do this kind of workout every day. Two to three time a week should be sufficient, but it's important to work all major muscle groups. Strength training means doing exercises like squats, leg lifts, push-ups, and so on; weight lifting requires you to actually lift weight.

If you're female, don't be nervous about lifting heavy weights. For years. the consensus was that women should do more reps and lift lighter weight so as not to bulk up, but more recent evidence indicates that if you want to tone up, you should do what the guys do: lift large amounts of weight fewer times. A 2002 study showed that women who did two sets of eight repetitions at 85 percent of their maximum ability had the biggest boost in their metabolism, and another revealed that lifting more weight less times was the most effective in reducing overall body fat.

"I would concentrate on making the perfect omelet. It was important to me to be able to make a perfect omelet with nothing in it."

—Mario Batali

Eat Foods High in Vitamin E

To boost your memory and prevent cognitive decline, snack on foods that include vitamin E, such as eggs, asparagus, beans, avocados, and leafy green vegetables. Within the body, vitamin E also acts as an antioxidant, removing free radicals and preventing against infertility and against heart disease that can be caused by saturated fats. If you want to take a vitamin E supplement, take it along with the mineral selenium for the best effect, and don't take more than 1,000 mg per day.

GO NUTS FOR VITAMIN E

If you like nuts, it's really easy to get enough vitamin E to meet the recommended daily amount of 14 mg. Just take a look at these numbers provided by the National Institute of Health and you'll see where they stack up in the daily value you'll receive.

20–24 almonds—40% DV
¼ cup sunflower seeds—30% DV
12 hazelnuts—22% DV
2 tablespoons peanut butter—15% DV
½ cup spinach—10% DV
1 kiwi—6% DV

---

*"To take wine into our mouths is to savor a droplet of
the river of human history."*

—Clifton Fadiman

Drink a Glass of Red Wine or Beer a Day

Though it's not wise to drink in excess, it can be good to drink in moderation. According to some studies, having a glass of red wine a day can reduce the risk of certain cancers, and heart disease and slow the onset or progression of Alzheimer's and Parkinson's disease. These health benefits are tied to a type of antioxidant called flavonoids and to a nonflavonoid known as resveratol. Reserveratol, which is found in the highest concentrations in red wine and dark grape juice, is the chemical in these beverages responsible for lowering LDL cholesterol, preventing blood clots, and reducing the risk of certain cancers.

Recently, scientists discovered that red wine isn't the only alcohol that offers health benefits. Light and medium-bodied, malty, hoppy, barley-based beers, such as India Pale Ale, have been shown to be high in silicon and by drinking these in moderation you might be able to guard against osteoporosis. Previous studies have revealed that drinking beer in moderation can also guard against type 2 diabetes and kidney and gall stones and protect against cancer. But be careful not to drink too much or you'll end up with a beer gut—or worse, as overindulging in beer, wine, or any alcoholic beverage can wreak havoc on your health!

"For women the best aphrodisiacs are words. The G-spot is in the ears. He who looks for it below there is wasting his time."

—Isabel Allende

Share Some Sexy Foods

Maybe the true road to love is through the stomach. Though most aphrodisiacs (named after Aphrodite, the Greek goddess of love) likely succeed because of the placebo effect, raw oysters might be an exception. These tasty shellfish are high in zinc, which may improve sperm in men and testosterone production in both men and women. Among its many effects, testosterone is known to increase sex drive and arousal. At the very least, the two of you will have fun slurping down these ocean-dwelling creatures (sorry, vegetarians), which resemble the female genitalia and might lead to some other kinds of excitement!

While oysters may be a powerful aphrodisiac, they're not the only one. Here are some others you might want to try

- Almond
- Asparagus
- Avocado
- Banana
- Basil
- Caviar
- Cayenne
- Chocolate
- Clove
- Egg
- Fig
- Ginseng
- Kava kava
- Kelp
- Maca
- Mango
- Pumpkin
- Tangerine
- Tomato
- Vanilla

The good news? Even if these edibles don't arouse you sexually, many of these are still very good for your body.

"Between whom there is hearty truth, there is love."

—Henry David Thoreau

Tell the Truth, Even If It's Hard to Do

One way to reduce the stress in your life is to tell the truth. It feels good to be honest—though not brutally so—to those around you. Telling the truth builds trust between partners, family, and friends and leads to longer-lasting, more meaningful relationships. Though sometimes telling the truth can be difficult to do, especially if you've done something you're not proud of, it prevents you from having to deal with the guilt of lying and the potential need to create more lies to cover up that one lie.

In addition to telling the truth, speaking up with the truth is important to being a better friend and partner. If someone you care about in your life is doing something that is harmful to herself or himself, try to be strong enough to approach that person and to speak honestly of the situation, whether it's to express your opinion that this person needs to leave a bad relationship or to stop drinking. Though you might need the help of other friends and family members to do this, your loved one is likely to appreciate your concern in the long run.

"When we are prepared for a thing, the opportunity to use it presents itself."

—Edgar Cayce

Follow the Five Steps of Manifesting

When there is something you desire, consider using the tool of manifestation to make it appear in your life. By manifesting, you set your intentions on a goal, and your mind (and, depending on your set of beliefs, the divine) guides you so that you reach it, whether that goal is to lose weight, find a more fulfilling career, or find a great partner.

There are five basic steps to effective manifesting that you should repeat daily until your intention has been fulfilled:

1. **Free your mind of negativity**. Have a clear understanding of your intention.
2. **Set forth your intention**. Verbally and mentally articulate what you desire and wish to manifest.
3. **Expect to receive what you desire**. Believe that you deserve it and that it is already yours.
4. **Envision your desire**. Visualize yourself already having what you wish to manifest.
5. **Be grateful**. Feel and express gratitude for what you already have.

"Love is the big booming beat which covers up the noise of hate."

—Margaret Cho

Become More Tolerant

Letting go of your habit of judging others for having a different lifestyle than you will lift a burden off of your shoulders. Dislike of another can come from what your parents or the society in which you were raised in taught you. You believed them either because you were too young to have a reason to disagree or because you wanted to fit in. Now, you're old enough to revisit your beliefs and to see if and why they still hold true for you. Challenge yourself to find holes in your intolerant beliefs and to be open-minded to hearing the opinions of someone whom you see as the other. You'll probably find the two of you have more in common than you thought.

As you work to become more tolerant and accepting of others and their beliefs, you will become smarter because you'll learn about other ways of life and you'll become happier because you will no longer walk around holding onto anger. Being open-minded to having friends who differ from you in their race, religion, political beliefs, sexual orientation, and other ways can enrich your own life because it allows you the opportunity to see things from another's point of view.

For more tips on how to be tolerant, go to *tolerance.org*.

"It's simple. If it jiggles, it's fat."

—Arnold Schwarzenegger

Strengthen Your Core

A toned core is not only sexy, it's also good for you. As you strengthen your abdominal and back muscles, you'll automatically improve your posture, prevent future and relieve existing back pain, and help your overall balance. Plus, you'll look even hotter than you do now.

The best exercises for strengthening the core muscles are those that require you to engage the muscles and move them around. Activities such as Pilates, yoga, boxing, gymnastics, dancing, and basketball are all excellent core exercises, as are targeted strength-training exercises. While you cannot spot-train to reduce fat, you can spot-train to increase and tone muscle. So if you need to lose body fat, make sure to burn off extra calories through aerobic activity and to strength train your core muscles so that when the fat is gone, you'll have something sexy to show for your hard work.

GREAT CORE MOVES

To improve your core muscles and posture, add the following strength training exercises to your routine:

- Crunches
- Bicycle
- Vertical Leg Crunch
- Plank
- Side Plank
- Bridge
- Reverse Crunch

"Caffeine. The gateway drug."

—Eddie Vedder

Limit Caffeine

In small doses, caffeine can be good for you. It makes you temporarily more alert by raising blood pressure, speeding up your heart rate, and increasing the amount of serotonin in the brain. If ingested before exercise, it can lessen the pain of the workout. But an addiction to caffeine can be detrimental to your health and to your mind, because it can cause dehydration, ulcers, anxiety, insomnia, and jitteriness. Within the brain, caffeine may negatively impact short-term memory.

Caffeine can also prevent the neurotransmitter adenosine from reaching its receptor cells; in response, the brain builds more of these, which results in you needing to consume more caffeine for it to have the same effect. When you try to withdraw or cut back your caffeine intake, the adenosine dilates the blood vessels in the brain and you get a headache. Your serotonin levels also plummet, making you feel groggy, irritable, and less motivated. The good news is that, after five days of reducing or ceasing your caffeine intake, these effects usually subside completely, even if you're a hardcore caffeine addict.

To stay healthy, keep your caffeine consumption to below 300 mg a day. In the following table, you'll see how much caffeine you're consuming in a single serving of popular caffeinated beverages:

DRINK	CAFFEINE	DRINK	CAFFEINE
Coke	35 grams	Red Bull	115 grams
Espresso	30–90 grams	Monster Energy	160 grams
Generic Instant Coffee	30–170 grams	Grande Starbucks Coffee	320 grams
Tea	40–120 grams		

"Yoga is the fountain of youth. You're only as young as your spine is flexible."

—Bob Harper

Improve Your Flexibility

Joke all you want about how being flexible will help you in bed, but flexibility is one of the best ways to keep your body young. The best way to become more flexible is through daily stretching and stretching after you work out. Certain exercises, such as running, can cause muscles to tighten up after you finish your workout, so it's important to stretch them back out to avoid post-workout soreness and improve your flexibility. When you stretch, make sure to hold each position for at least 30 seconds and do not bounce. Bouncing tears the muscles and causes scar tissue, which causes you to be less flexible. Also, never stretch before you warm up as you can injure cold muscles. It's best—if you can—to do a short, five-minute warm-up, to stretch, and then to continue with your workout. When you complete your workout, stretch again.

When your body is flexible, your blood circulates better so you can heal faster after injuries and be less sore after workouts. It can also improve your balance and make you less prone to falling. As we age or become less active, our muscles become shorter and less flexible. This decreases our range of movement and makes it harder for us to be active. Stretching breaks that cycle and can reverse this process.

FLEXIBILITY EXERCISES

Enrolling in yoga or Pilates classes helps improve your flexibility. No matter what your natural level of flexibility, you'll be impressed with the results after just a few weeks of training twice a week. You'll likely see your stamina, posture, and flexibility improve and find yourself looking longer and leaner.

"For those of you who like to scarf your popcorn in the sack, the good news is that Newman's Own contains an aphrodisiac."

—Paul Newman

Try a Sexy Herb from Peru

The power of most aphrodisiacs is in the placebo effect, or because they help to get the minds of those eating them thinking in sexual ways. But maca, an herb that hails from the Andean mountains and is served in many different ways within Peruvian culture, is considered an effective aphrodisiac.

If eaten in large quantities, maca can lead to the formation of goiters, because it is very high in iodine. But you can take maca extract in moderation to enhance your sex life without worry.

Though no large-scale tests have yet been performed on the efficacy of this extract, the completed studies have shown that it can enhance libido and sperm production in men. Trials have not yet been conducted to show if maca has an effect on female libido or fertility. It should be noted that the studies showed no improvement in the areas of impotence, which means that maca is unlikely to become an alternative to Viagra. Otherwise, if you want to enhance your desire and really want to pounce on your mate or your partner to pounce on you, consider taking a 1,500 mg to 3,000 mg supplement daily.

"Serenity is not freedom from the storm,
but peace amid the storm."

—Anonymous

Avoid Chronic Stress

Unlike acute stress, which we all experience from time to time when we have an important event, like a job interview, or something unexpectedly intense happens in our lives, chronic stress occurs when you feel stressed for long periods of time and feel that the situation is interminable. Chronic stress can occur when you are managing too many responsibilities or when you're working on what feels like an endless project at the office. With acute stress, the feeling of fight or flight dissipates rather rapidly and you come back down to feeling normal again. But with chronic stress, the body reacts very differently. You may find you have trouble sleeping or you might feel fatigued or have strange pains in your neck and back. Depression, anxiety, or even feelings of aggression might start to derail your emotional well-being.

When chronic stress is combined with a diet high in carbohydrates and saturated fat, you really put yourself at risk. By learning how to first say no and not take on more than you can handle, you can try and stop stress before it starts. If that's not possible, do your best to mitigate its effects through relaxing activities, exercise, and a healthy diet. You'll learn some calming techniques in the weeks ahead that will help you get this stress under control so it doesn't control you.

"He who does not economize will have to agonize."

—Confucius

Master the Ten-Second Rule

This is definitely a tactic you'll want to try if you have a habit of spending money most of the times when you leave the house. Every time you get ready to purchase an item, hold it in your hand for ten seconds and ask yourself if you really need it. You may want it, but would you rather spend that money on something else—say, on a bigger purchase? While little purchases don't seem like much at the time, they add up. If you want to see your money really grow, write down the amount you were going to spend and transfer it to your savings.

WEEK TWENTY-FIVE

"Friendship improves happiness, and abates misery by doubling our joys and dividing our grief."

—Joseph Addison

Build a Strong Support System

Though some people are natural loners, most of us require social contact to lead a happy life. These social connections and support systems can include your partner, your family, your friends, your coworkers, and other people you meet through various activities. These are the networks you can turn to when you're troubled and need to talk; these are the people you can spend time with when you need to take a break from a draining experience. Maintaining numerous support systems can help you cope better when times are rough and allows you not to put an undue burden on one person.

Studies have shown that having these support systems can help protect you from stress-related conditions and may help people with mood disorders to better deal with them. When you have strong social connections, you also tend to recover faster and to take better care of yourself following an illness or hospitalization and you require less pain medication after surgery. Plus, scientists have found that whether you're an extrovert who likes to be around people or an introvert who likes spending time alone, you might actually be measurably happier when you spend time with those with whom you have close, positive relationships.

"Physical fitness is the attainment and maintenance of a uniformly developed body with a sound mind fully capable of naturally, easily, and satisfactorily performing our many and varied tasks with spontaneous zest and pleasure."

—Joseph Pilates

Practice Pilates

Looking to be long and lean? Sign up for a Pilates class. Pilates, developed by Joseph Pilates in the early 1900s, involves putting the body through a series of exercises that help you to develop more flexibility, balance, and better posture. As with most types of yoga, Pilates is not a high-intensity aerobic exercise. Instead, this low-impact exercise will put you in tune with your body as you focus on doing each movement slowly enough to be controlled. But it's not easy. These graceful motions help tone your core and burn calories because you'll have to work hard against the resistance of your body (or a machine) to hold the positions.

Though you can practice Pilates at home, it's a good idea to learn the basics with a teacher. That will ensure you are doing the positions correctly and getting the most out of each movement. When you start to look for Pilates classes nearby, you'll find there are two primary types: those that use a mat and those that use machines, such as the Pilates Reformer. You can start out with either, though it may be easier for you to get a handle on the positions on a mat before adding the bells and whistles of the machines. Also, mat classes are less expensive because you're not helping the studio pay for the price and upkeep of the machines, so if cost is an issue, definitely start with mat courses before investing in the Reformer classes.

*"Always do sober what you said you'd do drunk.
That will teach you to keep your mouth shut."*

—Ernest Hemingway

Minimize Alcohol Consumption

Alcohol, if consumed in moderation (one or two drinks a day), isn't likely to have a negative effect on your long-term health unless you have certain conditions like diabetes or hepatitis. But when you have more than two drinks, and especially if you do this on a regular basis, your brain will suffer. Excessive alcohol consumption can cause your brain to physically shrink, and because it's a neurotoxin, it also kills brain cells. Scientists have studied the brains of alcoholics and found that the cerebellum, the primary coordination center, has been negatively affected and that alcoholics also have a harder time forming new memories. Since alcohol's impact on the brain is so strong, it should come as no surprise that heavy drinking can lead to dementia and decreased cognitive function.

WHAT IS ONE DRINK?

At your annual checkup, your doctor may ask you how many drinks you have per week. And, we're recommending you only have one or two drinks at most daily. But, because alcohol differs in potency, drinks aren't of equal volume. According to the CDC, a standard drink is 13.7 grams of pure alcohol or:

- 12 ounces of beer
- 8 ounces of malt liquor
- 5 ounces of wine
- 1.5 ounces/one shot of 80-proof distiller spirits or liquor such as rum, vodka, whiskey, etc.

"You cannot do yoga. Yoga is your natural state. What you can do are yoga exercises, which may reveal to you where you are resisting your natural state."

—Sharon Gannon

Practice Yoga Stretches and Poses

As you age, you can become less flexible and your posture can start to slip. Yoga will help reverse those processes. In Eastern culture, where yoga was developed, this ancient practice consists of eight different attributes, or "arms":

1. How we act toward others and ourselves
2. The breathing practice
3. Concentration
4. The withdrawal of the senses
5. Enlightenment
6. Meditation
7. The poses

In Western culture, however, we focus mainly on the poses, though some classes are guided with a spiritual bent and some Western practitioners of yoga believe it is a way of life. But for the most part, in this part of the world, yoga is thought of as an exercise routine. Even if you find you have no spiritual connection to the practice, you can still reap its benefits. Yoga forces you to get in touch with your body, because you learn to breathe through the pain of difficult poses as you push yourself further physically. This forces you to slow down, to focus on your breath, and to allow the rest of the world and any troubles you have at the time slip away.

Yoga doesn't just help you relax. It's also an excellent strength-training exercise that improves circulation, posture, muscle tone, and flexibility. One more added bonus? It can actually reduce the appearance of cellulite by relieving the pressure caused when the fibrous connections in skin are pulled too tightly.

*"The true feeling of sex is that of a deep intimacy,
but above all a deep complicity."*

—James Dickey

Enhance Your Intimacy

You and your partner learned how to find comfort and love in each others' eyes in Week 11. With this exercise, you can give your newfound intimacy voice.

Hand-on-Heart/Soul Sharing: Opening up about your feelings and fears is one of the best ways to become closer to one another. If one of you has been holding in a lot, that might be what is causing the separation. While this exercise might feel scary, it's important to let those things out in order to heal you and your partner's wounds.

With this exercise, your partner lies on the floor or bed while you sit next to him, and the two of you put your hand on one another's heart. When you're ready, open up and share how you're feeling with your partner. Speak from your heart, but be careful not to hurt your lover, at least intentionally, by using nonblaming words and choosing "I" statements over "you" statements. Your partner, as the listener, should strive to be nonjudging and empathetic, even if what you are saying is difficult for him or her to hear, because the purpose here is to connect, not to react or judge. If your partner starts getting emotional, it can help to take some deep breaths and allow those feelings to pass, so he or she can continue to be a supportive listener for you.

When you've said what you needed to say, thank your partner for listening. Then switch places and be your partner's listener as he or she becomes vulnerable and opens up to you. When finished, thank each other for sharing these feelings and thoughts—even if they're difficult to hear.

"Yoga is a way to freedom. By its constant practice, we can free ourselves from fear, anguish, loneliness."

—Indra Devi

Practice Yoga Meditation

Whether or not you are interested in practicing yoga, you can use yoga for meditation. Remove your shoes and sit cross-legged, if you can, or in the position known as half-lotus, with one foot up on the opposite thigh. Place your right hand, palm up, on your right knee and your left hand, palm up, on your left knee. Keep your palms open or touch your thumb to your middle or index fingers. Move your hips around until you are comfortable, and then lengthen your spine to achieve a good posture. You don't want to meditate hunched over, because although you might feel more at ease at first, you'll become uncomfortable very quickly.

Close your eyes and begin to take slow, deep breaths. From here, you can choose to focus on your breath alone or to combine this with a mantra, mandala, or internal visual meditation. Start with a five-minute meditation and work up to a half-hour or an hour as you become better at the practice.

"I believe that thrift is essential to well-ordered living."

—John D. Rockefeller

Go Coupon Shopping

Not long ago I was standing in line at Target when the woman in front of me pulled out a huge stack of coupons. As the cashier scanned each, I watched her bill plummet by over a hundred dollars. Her money-saving tool? The Sunday paper and a pair of scissors. With a little effort, you, too, can save this kind of cash on your next outing. Subscribe to the Sunday paper—this is usually less expensive than buying it off the newsstand—and each week, clip out a coupon for each product you think you might use. Tuck these coupons into your wallet, or even better, into a coupon book to take with you to the store. Even if you prefer to shop at boutique stores or to buy online goods, you will probably be able to use coupons for item you can purchase anywhere—dishwashing soap, for example. For extra savings, look in grocery store and drugstore flyers for coupon matches that you can use in conjunction with the coupons in the Sunday savers.

If you own a printer and want to spend a little longer stocking up on savings, visit coupon sites such as *www.coupons.com* and the websites for the products you often purchase to see whether either has a manufacturer's coupon that you can combine with a store coupon. If you're savvy, you might find yourself saving as much as that woman in Target or even more!

"All well-regulated families set an hour every morning for tea and bread and butter."

—Joseph Addison

Make Time for Family

No matter how busy you become with your work and social life, it's always important to find time for your family. They will help ground you and allow you to be yourself. By supporting your family in the things they enjoy and asking them to support you, you will become closer as a unit and you will personally feel happier, because you know you have a support system to fall back on. Make sure that even if each member of your immediate family has outside responsibilities, you all come together at least once each day, whether it's for breakfast or dinner. If you have multiple children, find ways to connect with each of them on an individual level as well.

And don't just limit your attention to your immediate family. Spend the time to call your other relatives, to write letters, and to bring everyone together as often as you can.

SIMPLE WAYS TO CONNECT

Here are some ideas on how to connect with your immediate family more regularly:

- Plan a weekly movie night. Whether you go out or stay in, each week alternate who gets to pick the movie.
- Schedule one night or one day a week for exercising together. Go bowling, hiking, play soccer, go to the batting cages, but do it together as a family.
- Celebrate accomplishments. Show your family members that their successes mean something to the family unit, whether it's with a high-five, a big hug, a toast, or a small token of your love like a bouquet of flowers.

"Durability is part of what makes a great athlete."

—Bill Russell

Improve Your Stamina

The longer you can exercise, the more calories you'll eventually burn. While interval training is an excellent weight-loss tool and doesn't require as much of a time investment as other types of exercise, you'll need enough stamina to push through the pain. As you build your endurance, you'll find it easier to stay in motion, because your heart and lungs won't have to work as hard.

To increase your stamina, exercise at least five times a week and alternate harder days with easier ones so you won't overwork your body and can allow it to recover on the lighter days. Each week, try to do a little more. An easy way to do this is to keep a log of your exercises. If you did three sets of ten reps one week, then up the weight or up the reps the next week. Or if you were able to bike for 30 miles last week, make the next week's goal 35 miles. As you continue to push the limits of your body, you'll become stronger, healthier, and leaner.

BUILD IN REST DAYS

When you're training hard to improve your stamina, it's very important to build hard, easy, and rest days into your schedule. By alternating between hard and easy workouts, you'll give your body enough of a break to recover for when you need to push it to the max and the rest days will help prevent injury from overuse.

---

*"A woman is like a teabag. You never know how
strong she is until she gets into hot water."*

—Eleanor Roosevelt

Make Herbal Tea

Green tea offers incredible health benefits, but sometimes, you might not be in the mood for green tea. When you want a hot drink, but want a different flavor than what green tea or coffee offers, reach for herbal tea, more accurately known as tisane. Herbal teas are made mostly from the dried flowers, leaves, stems, or other parts of various plants. Because their base does not contain the tea plant, many herbal teas are caffeine free. There are many varieties of herbal tea, but here are some you might want to try:

- **Bilberry.** May improve circulation, lower blood sugar levels, and reduce inflammation
- **Catnip.** Acts as a relaxant and mild depressant
- **Chamomile.** A soothing tea that promotes sleepiness and relaxation
- **Chicory.** May normalize liver function
- **Dill.** May calm the stomach
- **Ginseng.** Can help you battle the effects of stress
- **Gotu kola.** Can act as a sedative but can also help strengthen brain functions
- **Hawthorn.** May improve heart conditions
- **Rooibus**. Though caffeine free, this red tea offers many of the same benefits as green tea
- **Yerba mate**. May boost metabolism, reduce fatigue, and sharpen the mind.
- Caution: If you are pregnant or have a medical condition such as high blood pressure, check with your doctor before drinking any herbal tea.

*"Enthusiasm is the yeast that makes
your hopes shine to the stars."*

—Henry Ford

Try Some Kombucha

Kombucha, a fermented tea made from a bacteria culture, yeast, and black tea has recently gained attention because its fans claim it can do everything from cure cancer to improve your eyesight. While the FDA and the scientific community have yet to weigh in on whether kombucha can fight cancer cells; improve the rods and cones in eyes; or help with arthritis, obesity, constipation, impotence, and so on, what we *can* tell you is that most kombuchas do carry B vitamins, and B vitamins are great for your skin, hair, and nails as well as for your mood and metabolism.

If you have a healthy immune system, aren't pregnant, and aren't suffering from any bacteria-related diseases, you might want to give kombucha a try. I recommend a daily four-ounce serving. It's found in the refrigerated section of most health food stores and the carbonated drink has both a sweet taste and a sour, vinegar-like tang.

MAKE YOUR OWN

Kombucha is healthy (and delicious!) but it can also be expensive, sometimes costing upwards of $3 for sixteen ounces. To cut down costs, brew your own. You'll need black tea, sugar, a jar you can seal, and a SCOBY (a yeast and bacteria culture obtained from a kombucha "mother"). Happy Herbalist sells these and they have a great step-by-step guide on how to brew this fizzy drink at *www.HappyHerbalist.com/kombucha_brewing_guide.htm*.

"An oil massage, a hot bath, a good night's sleep, soft smells and music, and clothes with soft textures denote sensuality to me."

—Padma Lakshmi

Share an Erotic Massage

If you want to get your partner seriously turned on, try giving him or her an erotic massage.

Have your partner lie face down on a flat, comfortable surface. Start with light, relaxing caresses. As you work over your partner's body, bring both hands gently down on either side of his or her spine, and with soft, broad strokes, glide your hands from the top of the back down to the small of the back, and over the hips.

Extend the strokes gradually to cover the butt, the sides of the hips, and the arms, and then move down the legs, gliding over the calf, the back of the knee, up the hamstrings, and over the butt. Continue up the side of the back, over the shoulder, and down the arm on the same side. Repeat the sequence over the other side of your partner's body.

Gently ask your partner to turn over so you can attend to the front. Start the movement by gliding over the shin and across the top of the thigh and down the other side of the leg all the way back to the ankle. Allow your fingers to come close to your lover's genitals and even linger nearby, but don't actually touch them. The inner thighs are creases where the thighs end and are extremely sensitive; you can build sexual tension by stroking them.

"If there is light in the soul / There will be beauty in the person. If there is beauty in the person / There will be harmony in the house. / If there is harmony in the house / There will be order in the nation. If there is order in the nation / There will be peace in the world."

—Unknown

Follow Some Feng Shui Tips

If you want to Feng Shui your home to the fullest, you're probably going to need an expert. But you can make some adjustments on your own that will help improve your home's positive energy:

- Clear out the clutter. Not only can clutter be stressful, it also prevents energy from flowing well.
- Add mirrors to create a feeling of more space, to double good energy, and to deflect negative energy.
- Don't hang a mirror so that you can see yourself when you walk in the door. This will send the positive energy right back outside.
- Place a water fountain in a section of your home where you want to attract positive energy.
- Keep only positive images in your home
- Open the windows in the house each day to let fresh energy and oxygen into the home, but only keep them open for a little while if it is cold outside.
- Use pairs in your bedroom (candlesticks, photographs, nightstands on either side of the bed) to welcome in and enhance love.

"I have always imagined that Paradise will be a kind of library."

—Jorge Luis Borges

Check Out the Library—and Not Just for Books

If you've exhausted your personal DVD library, are looking for new music to listen to, and can't bear to watch one more show on Hulu, head over to your local library. Libraries aren't just great places from which to borrow books anymore. Many libraries now also house impressive DVD and audio collections, so once you've signed up for a library card, you can get a movie to watch for the night without spending a dime.

As an added bonus, some libraries host film nights, and local special-interest groups might meet at the library for their get-togethers or may post invites to their meetings on the library's bulletin board. So if you're looking for a knitting circle or friends to garden with, the library's bulletin board might be worth a look.

"The one thing I remember about Christmas was that my father used to take me out in a boat about ten miles offshore on Christmas Day and I used to have to swim back. Extraordinary. It was a ritual. Mind you, that wasn't the hard part. The difficult bit was getting out of the sack."

—John Cleese

Start a Tradition with Your Family

When you were growing up, I bet your family had traditions, or you wished they had. Now is the time to carry on these beloved traditions, or to start new ones, with your own family. Sit down with your partner and brainstorm some ideas that can help bring your family closer together. The tradition can be something you do weekly or annually during certain holidays or other special events, like birthdays or your anniversary. If you put your heart into these activities, you and your family will eagerly anticipate each week, month, or holiday, and your kids might even pass them down to their children.

If you don't have children yet, you can create new traditions with your partner. Make a plan to share a bottle of wine and make dinner together on Sunday nights. Be active together on Saturday mornings. Schedule a weekly brunch with your friends, trading hosting duties each week. Whomever you plan your traditions with, strive to make sure everyone is fully involved, which means laptops and cell phones are off or put away. The possibilities are endless.

"There are no bungs in football, only presents."

—Eric Hall, football agent

Be Active with Your Family

Exercise doesn't have to be a solitary activity. It can be a great way to spend time with your family or your partner. Instead of planning yet another movie outing, teach your children how to play soccer or take them on a hike or a bike ride. Engaging in team activities helps them to understand cooperation, respect for the rules, and good sportsmanship, and can improve their overall self-esteem and confidence. These outdoor activities not only burn calories and show your family that exercise can be fun, they also allow for more family bonding, as they require you to interact with one another in passing the ball or pointing out wildlife. The earlier you can instill an interest in physical activity in your children, the more likely they will be able to stay on this healthy path throughout their lives.

ACTIVITY IDEAS

Stuck on what to do? Here are some fun ideas that can get you and your family moving.

- Throw sports parties at roller rinks, laser tag courts, paintball fields, baseball diamonds, or anywhere else your family and their friends might have fun.
- Play active video games. With the Wii, the Xbox 360's Kinect, and the PlayStation's Move you and your family can play games together and burn calories.
- Join a race together. Whether it's a 5K or something longer, sign your family up for a race and start practicing together as a team so you can motivate each other.

"Tea is drunk to forget the din of the world."

—T'ien Yiheng

Drink Green Tea

It seems that each day scientists discover a new benefit that green tea can provide—from lowering your risk of cancer to inhibiting the growth of bacteria that causes periodontal disease and cavities. Here are just some of the benefits this impressive little leaf offers:

- Drinking five cups or more a day can reduce the risk of stroke by half in women over forty.
- Green tea can help prevent heart disease and atherosclerosis.
- Drinking more than ten cups can protect against liver damage from alcohol.
- The ECGC contained in green-tea leaves can aid in weight loss.
- Green tea may lower bad cholesterol levels.
- By absorbing free radicals, green tea protects your skin against damage from the sun.
- Green tea protects against age-related cognitive impairment.

Though green tea is great, do keep in mind that it does contain caffeine, and too much caffeine is not good for you. Each eight-ounce serving contains between 30 and 60 mg of caffeine, so you shouldn't drink more than five cups a day without consulting a doctor.

"If you don't like what you're doing, you can always pick up your needle and move to another groove."

—Timothy Leary

Try Acupuncture

It might sound like science fiction, but having needles stuck in your face might be the key to looking younger. And by needles I don't mean Botox; I mean acupuncture. Acupuncture is a traditional Chinese medicine practice that involves inserting very thin needles into acupuncture points in the body to help the *qi* ("life force") flow properly again. While the American Medical Association doesn't hold much faith in the power of acupuncture, in 2003, the World Health Organization stated that acupuncture has had a positive effect on diseases ranging from strokes and headaches to rheumatoid arthritis and depression. It also has been touted as a weight loss tool and a way to increase metabolism. In 2009, it came to light that getting facial acupuncture may reduce the appearance of fine lines and wrinkles, because the needles may stimulate the production of collagen and elastin, which help to give your skin that plump, young look.

If you are going to have acupuncture done, only go to a practitioner who has been licensed by the National Certification Commission of Acupuncture and Oriental Medicine.

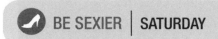

"True love begins when nothing is looked for in return."

—Antoine de Saint-Exupery

Place a Note under Your Partner's Pillow

For a truly *aww* moment, write your significant other a love note and tuck it under his or her pillow. It can be something as simple as "I love you," or you can try writing a love poem or giving your lover a small card with a list of all the reasons you love him or her on it. Even if you're not around when your partner finds your love letter, rest assured you'll have made your partner's day and he or she will be beaming and ready to shower you with love and kisses the next time you see one another.

A sweet thing you can do if your partner is traveling out of town is to sneak an "I love you" or an "I miss you" note into his or her suitcase, along with a smiling photo of you or the two of you together. When your lover discovers your little gift while unpacking, it will make him or her feel loved and excited to get back home to see you!

"Noble deeds and hot baths are the best cures for depression."

—Dodie Smith

Take a Warm Bath

Soaking in a bath after a long day or a hard workout can be just the ticket to finding peace and relaxation. If you've been suffering from insomnia, a warm bath an hour or two before bedtime can help you sleep. To create a relaxing environment, turn down or turn off the lights and illuminate the room with candles; bring in a book or magazine you enjoy, if reading helps take your mind off of things; play soothing music; put a thick, rolled-up towel behind your head; and use a space heater, if you have one, so you can stay warm after you leave the water. You can use aromatherapy—for example, adding a few drops of essential lavender oil to the water—to further relax you, or if you're extra sore, drop two Epsom salts into the water to ease the tension in your muscles.

For an even more luxurious experience, consider a milk and honey bath, like Cleopatra used to enjoy. Not only will you feel like royalty, you'll also be rewarded with soft skin. Combine half a cup of honey with two to three cups of powdered milk and add these to the bath once the water has been turned off. After the milk-and-honey mixture dissolves, sprinkle in some rose petals or lavender buds.

"A man who does not think and plan long ahead will find trouble right at his door."

—Confucius

Plan Ahead for Big Purchases

For many people, it isn't until it's time to buy a car or to start planning for some major expense, like a wedding or extended vacation, that they start thinking, How am I going to pay for this?

To avoid this dilemma, start planning for the big events and purchases in your future now. Make a list of all the big-ticket items you think you might want to do in the next five, ten, or even fifteen years. Do you eventually want to get married? Do you plan to own a house someday? Would you love to take a long trip overseas? Is owning a sports car or a pair of Christian Louboutans on your wish list? Do you have kids who might need braces or who want to go to college? Once you've made your list of all the items you want to save for, decide how much of a percentage of your savings should be allocated to each. Then, each time you put away savings, put that percentage into the appropriate bin.

This way, instead of panicking when the moment comes when you need to buy something, or feeling that you'll never get to purchase what you want, you'll have already stored up a large portion (if not all) of the funds you need to put down for that car loan or to purchase that high-ticket item you've been lusting after without having to worry about high loan payments or credit card debt.

"Family and friends are hidden treasures.
Seek them and enjoy their riches."

—Wanda Hope Carter

Make a Video of an Older Family Member Sharing Memories

Today's digital tools permit us the chance to capture our loved ones on film. Before parents, grandparents, or any other relatives get any older, sit down with them and videotape a conversation. They might feel weird at first, but assure them that you are doing this so you can watch it when you're not together and that you're not planning on posting it on YouTube. If there is a particular story you'd like to hear again or one you'd like to learn more about, start there. Ask them about their parents, their childhood, their adventures. Ask them about living through the war, the depression, the free love era. Did they fight in any wars? Did they go to Woodstock? If there's an item of jewelry someone has always worn, ask her or him about the story behind it. Pretend you're a journalist digging for a good story, ask questions and listen attentively, and you're bound to hear, and record, many great stories.

"A computer once beat me at chess, but it was no match for me at kickboxing."

—Emo Philips

Take a Kickboxing Class

To really rev up your calorie-burning potential, sign up for a kickboxing class. Learning to jab, uppercut, roundhouse, and more is sure to boost your self-esteem and confidence, plus it will give you some self-defense skills and melt away those pounds. You'll be working your entire body intensely for forty-five minutes to an hour in an interval-style workout that will burn calories with cardio and require you to engage in strength training moves that will tone your arms, legs, core, and butt. Stressed about your job or anything else in your life? This is a great, positive place to let all of that anger out.

KICKBOXING STYLES

There are many different styles of kickboxing that you can learn, but here are some of the most popular.

- **Muay Thai:** This form uses punches, kicks, elbows, knee strikes, clinches, and foot stomps to allow you to connect with your opponent in eight different ways.
- **Lethwei:** This Burmese style uses punches, kicks, elbows, knee strikes, head butts, and bare knuckle strikes.
- **Taekwondo:** This Korean style uses punches, kicks, blocks, throws, and open-handed strikes.

"All you need is love. But a little chocolate now and then doesn't hurt."

—Charles M. Schulz

Eat Chocolate

Improve your intelligence by indulging in chocolate—in moderation, of course. Make sure to eat only high-quality dark chocolates that are made from real cocoa butter and a minimal amount of sugar. Cheaper dark chocolates may contain wax, hydrogenated palm oil, preservatives, and lots of sugar, and those ingredients counteract chocolate's benefits, which include lowering blood pressure and decreasing LDL cholesterol levels.

Quality dark chocolate also does an excellent job of protecting your brain and body from free radicals, because it is packed with more antioxidants than any other fruit or vegetable. In fact, it has twice the amount of antioxidants than what is found in red wine and up to three times the amount found in green tea. Researcher Henriette van Praag has also discovered that epicatechin, a compound found in cocoa, can improve the brain's learning and memory capacities, which may be due to the fact that this same chemical also increases the blood flow to the brain.

It doesn't hurt that chocolate is also delicious.

"But you're saying a foot massage don't mean nothing, and I'm saying it does."

—Vincent Vega, in *Pulp Fiction*

Try Reflexology

Reflexology is similar to acupuncture in that the idea is to remove blockages throughout the body so that the *qi* can flow freely. Unlike acupuncture, reflexology uses no needles, and nothing is inserted into the body. Instead, a reflexologist puts pressure on different spots of your feet or hands that connect to zones on your body. For instance, the pressure point for your heart is located on the ball of your foot, so if you were having trouble with your heart or cardiovascular system, a reflexologist might concentrate on this area.

Though science has yet to prove the benefits of reflexology, it is, at the very least, an effective stress-relieving activity. Having your hands and feet worked on by a master reflexologist is akin to getting a great massage, and you're bound to come out of the office feeling refreshed.

If you're interested in learning more about reflexology, you can find a chart online at Ofesite.com.

"What comes first in a relationship is lust. Then more lust."

—Jacqueline Bisset

Take a Steamy Shower Together

When the feeling of being enveloped by a large body of water, such as a pool, lake, or even the ocean, is combined with sex, the feeling is incredible. But if you don't have easy access to a natural body of water, you can recreate part of that feeling in the shower.

The next time your partner takes a long shower (not the five-minute kind, where he has to run to work right after), wait a few moments and then step into the shower with him. Soap up your lover's back, legs, and shoulders, and then slowly start to move your hands to lather up his nether region. Kiss his wet skin and pull him under the falling water to steal a passionate, underwater-like kiss on the mouth.

If the two of you have the time, consider going down on your partner or try having sex while the water rushes down on the two of you. Few intercourse positions work well in the shower because of the slipperiness of the wet shower surfaces, a standing version of rear entry is a good starting position to try. Or you can plan ahead and pick up some shower adhesives so the two of you can have more grip to attempt other angles.

"What my mother believed about cooking is that if you worked hard and prospered, someone else would do it for you."

—Nora Ephron

Assign Each Household Member a Night to Cook

For some of us, cooking is a great way to unwind after a long day at work. The time spent preparing a dish allows us to decompress because we have to put aside our stress from the day and focus on executing a tasty meal. But for others, it's just another thing that must be done before we can finally relax. If you're the latter and you have a partner, a family, or share your home with a roommate who tends to be around at night, consider splitting the kitchen duties and assigning each member of the household a night to plan and cook a dinner. This will allow you time away from the kitchen, and especially if you have children, allow the other members of the household to learn how to cook.

You'd be surprised at the meals even small children can prepare. Though an adult should always supervise younger kids in the kitchen and even tweens may need supervision or help with cutting something or using the stove or oven, most kids can make sandwiches and salads on their own. Start with teaching them how to make peanut butter and jelly sandwiches and work your way up to Cuban sandwiches and salads with apples, cheese, walnuts, and balsamic dressing. You'll soon have a little gourmet chef on your hands!

"We must make the best of those ills which cannot be avoided."

—Alexander Hamilton

If You Go over Your Cell Minutes, Upgrade Your Plan

It may seem counterintuitive, but if you've been going over your cell phone minutes or texting limits regularly, it's time to upgrade your plan. This is something I personally resisted for months. But take a look at your cell phone bill. If you're always over, or nearly over, your maximum number of minutes or texts, determine how much you're paying in those extra minutes versus how much the next plan up would cost. You'll probably realize you'd be spending less money in the long run—and you'll certainly be less stressed about your minutes—if you upgraded to the next size plan.

Another option is to speak to some of the people you call regularly to see if they'd be willing to switch to your network, or you could consider switching to theirs. If you're the only person in your immediate circle who is on another network, consider switching so that your regular phone calls don't eat up any of your minutes.

WEEK TWENTY-NINE

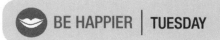

"Families are about love overcoming emotional torture."

—Matt Groening

Schedule a Family Meeting Each Week to Air Grievances

Though some experts disagree, most psychologists and behavioral therapists believe that holding in emotions can lead to feelings of depression, anxiety, and stress and even cause insomnia. It's important to share feelings constructively, not only with your partner, but also with other members of your immediate family.

Schedule a time each week for the family to come together, and allow members to talk about anything that has been bothering them. Perhaps they're going through something at school, or perhaps they're angry with you for not doing x, y, or z. No matter who is at fault, set a good example for the rest of the family by first being empathetic to whoever has an issue to air. Then take the time to discuss the problem and offer constructive solutions. Allow other family members to offer their ideas, if appropriate, and calmly state your piece as well. If you have children who have a tendency to interrupt each other, make a rule that whoever is holding the talking stick (or other object) is the only person allowed to speak.

By making these sessions a regular part of your family interactions, you'll teach your children how to discuss difficult issues in a constructive manner. This will serve them well in the future when they face problems at work or in their own relationships. In addition, by being empathetic and nonjudgmental, you increase the bond between you and your child, and they'll be more likely to be open and honest with you about what is going on with their lives.

"If you can keep playing tennis when somebody is shooting a gun down the street, that's concentration."

—Serena Williams

Sign Up for Tennis Lessons

Playing tennis, either with friends or through a lesson, is a great workout. It will improve your eye-hand coordination, burn serious calories, and if you're playing doubles, you may learn how to work better as a part of a team. If your spouse needs to lose a few pounds, it's perfect, because unless you are practicing against a wall or with a ball machine, you're going to need a second person. You'll soon discover that tennis uses all the major muscle groups, and because of that, it shouldn't be played daily. However, unlike some heavy-contact sports, it is an activity that can be enjoyed throughout your lifetime.

If it's been some time since you've played tennis, consider taking a lesson. A lesson can help you unlearn bad habits you may have picked up. You'll also learn the best ways to move on the court, how to position your body, and how to swing properly so you have a powerful serve or return and don't hurt yourself.

As you play tennis, don't be surprised to find that not only are your tennis skills improving but your overall stamina, speed, coordination, agility, and flexibility are improving as well. According to Harvard's Dr. Ralph Paffenbarger, individuals who play at least three hours of tennis a week cut their risk of death from *any* cause by half. Maybe that alertness really does come in handy if there's a bus approaching.

"Memory is the mother of all wisdom."

—Aeschylus

Eat Blueberries

Blueberries are one of Dr. Oz's favorite foods. They should also be one of yours. The tiny berry is high in fiber, has the highest concentration of antioxidants of all fresh fruit, and can aid in reducing belly fat and heart disease. This tart fruit can also help your vision by preventing or delaying the onset of cataracts, macular degeneration, and myopia. In a nutshell, they'll help make you thinner, healthier, and younger. What's not to love?

Blueberries are also good brain food. According to Dr. James Joseph, a neurologist at Tufts University, blueberries are able to *reverse* short-term memory loss and slow the effects of aging by reducing cell damage done by toxins. They also strengthen the signals fired between neurons, which keeps cognitive functioning high. For the greatest impact, eat half a cup of fresh blueberries a day or use half a cup of frozen blueberries along with fat-free milk to make a smoothie.

BLUEBERRY RELATIVES

Blueberries are powerful little berries, but they're not alone. Within the *Vaccinum* family are other healthy berries you might want to check out. These include the huckleberry, lingonberry, cranberry, gooseberry, and the bilberry, which is very popular in Russia and can help prevent eye disorders like cataracts.

"When I want to reward myself, I get a relaxing massage."

—Eva Longoria Parker

Get a Massage

If you're an athlete or a fitness buff, a post-workout massage can relieve the soreness within your muscles so that you aren't in pain for days and can continue to push yourself in your workouts. But massage is great for non-exercisers too. It allows the body to relax, which helps reduce blood pressure and the amount of the stress-hormone cortisol in your blood. Just by experiencing this touch, you're protecting yourself from heart disease, stress-related diseases, and possibly from catching a cold. If you've been feeling stiff because of a disease, bad posture, or stress, a massage can help your muscles and joints regain more mobility and allow you to be more active.

There are many types of massage. These are some of the most common:

- **Swedish**. Features long, flowing strokes and can reduce pain and improve circulation
- **Shiatsu**. Mixes acupressure and stretching together to relieve tension
- **Deep tissue**. Works the muscles that lie below the first layer of superficial muscles and is excellent for relieving or reducing chronic pain
- **Thai**. Blends yoga poses with traditional massage techniques. During a Thai massage, you remain fully clothed and no oil is used.

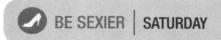
"People don't want to see me having sex . . . I'm the queen of the 'kiss, foreplay, dissolve.' And then the 'Whoo! Good morning, tiger.'"

—Julia Roberts

Don't Skip Foreplay

Though it might be tempting to jump right into sex, make quickies the exception and make building up the anticipation through foreplay the norm. In doing so, you and your partner will spend more time getting to know each other's turn-ons and turn-offs, and you'll be able to connect with each other better in the bedroom and out of it.

Instead of seeing foreplay as a chore, use it to tease your partner and get him so turned on he can't take it anymore and has to have sex with you then and there. It's up to you and your lover as to whether orgasms are a part of foreplay or if you want to get him almost to the point of orgasm before leading into intercourse. According to a recent study by the University of New Brunswick, the average length of desired foreplay is only eighteen minutes long. So there's no reason why you can't fit in foreplay, to get your partner all revved up to go, before you have intercourse—especially since you're both likely to have an enjoyable experience, and that leads to a healthier sex life in the long run.

"Every once in a while, a girl has to indulge herself."

—Sarah Jessica Parker

Take a Spa Day

Save up for a spa day. For both men and women, the experience of pampering yourself at a luxurious spa can be a very relaxing experience as long as you schedule it on a day when you are free of to-dos and can fully immerse yourself in the experience. Depending on the spa, a typical day package might involve a massage, a facial, a light lunch, access to a sauna or aromatic steam room, a manicure, and pedicure. You'll leave the spa after a few hours feeling relaxed and refreshed.

If you can't afford a spa day, create your own with a friend, family member, or lover. Set up your bedroom with candles, put in a relaxing CD or play list, and cover your bed with a super soft towel. Pick up a bottle of unscented massage oil or a massage oil that has the essence of lavender, rose, jojoba, or another relaxing scent. Have the person receiving the massage lie down on the bed, put some oil in your hands to warm it up, and start working on your partner (or friend). Make sure to go slowly and cover all the parts of the body that the other person is comfortable with you massaging. After you're finished and your partner (or spa buddy) has taken a few moments to enjoy the feeling of his or her body post-massage, switch places. If you want to really make it feel like a spa, have some cucumber slices and other items on hand for make homemade facial masks, and consider giving each other manis and pedis. Men can enjoy those as well, even if they opt for no polish.

"Beware of little expenses; a small leak will sink a great ship."

—Benjamin Franklin

Cut Back on Your Lattes

How serious is your latte habit? Do you stop for a cup of joe every day or most days of the week? Is getting your morning brew a ritual that brings you pleasure? Have you gotten to know the barista and some of the regulars? Do your coffee runs serve as part of your social interaction for the first part of the day, as it does for some people, such as those who work from home? Or is it simply utilitarian? . . . You need caffeine; the experience isn't that important.

If you're the latter type, consider swapping out this expensive habit with an investment in a home espresso machine or buying better coffee to brew and drink at the office. Take the money you would have spent buying coffee or tea out and add it to your automatic savings account. If you're spending three dollars a day on coffee, you could save up to a thousand dollars a year.

Another way of saving money when you go out is to look at your restaurant habits, especially if you run over your entertainment budget. Instead of telling your partner and friends you can't go out, replace any sodas you might have had with water and lemon. (If you want to get in shape, you shouldn't be drinking soda anyway.) Rather than ordering an entrée yourself, split an entrée with a friend or order two appetizers. Considering the portion sizes in most of today's restaurants, you certainly won't go hungry.

"We were born to unite with our fellow man, and to join in community with the human race."

—Marcus Tullius Cicero

Join a Travel Club, Cooking Group, or Service Organization

Expanding your social circle can make you happier. A great way to do that is by joining or starting a group that is centered around something you are interested in or care about. Start by finding out what is already available in your area through a site such as *www.Meetup.com*. Search for an interest you have—hiking, bowling, cooking, traveling, volunteering etc.—and see if there are any established groups that you could join. If there aren't, start one of your own and let your community know that you're looking for members.

By doing this, you're now making yourself and your own interests a priority. This is especially necessary if you have a habit of putting others first and don't address your own needs. As you start to go to more of these group events, you'll become more committed to taking time for yourself and you'll likely feel happier and mentally recharged after these meetings. Plus, you'll probably make some new friends! That's because making friends within these groups can be easy, as you are meeting people with whom you already share at least one similar interest and you can use that topic as a jumping-off point for conversations.

"I haven't had sex in eight months.
To be honest, I now prefer to go bowling."

—Lil' Kim

Join a Softball or Bowling League

Softball and bowling are not the most aerobic of sports, but they will get you moving, and something is better than nothing. By signing up for a league, you'll be responsible for showing up for league play every week and expected to do your best. That pressure might inspire you to head to the lanes or the batting cages during the week to practice in anticipation of the upcoming game. Invite your friends out to watch you play if you need a little more incentive to play well. As you strive to get a home run or increase your strike potential, you'll probably start working out a little more often on the side.

If you've had a hard time staying committed to exercising, joining one of these leagues means you'll be burning extra calories at least one day a week. That, hopefully, will help convince you that burning calories doesn't have to be a chore and can involve bonding, friendship, and even laughter!

IMPROVE YOUR BURN

Just because these sports aren't the most high-intense exercises you could be doing (on average, a 160-pound person burns 365 calories in an hour of softball and 219 calories bowling), there are things you can do during play to boost those numbers. If you're playing a field position, squat when you're not running for the ball. It will keep you alert and you'll be ready to pop up for the ball when it comes your way. If you're bowling, consider doing lunges between turns. And, between events, think about practicing sprints from home to first base and back again or lifting weights so you can use a heavier ball and knock those pins down with ease.

*"Govern a great nation as you would cook
a small fish. Do not overdo it."*

—Lao Tzu

Eat Fish Low in Mercury Content

Unless you're vegetarian, I hope you've added fish to your diet so you can benefit from this lean protein's omega-3 fatty acids and other health benefits. However, you do need to choose your fish wisely, because some fish are high in mercury. Consuming too much mercury can result in mercury poisoning, which damages the brain, lungs, and kidneys and can result in sensory impairment, muscle weakness, and difficulty with coordination.

To avoid mercury poisoning, follow these FDA and EPA guidelines:

- Consume very limited amounts of or no shark, swordfish, king mackerel, or tilefish.
- Eat no more than 6 ounces (two servings) of tuna steaks, canned white tuna, lobster, halibut, or orange roughy a week
- Eat no more than 12 ounces (four servings) of shrimp, canned light tuna, salmon, Pollock, catfish, cod, crab, flounder, sole, grouper, haddock, herring, mahi-mahi, ocean perch, oysters, trout, sardines, scallops, or tilapia per week.

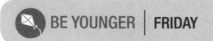

"Love is like seaweed; even if you have pushed it away, you will not prevent it from coming back."

—Proverb

Try Sea Vegetables

You might not think of eating anything that comes from the sea other than fish and shellfish, but some plants that thrive in the ocean water are also good for you. Seaweed and algae are high in essential vitamins and minerals and are present within the plants in a form that makes them easier for the body to absorb. These plants are very high in iodine, which helps the thyroid function properly, as well as folate, vitamin K, and lignans, a plant substance that may help protect the body from cancer. The brown sea varieties of kelp, wakame, and kombu contain a compound known as alginic acid, which can remove heavy metals from the digestive tract.

To indulge in sea vegetables, you can eat sushi, as it's wrapped in seaweed, munch on dried seaweed as a snack, or use the plants in a salad. Some people mix kombu with beans, as it is said to help reduce the flatulence beans can cause. Good for you and good for your company! It's a win-win.

"Eroticism is like a dance: one always leads the other."

—Milan Kundera

Tempt Your Partner with Kisses, Love Bites, and More

During foreplay or during sex itself, drive your partner wild by giving open-mouthed kisses all over. Trace over his erogenous zones with your tongue, and consider blowing on these areas to give him a rush of intensity. Draw a curving line from your lover's neck all the way down to his pubic bone, and you'll feel him give a pelvic thrust or a hand on top of your head signaling to you that he wants you to take your tongue just a little bit further.

You can also tantalize your partner with love bites. Bite his skin gently in the fleshy areas, and listen to him moan. If he likes it, you can bite harder, but make sure to ease off if your partner says "ow" or indicates pain. Scratching is another technique you can use that some people love. Start by scratching lightly, gently drawing your nails along your partner's thighs, back, or arms, pressing harder if asked. The red marks will fade in moments, but the fun memories will last much longer.

"A hunch is creativity trying to tell you something."

—Frank Capra, film director

Try Creative Therapy

When you tap into your creative conscious, you can unlock pathways that have blocked you and start to see the world in a different light. By allowing yourself to create without judgment and without censoring your creative expression, you can begin to work through stress, depression, grief, and other negative emotions that have prevented you from moving forward. This type of activity stimulates a different part of your brain than you're accustomed to using and can provide you with a more well-rounded perspective.

Creative therapy can also help you when you're not feeling "stuck." By engaging with that part of your brain and allowing your inner child to run wild, your brain may start to generate new positive ideas of things to build and create and paths to travel. Try to engage in creative therapy for at least thirty minutes two to three times a week so you can really get in touch with your child-like self. You can do anything that you find stimulates your mind, whether it is painting, playing a musical instrument, constructing pottery, knitting, writing, acting, or dancing. The point is to shake you out of your routine and have your thoughts follow a new track.

"When one tugs at a single thing in nature, he finds it attached to the rest of the world."

—John Muir

Install a Programmable Thermostat

If you operate your house temperature using a thermostat, consider installing a programmable one. They're available at most hardware stores, and though installing it requires a little technical know-how, it's not very difficult. If you have the basic, manual wall thermostat, all you'll need is a screwdriver to remove the old one, a drill to mount the new one, and the ability to tell red wires from whites so you can attach them to the correct places on the new device after you've temporarily turned off the power to them.

But what do you get for your efforts? You'll be able to set the thermostat so that the air conditioning or heat isn't running as high when you're away at work, but will reach the perfect temperature again by the time you walk back in the door. For instance, in the winter, you could program it so the heat dropped while you were out of the house but then rose to a comfortable, inviting temperature to warm you when you arrive in from the cold. Previously, if you were trying to save on heating during the winter, you might arrive home to a chilly house and run freezing to turn up the thermostat. This way, you and your wallet will be comfortable.

"A friend is a present you give to yourself."

—Robert Louis Stevenson

Make Friends

No man or woman is an island. Even famous recluses like the late J. D. Salinger had friends within the small town of Cornish, New Hampshire. Humans are, by nature, social animals. We live close to one another in cities; we work together in groups; and even though we may complain or begrudge them at the time, we tend to (perhaps secretly) enjoy ourselves at neighborhood block parties and family reunions. These social connections make us happy not only because our relationships can lift us up when we're feeling blue, but also because, as studies have shown, when we have happy friends, we become happier ourselves. According to a study conducted by James Fowler of UC San Diego and Nicholas Christakis of Harvard University, each happy friend increases our own happiness at an average rate of 9 percent, while each unhappy friend can decrease it by 7 percent. This, of course, doesn't mean you should abandon your friends when they're unhappy. By standing by them and helping them work through their problems, you can increase their happiness and your own. It's a win-win in the long run.

If you've been having a hard time making friends, you could join or start a group that revolves around an interest of yours. Make sure you speak nicely about others so that the person you are speaking with doesn't unintentionally take the negative traits you're espousing about another and attach them to you through what psychologists call "spontaneous trait transference." Force yourself to smile so that others think you are friendly. You might be upset that no one is talking to you at an event, but scowling about it isn't going to help your cause. What will are smiling and, if you can, introducing yourself to others.

"The dancer's body is simply the luminous manifestation of the soul."

—Isadora Duncan

Get Out on the Dance Floor

Exercise is allowed to be fun! And when it comes to expressing yourself and burning calories, not much beats dancing. Whether you enroll in an organized class, such as ballet, jazz, tap, swing, salsa, or country line dancing, or shake your groove thing at a dance club, you'll be sweating to the music and getting fitter as you have fun. Need proof? Just take a look at the before and after photos of the contestants who've twirled their way to the finale on *Dancing with the Stars*. They'd surely agree that dancing is an incredible cardio workout and can help you release stress and tone your whole body through movement. Even if you start out with two left feet, after a handful of weekends out dancing at a club or in a scheduled course, you'll start to have some rhythm and more confidence out on the dance floor.

BURN, BABY, BURN

Go out for an evening of dance and try to put in at least an hour on the floor. Because whether you have enough stamina to keep it up for an hour or you need to slow down your moves from time to time, you'll be lighting those metabolic fires. Take a look at what a 150-pound person burns on average for an hour for these different dancing styles:

- Aerobic dance/nightclubbing: 442 calories
- Fast Ballroom: 374 calories
- Ballet, Jazz, or Tap: 326 calories
- Medium-Speed Ballroom (Polka, Line): 306 calories
- Slow-Speed Ballroom (Waltz, Tango, Mambo): 204 calories

"A great introduction to cultures is their cuisine. It not only reflects their evolution, but also their beliefs and traditions."

—Vikas Khanna

Eat Chicken Vindaloo

According to UCLA, the spices used to make the tasty Indian dish known as chicken vindaloo can slow the impact of Alzheimer's disease, because the curcumin found in those spices helps remove amyloid-beta plaques that build up in the brain of those afflicted with the disease. Turmeric, one of those curry spices, also prevents against memory loss by slowing oxidation in the brain, and it aids in digestion by simulating the flow of bile and the breakdown of dietary fats.

SPICE SHOPPING Every recipe for this classic Indian dish is a little different, but here are the ingredients you'll need to have on hand to create the curry base that gives the dish its flavor. If you're having a hard time finding some of them, look for an Indian specialty store or try your local World Market.

- onions
- tomatoes
- white vinegar
- ginger
- garlic
- garam masala
- ground turmeric
- paprika
- coriander
- cayenne
- cardamom
- mustard seeds
- whole cinnamon sticks

"Shallots are for babies, onions are for men, garlic is for heroes."

—Author unknown

Pile on the Garlic

Garlic not only tastes great, it also can help you feel healthier and live longer. This popular culinary herb can lower cholesterol levels, act as a blood thinner and prevent clots from forming, kill harmful bacteria within the body, reduce blood sugar levels, reduce the risk of some cancers, and improve metabolism. Unless you have a garlic allergy, aim to eat two to three cloves of garlic daily—which is easier than it might sound. Garlic bulbs can be roasted in the oven with olive oil and then squeezed out onto bread to create homemade garlic bread, and they can be used to flavor everything from asparagus to chicken. There's even garlic ice cream!

One thing garlic doesn't do, though, is help your breath. So if you're planning on going to a meeting or on a date, munch on a sprig of parsley.

GROW YOUR OWN

While most of the garlic used in the United States comes from Gilroy, California, the world receives most of its garlic supply from China. But, if you don't live near Gilroy and you want to eat locally, you can always grow your own. To do so, plant a single, peeled garlic clove vertically an inch under the surface of the soil in a very sunny area of your garden or yard just after the first frost. If you're planting more than one clove, plant them four inches apart. When the leaves turn brown and die, go ahead and harvest them and hang them to dry in a cool, dry place so they don't rot.

"Everything about my husband is sexy, especially his lips."

—Kelly Preston

Talk Dirty

Talking dirty before sex can help build sexual tension; doing it during sex can turn on your partner even more by letting him know just how you feel in explicit terms. If you're a bit shy about talking dirty, start slow. Tell your partner how attractive he looks to you or how much you love kissing his skin or feeling his hands on your body. As you become more comfortable talking to and complimenting your partner during intimate moments, you can start to be more open with him about what you want to do to him, what you want him to do to you, or just how good he feels when you're engaged in mutual masturbation, oral sex, anal sex, or vaginal sex.

Not sure what sorts of words to use? Flip through a romance novel or a book of erotica, and you're sure to find plenty. As long as you speak confidently and aren't using terms that you know offend your partner, you'll be in the clear, even if you feel a bit out of your element.

"Meditation helps you do less and accomplish more."

—Deepak Chopra

Practice Mandala Meditation

Not all meditation involves sound. Some involves focusing your mind on visual images, either in your imagination or in the physical world. Eastern cultures sometimes use a mandala—an ornate, often circular image, filled with geometric designs—to concentrate on during a meditation.

To practice mandala meditation, find a mandala that speaks to you. They are available in books, in shops that sell spiritual or metaphysical products, and stores that carry Eastern goods. You could also create your own if you have some artistic talent. Then hang or place the mandala at eye level four to eight feet away from where you want to do your sitting meditation.

When you are ready to meditate, close your eyes and take ten slow, deep breaths or as many as you need until you are fully relaxed. Visualize your heart connecting with the mandala, and when you feel ready, open your eyes and look directly at the mandala with slightly unfocused eyes (the point is not to stare). Take in the colors and images without permitting them to engage you. Stay in this state for as long as you feel comfortable.

"Conservation is a state of harmony between men and land."

—Aldo Leopold

Open and Close Your Drapes with the Seasons

Drapes and blinds aren't there only to block out the sun and the nosy eyes of your neighbors. They can also be used to adjust the temperature inside your home. Though it might seem counterintuitive, to keep your house cool in the summer, keep the blinds and drapes shut during the day so the hot sun can't sneak in and heat up the rooms. In the winter, you'll also want to keep the drapes closed except during the part of the day when the sun is falling directly on the window. Then, you'll want to open the shades to allow the sun to penetrate and warm up the house. In the spring and fall, open the windows and drapes on warm days to allow fresh air to sweep through the house and to allow in the sun's rays.

Of course, you don't have to do this all of the time, and you certainly don't want to feel like you're living in a dungeon. But by using your drapes and blinds in this way (even if you only do it when you're away from the house), you'll be able to save on your heating and air conditioning bills, especially if you choose heavy drapes and blinds that provide significant insulation.

"It is one of the blessings of old friends that you can afford to be stupid with them."

—Ralph Waldo Emerson

Stay in Touch with Old Friends

As you make new friends, stay in touch with your old friends. As you get older and your circumstances change, it's easy to lose touch with people with whom you were once very close. After a decade or more out in the "real world," you might find that you no longer have as much in common with your best friend from high school or college. However, the more you two have stayed in touch, the less likely this will be.

The digital age has made keeping in touch with old friends much easier, as you can reach out to them through a social media site like Facebook or through e-mail. But to keep these relationships as strong and as healthy as they could be, you're going to need to do more than just forward along an e-mail once in a while or accept their Facebook friend request. You'll need to put in the effort to call, make plans to see each other, write real letters, send birthday and holiday cards, and so on. By continuing to share the more intimate details of your lives, you'll be more likely to retain and strengthen your bond of friendship and to make it last a lifetime.

"I live by a hill. I began walking it and then I began jogging it and then I began sprinting it."

—Tea Leoni

Start a Running Program

Running or jogging is a great high-octane activity that will help you shed pounds and feel amazing. Ever heard of a runner's high? That's when the body releases endorphins, those "feel-good" hormones—after you've pushed yourself to the limit during a long, strenuous workout. Although you don't have to run to achieve a "runner's high," running does burn a lot of calories and will help boost your metabolism.

Running can, however, be hard on your body. It's a high-impact sport, so you'll definitely feel it each time you hit the ground, unlike the low-impact workout you would get on an elliptical. Because of that, you'll want to be smart about starting a running program. Start slow, maybe adding five or ten minutes of running to your walks. If you're not the walking type and are more eager to get going, try going for a mile or a half-mile run at a relaxed speed; as you get stronger, gradually increase the distance. If you ease into your program, stretch after each run, and plan rest days, you'll start to see results and you won't be prone to injury.

*"All the good ideas I ever had came to me while
I was milking a cow."*

—Grant Wood, painter

Drink Skim Milk

Choosing skim milk over other types of milk with higher fat content will help your waistline and boost your brain power. One cup of skim milk contains thirty-eight grams of choline, a water-soluble vitamin that can reduce your chance of breast cancer and improve your memory. Although the effects that nutrients have on rats don't always correlate with the effect those same nutrients have on humans, rats that received adequate amounts of choline in the womb did not develop senility as they aged. The few human studies that have been conducted show that choline can improve memory and cognitive functioning. There are other sources of choline besides skim milk, though that is one of the healthiest. Other sources include egg yolks, soybeans, peanuts, butter, potatoes, and barley.

BUT, DRINK CHOCOLATE MILK AFTER A WORKOUT

Skim milk is the healthiest type of cow's milk you can have when you're reaching for a glass of milk, but recent research from the Human Performance Laboratory reveals that chocolate milk is actually the best drink you can have post- or mid-workout. The protein, carbs, salt, and sugar in this childhood favorite help relieve sore muscles and can fuel you for your next workout.

"Yogurt is very good for the stomach, the lumbar regions, appendicitis and apotheosis."

—Eugene Ionesco

Eat Probiotic-Rich Yogurt

Every few years, there's a "new" nutrient or food that takes the spotlight. Recently, it's been probiotics' time to shine, with food manufacturers toting the probiotic content of their yogurts, drinks, and kefirs. But what is a probiotic? A probiotic is a live bacterium culture that assists with the digestion of food and the destruction of harmful bacteria. For those suffering from constipation or diarrhea, they can help alleviate those issues and get the digestive system back in sync.

However, different strains have different beneficial impacts, and when a food product claims it contains probiotics, it probably does, but it might not contain the ones you're looking for. The probiotic that protects against the common cold isn't the same biotic that reduces the symptoms of inflammatory bowel syndrome (IBS). The FDA hasn't yet proven the claims set forth by manufacturers that the probiotics in their products work to improve digestion, but eating a cup of yogurt for breakfast isn't a bad idea.

"I feel a lot healthier when I'm having sex. Physically. I feel all these jitters when I wake up in the morning. Just energy jitters. I take vitamins, I work out every day. When I'm having sex, I don't have that."

—Alyssa Milano

Have Sex . . . Regularly

If you're doing it right, sex feels amazing. Orgasms release the cuddle hormone oxytocin and feel-good endorphins, which help make you feel happier and emotionally closer to your partner. They also temporarily decrease feelings of pain by more than 50 percent. Oh, and they render the "I have a headache" excuse null and void, because orgasms can actually make your headache or migraine go away.

Having sex can also be a good aerobic workout, depending on how creative you are with your positions and how much you get into it. Even if you aren't having vigorous sex, making love three times or more a week can decrease your chance of heart attack or stroke by up to 50 percent, improve your ability to sleep, and lessen your chance (if you're a guy) of getting prostate cancer. Plus, you'll live longer! A longevity study by Duke University and another by a British organization revealed a strong correlation between patients who enjoyed sex and had it frequently and patients who lived a long life.

"The only lasting beauty is the beauty of the heart."

—Rami

Practice Open Heart Meditation

In the hectic life you lead, sometimes your heart's needs get put on the back burner. You may take things head-on with your mind and your gut, but keep your heart in silence, waiting patiently to be heard. Through an open heart meditation, you put all your focus onto listening to your heart and opening it up to feel those great feelings you can experience when you are most vulnerable and allowing yourself to feel and share peace, joy, love, calmness, and happiness.

Open heart meditations are often conducted in groups, and sometimes at the end of the meditation, the group channels Reiki together. But you can practice open heart meditations on your own as well. To begin, sit on the floor so that you are comfortable and sitting up tall. Place two or three fingers on the center of your chest, on your sternum, and close your eyes. Breathe deeply and visualize your heart opening. Smile to your heart. As you do this, you may find that you laugh or even cry. That is okay. As meditation continues, you can choose to say the open heart prayer, to what open heart meditators call the "true source," asking for the source to remove jealousy, arrogance, and other negative feelings from the heart. If you feel more comfortable replacing this word with another divine or spiritual word, please do. By practicing open heart meditations, you can reap the benefits of general meditation while also learning how to lead and listen with your heart.

If you are interested in trying the open heart meditation but cannot find a local group, you can download a guided meditation for free at *HeartSanctuary.org.*

"We won't have a society if we destroy the environment."

—Margaret Mead

Install a Low-Flow Showerhead

To be good to your household budget and to the environment, install a low-flow showerhead and make a conscious choice to take shorter showers. The combination will save you thousands of gallons of water a year.

Not long ago, showerheads used to deliver water at a rate of 5–8 gallons per minute. Showerheads are a lot more environmentally friendly than they used to be, and the average showerhead releases 2.6 gallons per minute. However, a low-flow showerhead permits only 1.5 gallons of water to flow through it per minute, and it's likely you won't notice the difference during your morning routine, whether you prefer pulsing jets or the feeling of rain in the shower.

Combine your new showerhead with even a slightly shorter shower, and you could save over 10,000 gallons of water a year. While the cost you save won't be significant, because water costs about $1.50 per 1,000 gallons, it will pay for the new showerhead, and the environmental savings will be great.

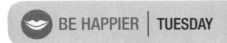

"A real book is not one that we read, but one that reads us."

—W. H. Auden

Be a Part of a Book Club

One activity that can make you both happier and smarter is a book club. Book clubs are great ways to meet and make friends with fellow bookworms and to connect with these people on a regular basis. Some book clubs are hosted by people with a similar career path—such as Ed2010.com's monthly book club for those who work in publishing—and can benefit you by opening a door to let you network with others in your field.

However your book club comes together and whether you discuss heady fiction, nonfiction, or pulp, the format is essentially the same. Between meetings, everyone reads the same book and then comes together at someone's house, a local library, or a coffeehouse to discuss it. As you talk about the events and themes of the book, you might find yourself feeling like you're back in one of those thrilling English class discussions, but this time you don't have to worry about a grade. You're sharing and bouncing your ideas off others and getting their input as well, which can give you a new insight into the book.

*"A lot of people run a race to see who's the fastest.
I run to see who has the most guts."*

—Steve Prefontaine

Sign Up for a Race

Sometimes, it's hard to push yourself to and to actually want to exercise. If you've struggled with trying to get in shape for months or even years, it's time to take a different approach, because yours isn't working. Wanting to lose weight to look better naked or for your health aren't bad goals, but if they aren't providing you with enough incentive, find something that will.

One way to motivate yourself to get into shape is to sign up for a race that you couldn't complete right now. Triathlon, 10K, and 5K races happen often all over the United States, and you can train for them year-round. Pick one far enough in advance to give yourself enough time to prepare but not so much time that you can delay your preparation if you don't feel like working out. Then, start telling people you're going to do it and ask them if they'll come out to watch you. Not only will you now have this added pressure, knowing you've paid for the race and told others you're doing it, but you'll also have a new built-in support team. You might even find that some of your friends or family members want to do it too!

As you work toward your goal, you'll be amazed at how your eating habits improve and how much more motivation you have to work out more often. And if you take a photo of yourself the day you sign up and then again on race day, you'll be quite proud of the results!

"That which, perhaps, hears more nonsense than anything in the world is a picture in a museum."

—Edmond de Goncourt

Take a Friend to a Museum

Museums aren't stuffy places built for field trips. They're architecturally interesting buildings that house some of the world's most precious creations. There are the incredible dinosaur skeletons in the Smithsonian's Natural History Museum, the original Claude Monet paintings in the Louvre, the interactive exhibits at your local science museum, and much more—all waiting to entertain and enlighten you. But museums are more than just their exhibits. Many also serve as the venue for talks by famous scholars, movie nights, and even dance parties.

Find out which museums are in your area and go visit them. There's bound to be one that has an exhibit open right now that piques your interest, and you might even enjoy it so much that you become a member. If you want to increase your enjoyment of the trip, consider bringing along a friend. Your friend may challenge you with a different interpretation of a piece of art or let you in on a fascinating tidbit of information on an artist or an object that the exhibit card doesn't mention.

"If carrots got you drunk, rabbits would be messed-up."

—Mitch Hedburg

Use Vitamin A

Most of the vitamins covered earlier and later in this book work best to improve your brain and body health if you ingest them. And don't get me wrong, it's important to get vitamin A in your diet. But if you want to look younger, you might want to consider putting it directly on your skin. According to a report published in 2007, by the University of Michigan Medical School, the participants in the study who put on a lotion containing .4 percent retinol (vitamin A) three times a week for a minimum of 24 weeks had noticeably fewer wrinkles, softer skin, and less signs of aging. The scientists tied the results to the fact that retinol increases the production of glycosaminoglycan and procollagen. Those two compounds help the skin retain water and create collagen.

Eating vitamin A is also good for you. It promotes the healthy development of cells and tissues, strengthens mucous membranes, protects vision, and stimulates bone growth. Healthy sources of retinol include carrots, broccoli, eggs, milk, sweet potatoes, kale, and pumpkin.

A RETINOL WARNING

Though ingesting vitamin A through the foods that you eat is healthy, using retinol products on your skin while you're pregnant can lead to birth defects. But you'll have that motherly glow instead, and you can still moisturize, which will help your skin during those nine months.

"He walked me home and made out with me. That was my second kiss and he got to second base too. Then there was Ben— he was my first dry hump."

—Charlize Theron

Do Everything but Sex

If you've been feeling like your sex life has been in a rut, go back to the basics. Try not having intercourse for a little while. Consider even putting a date on the calendar that's a few days or a week away. Though you may feel like you're a teenager again, this is a great way to reconnect with your partner. The two of you can still get off through mutual masturbation or oral sex, but you'll be forced to relearn your partner's body and how to make him moan with delight. Make it a point to lick, kiss, and caress areas that you know you haven't paid attention to in a long time, and see how your partner reacts. If he likes it, you can add this new move to your repertoire!

This exercise can be very helpful to couples who have been dating or married for years or decades, as your sexual desires and what feels good to you can change during that period. Since foreplay often gets rushed through by both men and women, this is a chance for you and your partner to find out what works for the two of you now. Plus, after a few days or more of these almost-there interactions, it's likely that your sex life will feel charged up again, and you'll be ready to start boinking like rabbits.

"The moment one gives close attention to anything, even a blade of grass, it becomes a mysterious, awesome, indescribably magnificent world in itself."

—Henry Miller

Practice Mindful Meditation

With everything you want and need to do in a day, it doesn't take much to get into a cycle in which you're rushing from one thing to the next, paying more attention to what's next on the agenda than on staying in the present. Afterward, you might look back with regret that a pleasurable moment has passed without you really exploring it. Without a time machine, you can't slow down or reverse the clock, but by using mindfulness meditation, you can get close to that.

When you're rushing during your leisure time, force yourself to slow down. Physically walk slower so that you have more time to observe your surroundings. Look at what is around you, listen to the conversations or sounds of nature, breathe deeply and take in the aroma of the place you're in. Instead of speed eating, put down your fork and admire your food. It may seem silly, but you took the time to come to this restaurant or to prepare this meal, and it's important to appreciate it. When you take your next bite, close your eyes and really taste the food. The more you practice mindful meditation, the more you'll appreciate your surroundings, the less likely your time will rush by, and the more relaxed within those moments you'll feel.

"By sowing frugality we reap liberty, a golden harvest."

—Agesilaus

Stop Services You Don't Use

Have you ever signed up for a service you don't need or a service you've never used? Of course you have. We've all done it. Now is a good time to take a look at the services you have and which of those you can eliminate to save money every month. If you hate television but love to watch movies, scrap the pricey cable service and sign up for an inexpensive DVD service. Consider ditching your landline and use Skype and your cell phone instead. Have you been exercising so much outside that you forget what the inside of your gym looks like? Then cancel your membership. Don't renew magazines you don't read. Clean your own house more often. See if you can share Internet services and split the bill with a neighbor, if you live in an apartment complex. Take the money you're saving from each cancelled service and invest it. In the long run, you'll enjoy that vacation more than you missed the cable.

"Lead the life that will make you kindly and friendly to everyone about you, and you will be surprised what a happy life you lead."

—Charles M. Schwab

Be the Kind of Friend You Want to Attract

A few months ago, we spoke about being the kind of partner you want to attract. To bring a good partner into your life, it's important that you treat others the way you want to be treated. The same goes for friends. If you work to make time for your friends, listen attentively when they express their joys and sorrows, are trustworthy with the information they tell you and don't gossip, and make an effort to have fun with them when you're together, you'll attract the same kinds of people to be new friends and strengthen the friendships you already have.

FRIENDSHIP NO-NOS

With a little work, it's easy to grow a great friendship. But you should also be aware of habits you might have that could sabotage even the best connections.

- Forgetting about your friends when you're dating someone new
- Only calling your friends when you need to vent
- Not showing interest in their problems or successes
- Never picking up the tab
- Sharing their deepest secrets with others

"Good communication is as stimulating as a cup of coffee,
and just as hard to sleep after."

—Anne Morrow Lindbergh

Have a Cup of Coffee or Tea Before Your Workout

The more hydrated you are before a workout, the more efficient your workout will be. But if you're already properly hydrated, consider sipping on a cup of tea or coffee before you head to the gym. Not only will you feel a little bit "wired" and have more short-term energy, you might also be better equipped to push yourself harder. After seven years of studying the connections between caffeine and exercise, Dr. Robert Motl of the University of Illinois has determined that having that cup of coffee or tea will reduce the amount of pain you feel when you exercise. Other researchers have found that having some caffeine following exercise can ease the soreness by helping with carbohydrate uptake and thus helping to direct more glycogen to your depleted muscles.

If you do choose to opt for the caffeine, don't overdo it; stick to only a cup before or after your workout, depending on what you're looking for. Don't load up your coffee or tea with cream and sugar, and drink more water during your workout to counteract the diuretic effect of your java. The goal is to deliver caffeine, not calories.

"A lecture is much more of a dialogue than many of you probably realize."

—George Ald

Attend Lectures

You might think that the last thing you want to do with your time off from work or school is to attend a lecture. But lectures (usually) are not as dry as you think they're going to be. In fact, many of them are a lot more engaging than the latest episode of a reality show you could watch on TV and just as long. If you're new to lectures, the key is to start with a topic that interests you. Would you like to learn more about photography? Go listen to a famous photographer speak about her life and how she created her photographs. Are you interested in space? Look to see if someone is giving a talk at a nearby planetarium or observatory. Does your favorite author have a new book out? Check out his website or the publisher's website and find his book-touring calendar, so you can hear the author read from his work when he comes to town—and maybe you'll even meet him. The possibilities are endless, but it's up to you to find the events.

Once you've attended a few lectures, consider going to one about a topic that you'd like to learn more about. If you continue to learn and challenge your brain throughout your life, you can help prevent it from deteriorating as you age.

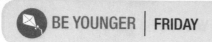
"The spice must flow."

—*Dune*

Grab Some Ginger

Looking to really stoke those metabolic fires? Then cook with ginger. An Australian study found that this spicy root can temporarily raise metabolic rates as much as twenty percent. And it's packed with as many antioxidants as a cup of spinach, assists with digestion, reduces inflammation, and can help prevent colorectal and ovarian cancer. All of that can help keep you more active and live a longer, happier life.

If you suffer from motion sickness, eating a few pieces of ginger, munching on ginger candy, or taking a ginger tablet can alleviate your nausea without making you drowsy like some over-the-counter motion sickness medications do.

GINGER-FRIENDLY RECIPES

Whether you enjoy it dried, candied, fresh, or pickled, ginger can be great for your body. If you're stuck on what dishes you could add it to, here are some ideas::

- Gingersnaps or gingerbread
- Carrot and ginger soup
- Spicy chicken wings
- Curries
- Stir Fries
- Sesame chicken
- Ginger steamed fish
- Sautéed broccoli
- Homemade ice cream

"Electric flesh arrows traversing the body. A rainbow of color strikes the eyelids. A foam of music falls over the ears. It is the gong of the orgasm."

—Anaïs Nin

Have Orgasms and Boost Your Self Esteem

Even before the scientists step in, it's easy to believe that having orgasms can make you feel good about yourself. Orgasms are intensely pleasurable, and you can't help but be impressed that your body is able to produce such sensations. If you're giving yourself an orgasm, your confidence should feel that much higher.

But having orgasms can actually improve your self-esteem because of the chemicals they release. During orgasm, blood flows into the prefrontal cortex of the right side of your brain. This part of your brain is responsible for decision making and personality expression, and when stimulated by the orgasm, it makes the body feel a profound sense of gratification. Orgasms also can reduce the effects of depression, because they release endorphins, hormones that improve mood.

To top all of that off, the German sex research Werner Habermehl believes that the more sex you have, the more intelligent you become, because adrenaline and cortisol are released during lovemaking.

"Is everything as urgent as your stress would imply?"

—Carrie Letat

Stop Junk Mail and Phone Calls from Telemarketers

Junk mail is annoying. Phone calls from telemarketers are worse. Instead of being laden with trash every time you open your mailbox and disturbed during dinner, do something about it. First, go online and sign up for the Do Not Call registry at *www.donotmail .org*. It takes only a moment to do so and entering your phone number into their database will prevent you from most, if not all, unsolicited calls from marketers.

Then, sign up for the Do Not Mail registry at *www.donotmail .org* and stop direct mailers from sending you flyers that just end up in your recycling bin. Not only does not mailing you cut down on their costs, it also helps the environment. Now the only thing left to aggravate you when you open the mailbox are those bills . . . but if you sign up for automatic, paperless billing, you won't have to see those either!

"We could have saved the Earth but we were too damned cheap."

—Kurt Vonnegut, Jr.

Use CFLs and LEDs to Reduce Your Energy Bill

Like it or not, the incandescent light bulbs most of us grew up with have gone the way of the buggy whip. Their replacement, the compact fluorescent (CFL), is up to fifteen times more energy efficient, but they have their downsides. The first versions emitted a cold light, as opposed to the warm light we were used to with the incandescent bulbs. Since then, these bulbs have been designed to give off warmer light, so you can feel good about saving money on your energy bill and enjoy the light in your home. But because CFLs contain a trace amount of mercury, you need to follow your state's laws for discarding them and the EPA guidelines for cleaning up fluorescent lighting if you break one.

A more recent addition to home lighting is the light-emitting diode, or LED. Developed in 1962, these extremely bright lights were originally used in handheld calculators but now can be used in your home. They use very little energy and are excellent for lighting small spaces. But they generate considerable heat, which restricts their size and use, and they are more expensive than fluorescent and incandescent light bulbs. Consider installing them in your closets, your basement or garage, or any small, infrequently used space where you need to see well. Each LED light will last between 25,000 and 100,000 hours, which means the next time you replace one might be next decade.

"Sticks and stones will break my bones, but words will make me go in a corner and cry by myself for hours"

—Eric Idle

Help a Friend Who Is Feeling Rejected

We've all been there. If you look back through your memories, you're bound to recall a time when someone—your partner, friend, boss, child—criticized you in a way that hurt you. Even if you're good at taking constructive criticism on the chin, there are times when you're just not prepared for it or when the comments feel less constructive and more like an attack. Some people are not very tactful when voicing their criticisms, and their words can really sting.

When this happens to a friend, be there for him or her. Help your friend to understand that the person who made the hurtful comment probably didn't intend for it to come across as it did, and that while the comment may have felt personal, it was probably about something larger, like a looming deadline. Or perhaps that person had been criticized earlier in the day and took it out on your friend. Being supportive of your friend will help her or him feel better and will bring the two of you closer, making it easier for you to turn to that friend in a time of need.

"The man who is prepared has his battle half fought."

—Miguel de Cervantes

Plan Your Meals Ahead of Time

When you take the time to plan ahead, you usually make better choices. This is true when it comes to your financial outlook and also when it comes to your diet. Instead of waiting until you get hungry and then ordering delivery or going to a restaurant or fast-food chain, make a plan for your week. To get you started in meal planning, the Mayo Clinic offers a Healthy Weight Pyramid on their site that will let you know how many calories you should be eating and how many servings of each type of food (fruits, protein, etc.) will help you reach your weight-loss goal. Then, using the clinic's guidelines, look through online recipe sites and cookbooks to come up with a list of healthy meals and snacks you'd like to have for the week and put together a grocery list.

By building in snacks and having a meal plan that includes foods you enjoy eating, it will be much easier for you to say no to unhealthy foods, because you're being good to your needs and your health. Plus, if you schedule one morning or afternoon to prepare as much as you can in advance for the week, you'll save yourself time later when you might be tempted to dial up the local pizza parlor.

*"Profanity is the attempt of a lazy and feeble
mind to express itself forcefully."*

—Anonymous

Limit Slang

As languages progress, there is a movement away from one way of speaking toward another. If you were to look back at the American lexicon, words that were deemed as slang in the past now dominate our vernacular. If you were to speak in only formal language, using the words and phrasing that those in Shakespeare's time preferred, you would certainly come off as odd, because we've invented new words to use in place of those and we no longer speak formally.

Some slang comes from subcultures that have had a profound impact on our culture. For instance, the words hip, cool, and baby all come from the jazz culture. New words are being invented all the time; twenty years ago, no one would have said the word e-mail, but everyone uses the term today and its now in the dictionary. This type of slang is common and accepted.

But some slang makes you sound uneducated, and it can also make your brain lazy, because you don't have to work to actually describe something. This type of slang is the four-letter variety. While these words can sometimes be useful in helping you express just how intensely emotional you feel, most of the time they're just a language cop-out. And slang terms that degrade others are just plain offensive and shouldn't be used under any circumstances. When you're about to spout one of the four-letter bombs, stop and think how you could phrase your thought in a way that is more profound.

*"Francine says you love her ginseng tea.
It's great for the sex drive."*

—From *Point of No Return*

Try Ginseng

For thousands of years, the roots of different varieties of ginseng have been used in Eastern medicine to heal a wide range of ailments. Herbalists and more modern naturopaths believe that American ginseng has a "cooling effect" and can be useful for fevers, while Asian ginsengs have a "heating effect" and are helpful for improving circulation.

If you want some scientific proof before adding this supplement to your diet, studies have shown that ginseng may help shorten the length of the common cold, improve blood glucose levels, lower LDL cholesterol, assist with erectile dysfunction, and reduce inflammation. If you are not taking anticoagulants, aren't pregnant, and don't suffer from hormone-sensitive diseases, you should be okay to consume up to 200 mg of ginseng per day. Check with your doctor if you have diabetes, are pregnant, have had breast or endometrial cancer, or are taking MAOI antidepressants before taking this root!

WHAT ABOUT SIBERIAN GINSENG?

Siberian ginseng, also known as eleuthero, isn't actually ginseng, though it does have many of the same health benefits and is also available as a supplement in most health food stores. The fleshy root can reduce inflammation, lower cholesterol, relieve stress, and may even be able to act as an antidepressant and with memory.

"Skill makes love unending."

—Ovid

Spice Things Up with New Positions

Sex is great until it becomes a bore. And one fast way for that to happen is to always use the same positions. Unless you have a medical reason for why you can't try a new position, switch things up to inject your sex life with energy. In the weeks ahead, I'll cover variations on the missionary positions, the woman-on-top position, the rear entry position, and others. But there are many more positions than I could possibly cover within this book. If you're looking for new ones, consider picking up Nerve's *Position of the Day Playbook* or downloading their smart phone app.

Some of these positions might include angles you're not used to holding your body in, so if anything becomes painful, stop. Don't be a hero and try to keep going, because you'll just hurt yourself and that will lead to less sex. Of course, if you want to increase your flexibility, you can add stretches, yoga, or Pilates to your life. What better inspiration to improve your fitness than the desire to be better in bed?

"I was angry with my friend: I told my wrath, my wrath did end. I was angry with my foe: I told it not, my wrath did grow."

—William Blake

Express Your Emotion to Lighten Your Load

How you feel emotionally can influence how you feel physically. If you're going through a rough patch, it can help to speak with a close friend, family member, or therapist so that you don't have to work through it all on your own and your feelings can be validated. As a recent study showed, sharing deep feelings and having meaningful conversations, rather than engaging in small talk, will help you feel happier and more connected with those you care about.

However, continuing to dwell on the same topic without resolution or forward movement can make you feel just as stifled. That's because when you constantly relive a difficult situation in your life, instead of coping with the problem, you also relive all those painful emotions associated with that situation time and time again. Eventually, there comes a point at which you have to either resolve the problem or, if you are unable to do that, just shelve the problem and move on. With time and experience, you might find that when you revisit a problem later, you have a solution and are able to put it to bed for good.

An extreme, unhealthy version of shelving an emotion is repression. Repression occurs when you bury negative feelings deep within your subconscious, but those feelings can still impact how you feel and act toward yourself and others. Therapy can be a very useful tool for unburying these emotions and learning how to work through them. I don't recommend you attempt to block out a troubling moment until you have "forgotten" the memory entirely, but if you're having trouble processing it, do take some time away from it and wait until you're more psychologically equipped to handle it.

"Always plan ahead. It wasn't raining when Noah built the ark."

—Richard C. Cushing

Start Saving for College as Early as Possible

If you have children and haven't started saving for their college education, start. If you don't have a child now but think you'll have one someday and you haven't started saving for your future child's college education, start. Though this latter advice might seem odd, that is what Ramit Sethi, publisher of *The Scrooge Strategy* (a paid subscription newsletter) and author of the book *I Will Teach You to Be Rich*, would advise you to do. He's doing it, and he doesn't have any kids . . . yet. This is because the longer you spend saving, the more interest your money will accrue and the less you'll have to pay over the long run. Here are two ways to start saving for your child's college education:

1. Add "College Education" as a section within your savings account and set up an automatic savings account that deducts money from your checking account and deposits a set amount into this account each month.

2. Consider a 529 savings plan. These plans can be used for either in-state or out-of-state colleges and can be prepaid or used like a 401(k) or IRA account so you can save over time. If you're concerned about the taxes you might pay on this money, know that the interest and savings on these accounts aren't taxed by the federal government while you're saving nor when you need to transfer money to the college.

"A single day is enough to make us a little larger."

—Paul Klee

Change Yourself to Change the World

Though it would be wonderful to snap your fingers and make the world operate the way you want it to, that's not possible—at least not yet. For now, the best thing you can do is to "be the change you want to see in the world" (Mahatma Gandhi). If you wish that more people were respectful, work on being more respectful yourself. If you wish more people smiled at each other, smile at more people. Whatever you feel is missing from the world, work on embodying that within yourself.

This type of worldly action is a way of life and of spiritual well-being for followers of the Hindu religion, who attempt to put this philosophy into practice in their daily lives with *ahimsa* (nonviolence), *dharma* (worldly duties), and *sadhana* (respect for all living things). As you make these positive changes within yourself and act kindly and respectfully toward others, you'll start to see that this attitude may have a domino effect within your social community.

PRACTICE GOOD KARMA

Hindus also believe in the power of karma, the idea that the actions you make not only have a positive or negative effect on the world around you but also will reflect back to you. In other words, if you do a good deed or are kind to someone, they believe that you will be rewarded for your action in a positive way. On the other hand, if you are cruel to people or harm them, they believe you will be punished for that action. But, it's not hard to see, even for non-Hindus, that acting lovingly toward those in your community and beyond will improve your life in the long run.

*"You better cut the pizza in four pieces because
I'm not hungry enough to eat six."*

—Yogi Berra

Learn to Eyeball Portion Size

Information is power. For instance, you may know there are 100 calories in every ounce of cheese, but how big is an ounce? Since we don't expect you to whip out a digital scale at a restaurant or your friend's house, it's important to know both the calorie content of food and what one serving of that food looks like if you want to lose weight.

Here are some helpful visual guidelines that will assist you in your estimating portion sizes:

- A 3-ounce portion of cooked protein should be the size of a deck of playing cards.
- A medium potato is about the size of a computer mouse.
- A cup of rice or pasta is about the size of a fist or tennis ball.
- A cup of fruit or a medium apple or orange is the size of a baseball.
- A half-cup of chopped vegetables is about the size of three regular ice cubes.
- A 1-ounce piece of cheese is the size of four dice.
- Two tablespoons of peanut butter is about the size of a golf ball.
- A thumb tip equals 1 teaspoon; 3 thumb tips equals 1 tablespoon; and a whole thumb equals 1 ounce.

*"Those who know nothing of foreign languages
know nothing of their own."*

—Johann Wolfgang von Goethe

Learn Another Language

When you learn a new language, you really challenge your brain. That's because a new language requires you to assimilate new information, practice your memorization skills, and relearn rules about grammatical structure. According to a University College of London study published in 2004, learning a new language not only allows you to converse with and connect with more people, it also builds the gray matter in your brain. The earlier in your life you can learn a second (or third or more) language, the more gray matter you'll gain. But no matter how old you are when you learn a new language, you'll still be able to increase the connections between your neurons in doing so.

As you're learning a new language, you're bound to get frustrated from time to time. When you feel that emotion creeping in, take a break and allow your unconscious mind to work through the knowledge you've gained. When you come back to your studies a few days later, you might find that you're able to get a grasp of what puzzled you before.

To learn a new language, consider enrolling in a continuing education class at your local community college. This will allow you to meet others, practice, and ask questions, and it will give you a structure so that you'll keep going with your practice. Once you can speak the language comfortably, reward yourself with a trip to that country and try out your new skills!

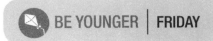
"A tale without love is like beef without
mustard, an insipid dish."

—Anatole France

Bring on the Mustard

Mustard is an incredible plant. One cup of its peppery leaves contains five times the amount of vitamin K you need, nearly 100 percent of your vitamin A, and over half of your vitamin C, not to mention it's also high in folate and vitamin E. Plus, a serving size of this antioxidant powerhouse has only twenty-one calories. Because of the vitamins and other nutrients within mustard greens, they can guard against heart disease and rheumatoid arthritis, support bone health, slow cognitive decline, and help alleviate the symptoms of asthma. To enjoy these greens, add them to a salad or sauté them to make a healthy side dish.

The mustard you most commonly think of is made from the seeds of the same plant. These seeds are high in selenium and magnesium and can help reduce inflammation and protect the body from gastrointestinal cancer. They'll also boost your metabolism. A study by the Oxford Polytechnic Institute found that eating a teaspoon of hot mustard will boost metabolism 20–25 percent for several hours. Try a spoonful of it before heading to the gym!

If you're the culinary type, you can also make your own mustard. Head to your local spice store or supermarket and buy whole mustard seeds. Grind these seeds using a mortar and pestle or coffee grinder, then add either vinegar, if you plan to store your mustard, or water, if you plan to eat it within hours, until it achieves the consistency you want. Then cover it and let it rest on the counter until it is as hot as you want. The longer you let it sit, the more fiery it gets.

"I've tried several varieties of sex. The conventional position makes me claustrophobic and the others give me a stiff neck or lockjaw."

—Tallulah Bankhead, actress

Try Variations on the Missionary Position

The missionary position may be the most common sex position, but it certainly isn't the most exciting. Here are some ideas for how to change it up

Coital alignment technique. After the man is inside the woman, he should move up about four inches on the woman's body and use a combination of small thrusts and his body to stimulate the first few inches of her vagina (where most of the nerve ending are) and her clitoris. It also puts pressure on the man and woman's pubic bones, which can help both reach orgasm through sexual intercourse.

Yawning position. In this position, the woman lies on her back and puts her legs up and over the shoulders of the man. This will allow for deep penetration, and depending on the angle of the woman's hips, G-spot stimulation. Doing kegel moves (the woman) while in this position can be an intense sensation for both partners.

Splitting the bamboo. Here, the man squats, kneels, or sits on his feet and tilts forward slightly while the woman's pelvis is supported by pillows. The woman should keep one leg bent and her foot on the bed and place the other on her partner's shoulder. As they thrust, the woman should switch her leg positions, which allows the G-spot to be activated as the man's penis moves inside her.

The Indrani. This position allows for very deep penetration and G-spot stimulation, but it allows the cervix to be undisturbed. To practice it, the woman should lie on her back and lift up her knees until they are at the level of her breasts.

*"Early to bed and early to rise makes a man healthy,
wealthy, and wise."*

—Benjamin Franklin

Sleep Away Your Stress

One of the first and most important things to do to build a stress-proof body is to get enough sleep on a regular basis. If you don't get enough sleep, you could experience the following:

- Increased irritability
- Depression
- Anxiety
- Decreased ability to concentrate and understand information
- Increased likelihood of making mistakes and causing accidents
- Increased clumsiness and slower reaction times (dangerous behind the wheel)
- A suppressed immune system
- Undesirable weight gain

Any of these effects of too little sleep could weigh you down in your daily life. Unfortunately, not sleeping may be the by-product of jet lag after business travel or your night-shift schedule. Sleep disorders—from snoring and sleep apnea to insomnia and restless leg syndrome—also often disturb our sleep, even if we go to bed on time.

Look carefully at what is keeping you awake—whether it's your own habits, your job, or a medical condition—and find ways to address the problems. Change your schedule; take the time to consult your physician; practice meditation. Once you've had a good night's sleep, you'll be more prepared to handle life's challenges and less anxious about meeting them head-on!

"The key to everything is patience. You get the chicken by hatching the egg, not by smashing it open."

—Arnold Glasgow

Don't Be an Early Adopter

You undoubtedly have friends who are proud to be early adopters. Let them have fun with their new devices *and* discover the bugs. Then, if it's a gadget you're interested in, wait until the second or third version, which is usually more reliable and definitely less expensive. You most likely won't have to wait for long. With today's fast-moving technology, it's usually only a few months until a newer, more reliable version is released. If you can hold out until the developers have created a more stable version of a new gadget, then you can also save money without missing out.

"You begin saving the world by saving one person at a time."

—Charles Bukowski

Be Friendly with the Homeless

When was the last time you came into contact with a homeless person? How did you react? Did you speak with him, ignore her, or were you antagonistic toward this person? Homeless people might make you feel uncomfortable or guilty about your place in life because you're in a financially better position than they are. But put yourself in their shoes for a moment, and you'll be able to see that if most people pretended you were invisible when you tried to speak with them, it could have a profoundly negative impact on your self-esteem. So even if you don't want to give money to homeless people, you can still give them a kind word, a smile, or sit down with them and have a conversation. Use your instincts as you would with anyone else and don't engage with someone you feel might be dangerous, but for the most part, you don't need to be afraid of learning their story. How did they end up here? Do they want to reconnect with their family? Have they had any luck with the local shelters? Do they have a plan to get back on their feet? If you are so inclined, you might be able to pool the resources of your community and help them get the life they hoped for restarted. These kinds of conversations and actions can help boost their self-esteem and get them moving in the right direction.

Instead of giving money, consider giving food. If you keep an extra energy bar, healthy snack, or new socks in your bag or car, you can offer any of these items to someone who's asking for change. When you go out to dinner and have your leftovers boxed, consider giving these to a homeless person you see on your way back to your car or home. Just remember, the homeless are people too.

"Animals are my friends and I don't eat my friends."

—George Bernard Shaw

Eat Vegetarian Meals

Vegetarianism is a way of life for some people. But if you want to lose weight, eating vegetarian meals as often as you can will help you achieve that goal.

Studies have shown that vegetarians have lower rates of obesity, high blood pressure, colon cancer, and diabetes. Plus, healthy vegetarian diets are lower in saturated fat and cholesterol because animal products are the main source for those substances. But don't fool yourself into thinking that just because you cut out meat you'll automatically start to lose weight. You still have to eat healthily, because a vegetarian diet can still include cookies, candies, sodas, and other unhealthy foods. However, if you choose to fill your plate with tofu, beans, whole grains, fruits, and vegetables, you're likely to lower your cholesterol numbers and lose weight.

VEGETARIAN ALTERNATIVES

Going vegetarian doesn't mean you have eat like a rabbit. There are vegetarian and vegan-friendly restaurants that create tasty dishes and you can make your own at home. Use tofu in your stir fry. Make pulled pork sandwiches using jackfruit instead. Use wheat-based proteins like seitan in chilies and in other recipes that call for meat.

"It allows you to adore words, take them apart and find out where they came from."

—Theodore Geisel, better known as Dr. Seuss

Study Latin

Latin, the language ancient Romans spoke, serves as the basis for the romantic languages: French, Italian, Portuguese, and Spanish. For centuries, Latin served as a way for scientists of different languages to communicate with one another. Although Latin is no longer spoken today, knowing Latin can give you a leg up in learning any romantic language. It will also help you to understand and use correct English grammar and to understand many of the roots of words in both romantic languages and English, which will improve your vocabulary. If you're going to medical, dental, or nursing school, a knowledge of Latin will help you learn all of the words for parts of the body and myriad other scientific and medical terms.

FAMOUS LATIN PHRASES

- **Carpe diem (Horace)** = Seize the day
- **Omnia vincit amor (Virgil)** = Love conquers all
- **Deus ex machina (Horace)** = God from the machine
- **Cogito ergo sum (Rene Descartes)** = I think, therefore I am
- **Sic itur ad astra (Virgil)** = Thus, you shall go to the stars
- **Si vis amari ama (Seneca)** = If you want to be loved, love.

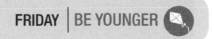

"Better beans and bacon in peace than cakes and ale in fear."

—Aesop

Fall in Love with Beans

When people go vegetarian, they look to beans to provide them with protein. But beans are great for vegetarians and nonvegetarians alike. With they're free-radical fighting powers, they'll help keep you young. But that's not all. They're also packed with fiber—one cup of beans contains about fifteen grams of fiber—so they help with digestion. And some beans, such as black beans, can help lower your cholesterol and keep your blood sugar in balance, making you at lower risk for heart disease and diabetes. Studies have shown eating beans regularly reduces your rate of obesity by 22 percent, probably because beans help fill you up with their fifteen grams of protein!

Aim to eat three cups of beans a week, but make good choices about the beans you buy. If you choose to purchase canned beans, look for low-sodium varieties and rinse the beans in cold water before you use them to wash away more of the salt. Look, too, for vegetarian beans, because they're not loaded up with lard or pork, which will add saturated fat to your diet.

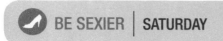

"Making love? It's a communion with a woman. The bed is the holy table. There I find passion—and purification."

—Omar Sharif, actor

Explore Variations of the Woman-on-Top Position

The standard reverse missionary (also known as the woman-on-top position) is fun, but if you're looking to spice up your sex life, here are some variations of this position:

Fluttering and soaring butterfly. The woman puts her feet on the bed and raises and lowers herself onto her partner's penis at the rate she enjoys. The man can help the woman steady herself and assist her timing, but this requires strong quad muscles on the woman's part. (Just one more reason to do squats.) A variation of this position is for the woman to put her knees on the bed and balance herself with one hand.

Alternating feet. The woman has one knee bent with her foot on the bed and the knee of the other leg rests on the bed. Should the woman want extra control, she can slide her hand underneath the man's pelvis and control his movements.

Reverse cowgirl. The woman sits on top of the man with her knees or feet on the bed but with her back to him. To change the angle of penetration, all the woman needs to do is lean forward or backward.

Both legs out in front. This position can be a bit tricky. The woman sits on top of the man, but instead of having her knees or feet under her, she straightens them out in front of her. Though the penetration isn't as deep in this position, it does allow for interesting sensations.

"Sleep is the best meditation."

—Dalai Lama

Get Eight Hours of Sleep Each Night

When you're fully rested, you're more equipped to handle what life throws at you. Think about it. After a few nights of mediocre sleep, do you feel less productive, easily frustrated, and like you're holding your emotional state together with a thread? Sleep not only helps your body physically recover from the day, it also improves your memory, lowers your stress levels, and decreases your chance of heart disease, and a full night's sleep might even help you lose weight. Aim to get between seven and nine hours of sleep each night, which means you might have to go to bed earlier than you usually do.

If you're having a hard time falling asleep at night, consider changing your nighttime diet. Foods that contain tryptophan—such as turkey, warm milk, honey, and bananas—help induce sleep, while alcohol, fattening or spicy foods, large amounts of protein, and of course, caffeine will keep you awake or prevent you from sleeping as well as you could.

"Nothing is so irretrievably missed as a daily opportunity."
—Marie von Ebner-Eschenbach

Mail That Rebate Form Immediately

From time to time, electronics items and big-ticket purchases, such as appliances, come with a mail-in rebate. The rebate is usually significant, but because you're required to mail it in and because you know you have to wait six to eight weeks for the rebate check to arrive in your mailbox, it's easy to forget about it. By doing that, you waste money and the manufacturers make more. The next time you purchase an item with a mail-in rebate, fill out the rebate as soon as you get in the car or on the subway. When the check arrives in six to eight weeks, you'll probably have already paid off the item, so take this money and invest it into your savings account.

Sometimes, though, the check doesn't arrive within the timeframe stated on the rebate form. Here are some steps you can take to ensure that you will get the money you're owed, as recommended by Consumer Affairs (*www.consumeraffairsusa.org*):

1. Make a copy of the rebate form after you've filled it in.
2. Return the rebate form by certified mail and request a return receipt. File this receipt so you have it on hand in case the check doesn't arrive so that you can prove the rebate was mailed. With it, keep the contact information that is printed on the rebate form.
3. If the company fails to send a check or to respond after you've contacted them, you can file a complaint online with the Federal Trade Commission (FTC)

"Life is too short to be small."

—Benjamin Disraeli

Be a Considerate Driver

Traffic is stressful for everyone. Make driving less stressful for yourself and for others by being a considerate driver on the road, and don't let your frustration get in the way. When drivers are moving too slow, go around them safely and don't glare at them as you pass. If someone cuts you off on the highway, ease off the gas or change to a different lane. If someone honks at you, consider whether you could do something differently, and if not, ignore the honking driver. Look for ways in which you can be a part of the solution instead of the problem. Not everyone is an expert or polite driver, but you can reduce your own stress and prevent derailing your own happiness if you don't allow yourself to get emotionally dragged into their poor driving or behavior.

Another way to reduce your car stress is to give yourself more time than you need to reach your destination. If it looks like you're going to make it to your meeting early, you can always relax in the car with some soothing music when you arrive or stop at a place that looks interesting on the way. If you do end up stuck in traffic and there are no alternate routes, play a game with yourself or with the other people in the car. Traffic is frustrating, but it's frustrating for every driver stuck in it, so remind yourself that it's not personal, it will end, and in the meantime, it's best to try and find a way to enjoy the moment alone or with your fellow passengers.

"All happiness depends on a leisurely breakfast."

—John Gunther

Eat Breakfast

Step away from the Egg McMuffin! But don't step away from breakfast altogether. Eating within an hour of waking up will kick-start your metabolism, and studies show that eating a high-fiber, low-fat breakfast can help you eat in moderation and consume less fat throughout the day. Breakfast also fuels your brain and helps you to be more productive. But you have to eat a healthy breakfast. Coffee and a biscotti doesn't count; a combination of protein, carbohydrate, and fat does. If the thought of eating within an hour of waking turns your stomach, reach for something small, like a piece of fruit or a slice of whole-grain toast, and then eat a proper breakfast an hour or so after that. This gives your body something to work with, and all you're essentially doing in that case is switching your late-morning snack with breakfast.

Here are some healthy breakfast ideas:

- An egg served with a slice of whole-wheat toast and vegetables or fruit
- A whole-grain waffle topped with peanut butter and berries
- Oatmeal topped with fruit
- Yogurt mixed with low-fat granola and fruit
- Whole-grain bread topped with low-fat ricotta and figs or tomatoes

*"It is exercise alone that lifts the spirits and
keeps the mind in vigor."*

—Marcus Tullius Cicero

Learn Five New Words a Day

Like the athlete who takes time to warm up and flex his or her
muscles before engaging in a strenuous activity, flexing your brain
cells every day keeps your mind sharp.

Pick up your dictionary and pick out five words you don't
know. Commit their definitions to memory and write five sen-
tences using them in different ways. See if you can recite their
definitions from memory the next day. And then learn five more. If
you're not in the habit of memorizing poetry, song lyrics, obscure
facts, or unfamiliar names, acquiring a new vocabulary can be a
challenge. However, "practice makes perfect," and as you persevere, you'll soon discover that the task of committing words
to memory will become increasingly easier to achieve and more
satisfying.

FIVE WORDS TO GET YOU STARTED

1. **chiack** 1. (v), to tease; 2. (noun) friendly banter
2. **countervail** (v) to counteract
3. **limbate** (adj), having a border of a different color
4. **peculate** (v) to embezzle funds
5. **scabrousness** (n) roughness

"It is not the horse that draws the cart, but the oats."

—Proverb

Eat Oatmeal

Oatmeal is a wonderful choice for breakfast or for a healthy snack. The soluble and insoluble fiber it contains allows it to be digested slowly by the body, and in doing so, it boosts your metabolism without causing blood-sugar levels to spike. The soluble fiber in oatmeal also helps to lower LDL cholesterol without negatively impacting your HDL level, because it forms a gel-like substance that traps the cholesterol-laden bile acids and transports them, along with other waster products, out of the body. For maximum effectiveness, it's recommended that you eat three grams of soluble fiber a day, which can be found in two-thirds cup of dry oat bran or one cup of dry oatmeal.

FOODS WITH HIGH-SOLUBLE FIBER CONTENT	
Plum	1.3 grams
Grapefruit	1.8 grams
½ cup cooked peas	2 grams
½ cup pinto beans	2.2 grams
1 potato	2.2 grams

*"All nature's creatures join to express nature's purpose.
Somewhere in their mounting and mating, rutting and butting,
is the very secret of nature itself."*

—Graham Swift

Try These Rear-Entry Positions

Rear-entry positions refer to vaginal intercourse, not to anal intercourse. Though you could use any of these positions during anal sex, rear-entry positions are those in which the man is behind the woman instead of in front of her during vaginal intercourse. While the clitoris isn't stimulated by any of these positions, the man or woman stimulate it in foreplay or manually if the position allows. These particular positions are good for stimulating the G-spot

Doggie style. This is the most well-known of all of the rear-entry positions. The woman (and sometimes the man as well) is on all fours while the man kneels behind her and penetrates her. For the couple's movements to be in sync, it is common for the man to hold the woman's waist as he thrusts.

Lazy dog. In this variation of doggie style, the woman puts her chest and arms on the bed but raises her butt high in the air. The man thrusts from the same position as in the doggie style or positions himself above his partner's legs so he is just over her butt. This allows for intense, but pleasurable, pressure for the man.

Elephant. The woman lies on her stomach with her legs stretched out, and the man lies on her back or kneels between her knees. In this position, he can penetrate deeply and her clitoris can be stimulated by the surface of the bed.

Inverted rear entry. It's a little tricky to get a rhythm going in this position, where the man lies face up on the bed and the woman lies face up on top of him. However, it allows the man to caress the woman as they try to move together.

"Don't let your mind bully your body into believing it must carry the burden of its worries."

—Astrid Aluada

De-Stress Before Bed

Help curb potential insomnia by releasing your stress before you slip between the sheets. Breathe deeply. Take a warm bath. Listen to relaxing music. Write in a journal. Discuss the day with a friend or loved one. Go for a leisurely stroll. Enjoy a glass of warm milk. Meditate. If you go to bed feeling stressed-out, you're more likely to toss and turn throughout the night or not be able to sleep at all.

STRETCH YOUR WAY TO SLEEP

Every night, take a few minutes to do these simple yoga stretches that will help you sleep.

- Rag Doll: Stand with your feet hip-width apart, bend over slowly, let your body and head go limp. Let your arms hang, feel the stretch in your lower back, relax your upper body.
- Dying Bug: Lie on your back, bring your knees into your chest, and grab the outsides of your flexed feet. Slowly pull your knees down to the outside of your body.
- Bridge: Lie on your back with your feet flat on the floor and lift your pelvis until your body makes a straight line. Walk your hands under your body and interlace your fingers.
- Seated Side Bend: Sit crosslegged, reach your hands toward the ceiling, and lean to the side, keeping your butt on the floor and your shoulders relaxed.
- Pigeon: Sit up, push one leg straight behind you, and bend the other so that your foot touches your inner thigh. Lie forward.

See these positions in detail at *www.FitnessMagazine.com/workout/express/10-minute/stretches-to-help-you-sleep*.

"Fortune favors the prepared mind."

—Louis Pasteur

Save Automatically for Those Large, Irregular Bills

When you think about paying the bills, do you remember the few you don't get *every* month? Tax bills, for example, often come annually or semiannually, as do insurance bills. If you're on a tight budget or have an unexpected need, these irregular bills can be devastating. Paying a big tax bill could force you to buy regular things like groceries on credit and then get saddled with finance charges as you pay the credit card back down.

The most effective method to handle bills that come irregularly is to automatically put away a fraction of the cost of that bill every month. Contact your bank and ask if you can set up automatic deposits into a savings account each month. For an annual bill, put away one-twelfth of the bill amount into a savings account each month. For a semiannual bill, put away one-sixth of the bill amount into a savings account each month. If you have your bank do this automatically, you'll barely notice that the money is gone, but when the bill comes due, you'll find you have the money already in a savings account, saving you the pain of having to scrape together the money for the bill. Even better, it will have likely earned a few dollars' worth of interest—an extra bonus for being smart about your bills.

"In every community there is work to be done. In every nation, there are wounds to heal. In every heart, there is power to do it."

—Marianne Williamson

Develop a Recycling Mindset

According to the United Stated Environmental Protection Agency (EPA), in 2008, Americans generated 250 million tons of trash, but only 83 million tons were recycled or composted. That means that, on average, each person in the U.S. generated 4.5 pounds of trash but recycled or composed 1.5 pounds of it.

If you want to start recycling yourself or you want to encourage others to recycle, the key is to make recycling easy. At work, request a meeting with your manager to discuss the option of starting a recycling program. Some states and cities offer businesses the opportunity to recycle their materials for free, which can be an incentive. Once your manager has agreed, work with the company to find places in the office that would make it easy for your coworkers to recycle. Put up signs, and let everyone know the company has launched a recycling program and would like all employees to be part of it. Let employees know which materials can be recycled and which cannot. If you're unsure, go to *www.RecycleStuff.org*.

At home, work with everyone who lives in the house to set up a recycling program. If you have children, explain to them why recycling is important. Check the trash occasionally to see if objects that could be recycled are ending up in there, and let the household know those items can be recycled. In addition, try to encourage a habit of reusing in addition to recycling. Be inventive and you might just start a following!

Purchase reusable bags to use instead of "paper or plastic" at the store, too.

"I don't always want a big meal after work—
just some crisps and wine!"

—Saffron Burrows, actress

Don't Skip Meals

Cutting calories by skipping meals might be tempting, but it's a no-no if you want to lose weight. Not only does skipping meals sap your energy and with it your productivity, it also makes you more likely to reach for an unhealthy snack or to overeat at the next meal. Plus, it slows down your metabolism. While you don't *have* to eat several small meals throughout the day as suggested in Week Forty, you can help keep those metabolic fires burning by consuming at least three meals and one or two snacks daily. Just make sure that most of the meals you eat are healthy and full of lean proteins, complex carbs, and healthy fats that will satiate you throughout the day.

PLAN AHEAD

When you make smart meal choices ahead of time, you can avoid gaining weight or slowing down your metabolism. Consider making a meal chart for the fridge of all the meals you want to eat that week—and if you have a spouse, kids, or a roommate, consider enlisting their help. By deciding in advance what you want to do you'll have healthy snacks and meals in mind so if you get hungry in the middle of the day, you don't have to feel guilty about reaching for a little pre-planned nosh. To make the meals come together that much faster, after you go shopping, do all the prep work that you can (chopping, making marinades, etc.) for the week.

*"When you look at my crumpled helmet, it's amazing
there's not one cut or bruise on my head."*

—Daniel Macpherson, triathlete

Wear a Helmet

Wearing a helmet is one of the smartest things you can do if you're engaging in any activity that could result in a head injury. Tour de France riders wear helmets, NFL and NHL players wear helmets, and Derby Dolls wear helmets for one reason: to protect their brains. A helmet greatly reduces the chance of you suffering a concussion if your head is hit, and in the event you do sustain a concussion, the concussion will be less severe if you are wearing a helmet at the time of impact.

Concussions are serious. In the past, they were brushed off as "just a concussion," but we now know that even minor head injuries can lead to serious problems down the road. The severity of your concussion can be measured by how you react after being hit. A grade-one concussion causes disorientation, trouble focusing, and confusion but is resolved within fifteen minutes. The symptoms are the same with a grade-two concussion, except it persists longer than fifteen minutes. A grade-three concussion means that you were knocked unconscious. Permanent brain injury can result from either a grade-two or grade-three concussion. Repeatedly sustaining grade-one concussions can also cause permanent brain damage or set you up for dementia or Alzheimer's later in life.

If you don't think helmets are "cool," then it's time you got back out there and saw what is on the market. Helmets come in a wide range of styles and colors these days, and some are built so they actually look like hats, with the helmet hidden underneath. It's time to give up the excuses and protect your brain.

"Weather means more when you have a garden. There's nothing like listening to a shower and thinking how it is soaking in around your green beans."

—Marcelene Cox

Ingest Chromium

Chromium is a shiny mineral that gives the "chrome" on cars their unique luster, but it is also useful for the human body. When ingested, chromium plays a role in the metabolism of fats and sugars while also lowering cholesterol levels. It can help keep the body young by protecting its DNA and RNA, and it may curb hunger and reduce cravings that can lead to overeating. While taking a chromium supplement is unadvisable, because high levels can be potentially dangerous, it is okay to eat foods that are naturally high in this trace element. These include whole grains, eggs, broccoli, green beans, seafood, meat, dairy products, orange juice, and grape juice.

"The great living experience for every man is his adventure into the woman. The man embraces in the woman all that is not himself, and from that one resultant, from that embrace, comes every new action."

—D. H. Lawrence

Try These Other Positions

To add to your sexual repertoire, here are some positions for sexual intercourse to inspire you:

- **Stand up and deliver**. The man stands and holds the woman underneath her butt. She wraps her legs around his to support herself as he thrusts.
- **Standing rear-entry**. The woman leans against a wall spreads her legs a bit wider than shoulder-width while the man penetrates her from behind.
- **The wheelbarrow**. This position requires balance and flexibility. The man holds the woman's legs from behind while she put her arms on the bed as he kneels between her legs.
- **The screw**. The man kneels on the floor next to the bed while the woman lies on the bed with her knees pulled to her chest as he thrusts forward.
- **Sit down**. The man sits comfortably on a raised surface, while the woman straddles him and faces either toward him or away from him.
- **The scissors**. The couple should lie on their sides facing each other, with the man perpendicular to the woman and with one of the woman's legs across the man's. This allows for clitoral stimulation and pressure on the penis.
- **Spoon**. The man lies behind the woman and penetrates her from behind as he wraps himself around her and caresses her body.

"How can you ever know anything if you are too busy thinking?"

—Buddha

Try Zazen Meditation

Zazen is the sitting meditation of Zen Buddhism, but it doesn't require any religious or philosophical affiliation. Zazen can be accurately defined as "just sitting." All it requires is the ability to apply the seat of the pants to the floor and stay there for a while, but it's not easy if you're more accustomed to accomplishing something every minute of the day!

To begin zazen, sit cross-legged or on folded legs, with a firm pillow under your hips so that you aren't sitting directly on your legs. Make sure you are wearing enough clothes to stay warm. Sit up straight, feeling a lift from the crown of the head toward the ceiling and an open feeling in your spine. Keep your shoulders back, your chest open, and place your tongue on the roof of your mouth. Your focus points should be slightly downward and your eyes relaxed. Now, unfocus your eyes just a little so that you don't really see what's in front of you. This will help you to focus inwardly. Rest your hands in your lap. Keep your mouth closed and breathe through your nose. At first, practice concentrating by counting each breath. In your mind, count from one to ten, with each full breath (inhalation and exhalation) constituting one number. Or, simply follow your breath, keeping your awareness focused on the sound and feel of your breath moving in and out of your body.

Like any form of meditation, zazen is most effective if you practice regularly. If you can make this—or any—kind of meditation a part of your regular routine, you'll find clarity, peace, acceptance, satisfaction, and a whole lot less stress.

"Leisure time should be an occasion for deep purpose to throb and for ideas to ferment. Where a man allows leisure to slip without some creative use, he has forfeited a bit of his happiness."

—C. Neil Strait

Step Away from Your Desk During the Workday

If you feel tense and exhausted at the end of a workday, then it's important to start incorporating some relaxation time into your schedule. Five minutes of deep breathing, lunch outside instead of at your desk, a walk around the block, a trip up and down the stairs, or even a half-hour power nap can make you feel refreshed and ready to work again. Your body isn't built for sitting all day. Your eyes don't deal well with staring at computer screens for eight or more hours a day. And you can't expect your brain to be as effective on hour seven as it was on hour one of your day if you haven't given it a rest and time to recharge.

Give yourself and your body a break. If you're not sure you have the time, work on cutting down the time you waste on the Internet or doing meaningless tasks, and use those extra minutes toward a bigger reward. By making it a habit to step away from your office or your cubicle throughout the day, you'll have more gas to pump out your best work when you're back at your desk.

Even if you don't work at a desk, make sure to take little breaks to recharge!

"How wonderful it is that nobody need wait a single moment before starting to improve the world."

—Anne Frank

Donate Your Old Eyeglasses

If you just got LASIK or your eyeglasses prescription is no longer valid, donate your glasses to someone who could use them. According to One Sight, a nonprofit organization that brings clear sight to millions of people around the globe, 314 million people worldwide cannot see clearly. Poor vision can affect a person's ability to learn in school, to succeed at work, and in some countries, to survive. According to the nonprofit Unite for Sight, blind people in Africa have a mortality rate that is four times higher than that of the average African.

To help those with impaired vision, you can donate your glasses, if they are still in good condition, to an organization such as One Sight, and they will hand-deliver them to someone who needs them but cannot afford them. If you don't wear glasses or want to help further, you can make a monetary donation to one of these organizations, which will help enable underprivileged sight-impaired individuals to get eye-care exams or to receive cataract or other eye surgeries as well as help to eliminate preventable blindness. Don't be one of the 4 million Americans who toss out their gently used glasses. Donate the gift of sight to someone in need.

*"Man may be the captain of his fate, but he is also
the victim of his blood sugar."*

—Dr. Wilfred Oakley

Eat Small Meals Throughout the Day

In place of three big meals a day, try grazing and eating several small meals throughout the day. Of course, you'll have to keep a strict eye on how many calories you're taking in, but fitness experts have theorized that when you eat healthily throughout the day your body burns more calories, because each time you eat you give it something to do, and that increases your metabolism.

Though the official ruling is still out on whether that is actually the case, grazing still has other benefits. When you keep your body busy with digesting calories, you're less likely to spike your blood sugar levels, and that means you'll maintain a stable energy level throughout the day. You're also less likely to put your body into starvation mode, where it holds on to calories more tightly, and so you're less likely to want to splurge on something unhealthy because you won't reach the stage that you're so hungry you'll eat anything.

"Shipping is a terrible thing to do to vegetables.
They probably get jet-lagged, just like people."

—Elizabeth Barry

Visit Your Local Farmer's Market

We've spoken about how eating organically is good for you and good for the environment. Taking it one step further and getting your organic produce from your local farmer's market is even better. By doing so, you are supporting your local farmers and their sustainable farming practices instead of buying from a faceless chain. You are also reducing your carbon footprint because you aren't buying produce that has been shipped from somewhere else in the world. And you might even save money. It's a smarter move overall.

If you have kids or friends who have never been to the farmer's market, take them. Introduce them to the farmers you buy from on a regular basis. If you make these outings fun for your kids (some have activity areas for youngsters), when they grow up and remember these outings, they'll look back fondly and be more likely to shop at them as well. After shopping at a farmer's market, make a meal from some of the ingredients that day so you can show newcomers to the market just how tasty those fresh ingredients are.

"Except the vine, there is no plant which bears a fruit of as great importance as the olive."

—Pliny the Elder

Munch on Olives

Olives and olive oil are high in fat—but it's good, monunsaturated fat. And they're also high in vitamin E. Monounsaturated fat helps to reduce LDL cholesterol levels in the blood, and vitamin E acts as an antioxidant, protecting the body from harmful free radicals and helping to prevent colon cancer. Plus, olives contain dietary fiber, so while you're unlikely to fill up on them, they make for a great snack.

Olive oil offers all of the same benefits as olives, but it is in a more usable form for cooking. If you want to be heart-wise, substitute olive oil in place of the other cooking oils. The consumption of olive oil might also help you live longer. Mariam Amash, an Israeli woman who claims to have been born in 1888, is still living and attributes her longevity partially to the fact that she drinks a glass of olive oil a day.

Olive oil is also found in some beauty products, as it can relieve dry skin and restore shine to dry hair, giving you a more youthful appearance.

"Sex is emotion in motion."

—Mae West

Find the G-Spot

The G-spot—or Gräfenberg spot, as it was named after gyne-cologist Ernst Gräfenberg, who studied the urethra's role in the female orgasm—is a small mound of erectile tissue that is located two to three inches within the vagina. The urethra, which carries the urine from the bladder out of the body, passes through this tissue, and it is theorized that this tube is also the delivery route for female ejaculate.

To find a woman's G-spot, wait until she's very aroused so the G-spot will be easier to find, because it will be filled with blood, and then insert a finger or two into her vagina. Use a come-hither motion against the front wall (the side toward her navel) once your fingers are one to two inches inside. Once you've discovered it, she may feel like she has to pee. Reassure her that she doesn't and that if any fluid does come out not to worry, as it's just added lubrication being excreted by her Skene's glands. If she enjoys the stimulation, play around with different pressures and strokes and tapping motions until she reaches orgasm.

"Tension is who you think you should be.
Relaxation is who you are."

—Proverb

De-Stress at Your Desk with Simple Stretches

You already know the importance of unwinding when you wake up, de-stressing before you go to bed at night, and taking your vacations, but you can also find peace in the middle of the day by taking the time to stretch. If you've just had an unpleasant interaction with your boss, or coworker, or even your partner over the phone or if you feel like you're drowning in work, take a moment to step away from the situation and release the tension.

Breathe deeply. Visualize an image that makes you feel grounded and at peace. Inhale deeply and stretch your arms up over your head, opening your fingers wide, and exhale. Bend slowly from side to side, allowing the tightness in your back to evaporate. If you are able to get up and do these and stretches that make your muscles relax, please do so a few times a day. If not, do what you can at your desk and allow yourself to take a break, even a five-minute one, to leave the office and center yourself.

"A first-rate organizer is never in a hurry. He is never late. He always keeps up his sleeve a margin for the unexpected."

—Arnold Bennett

Clean Your Workplace at the End of Each Day

When you come into work every morning, it's important to start with a clear head. And when your desk is cluttered with coffee cups, notes from the day before, and other accoutrements, it's easy to get distracted and lose that drive you walked into the door with. To start every day as productive as possible, take the time at the end of every work day to tidy your desk and your computer's desktop. That way, you'll always have the tools you need—pens, pencils, files, etc.—on hand because they're located in their proper place.

While you might be able to juggle multiple projects at once and still have a messy desk, your bosses might not know that. A clean desk shows them you're organized and able to handle several projects simultaneously without getting overwhelmed. If you're afraid of feeling like a nondescript "Dilbert" in your office or cubicle once you've decided to become organized, take the time to visit any big office supply store or art store. There, you'll find a wealth of organizational tools, such as file folders, task clips, and calendars, that will suit your style, whether it's comical or pretty.

"While the spirit of neighborliness was important on the frontier because neighbors were so few, it is even more important now because our neighbors are so many."

—Lady Bird Johnson

Help an Entrepreneur in the Developing World

One unique way to increase happiness around the globe is by helping an entrepreneur get off the ground in a developing country. In the United States, even in a depressed economy, it is relatively easy to start a new business, as entrepreneurs have access to grants, loans, and credit. In developing countries, it's not so simple.

In 1984, former Peace Corps member John Hatch founded the Foundation for International Community Assistance (FINCA) and used it to develop what he calls "village banks." These village banks provide community members in third-world countries in Africa, the Middle East, Latin America, and Eurasia with "microfinancing" to get their businesses started. In many of these countries, few salaried jobs exist, and between 30 and 80 percent of the population earn their living through self-employment, making this strategy very useful. FINCA also teaches business practices to recipients of microfinancing to help their microbusinesses succeed.

You can help these struggling businesspeople by investing in FINCA, volunteering, or making a small donation that will go into the village bank.

*"Happiness is a bowl of cherries and a book
of poetry under a shade tree."*

—Astrid Alauda

Include Snacks in Your Diet

Eating throughout the day is one way to prevent hunger pangs and to keep you from reaching for something to eat that you don't need. But if you still prefer to eat three square meals a day rather than several small meals throughout the day, at least help your body out by snacking. If you've already cut back on your calories, your body might be panicking and trying to go into starvation mode. One way to keep your body from doing that is snacking healthily throughout the day. To keep yourself satiated, eat snacks that are low in fat, high in carbs, and less than 150 calories. By eating in this way, you'll be less likely to overstuff yourself at dinner and your body will realize it's getting the fuel it needs, which will make it easier for you to burn off those last few pounds.

Here are some smart snack ideas:

- Half an English muffin with one tablespoon peanut butter
- Hummus and carrots
- Whole grain cereal and skim milk

"Memory is the scribe of the soul."

—Aristotle

Take Memorization Classes

You know it's important to improve your memory, but you've had a hard time motivating yourself to do the work it takes to rev it up. If that's the case, consider taking a memorization class. In one study, scientists challenged participants to memorize a list of random words. Prior to any memory training, the older subjects were able to recall less words than the younger subjects. But when given the test again after completing a handful of memory training sessions in which they learned skills such as chunking and acrostics, they tripled the amount of words they could remember.

Memorization classes might also help you to boost your overall IQ in addition to helping you find your lost keys. Children who were given memorization training saw their IQ test scores jump 8 percent, and while that study hasn't been conducted on adults, it wouldn't be surprising if learning these tools could improve your overall intelligence potential.

"Let's put some hummus on it. It cures everything."

—From *Date Movie*

Try Hummus

Finding satisfying snacks can sometimes feel difficult. But you can always turn to hummus. The Middle Eastern dish is made from chickpeas, olives, pureed sesame seeds, lemon juice, spices, and garlic—all ingredients that are very good for you. Many of these ingredients have antioxidant qualities, and most are known to boost the metabolism—helping you to maintain a youthful figure. If you're on a vegetarian diet, hummus combined with whole-grain bread will make a complete helping of protein. The dip comes in many flavors, from the original to ones that are flavored with olives, pine nuts, or extra garlic, and it's delicious on whole-grain bread or carrots. Be aware, though, that hummus is high in calories, so if you're watching your weight, scoop out only two tablespoons for a snack so you're not tempted to eat a lot of it. It's very tasty, so that can be an easy thing to do!

"It is not sex that gives pleasure, but the lover."

—Marge Piercy

Find the A-Spot

The anterior fornix erogenous zone, or A-spot, is a relative new-comer to the sex discussion, as it wasn't officially discovered until 1996, by Malaysian scientist Dr. Chua Chee Ann, when she was researching vaginal dryness. The A-spot is located on the anterior wall of the vagina just beneath the cervix. When it is stimulated, it releases fluid that lubricates the vagina and produces an intense orgasm.

One way to stimulate this spot is to insert a finger or two into your partner's vagina with your palm facing upward and your partner in a position that allows for deep penetration. Once your fingers are inside, make a scooping motion toward this wall. Use similar techniques as you would with the G-spot—rubbing, tapping, and stroking this area to find out what brings her to orgasm.

"You may delay, but time will not."

—Benjamin Franklin

Stop Procrastinating

Procrastinating feels great . . . in the moment, that is. But as one day of procrastination leads to the next, soon enough you'll be backed up against a deadline and your only choices will be to ask for an extension or stress yourself out trying to get it done.

For the most part, people procrastinate for one of two main reasons: the project isn't enjoyable or the project seems overwhelming. If you're avoiding a project because it's boring to you or you just don't like doing it, determine how long you think it will take you and schedule time to work on it. Make it the first thing you tackle each day, if you can. Tell yourself that after you've completed that day's portion you can treat yourself to something you do enjoy, like a walk outside or a cup of coffee, and that you'll celebrate in a big way when you've completed the whole project.

If you're delaying working on a project because it feels like too much to take on, that means you really need to stop procrastinating or else you'll really get buried. Take a moment and divide the project into pieces. Each day, try to accomplish one of those pieces until you've completed the entire project. When you look back, you'll be impressed with your efforts, and it will give you the confidence to take on another big project.

As you start to move away from procrastination and toward a more disciplined approach to tackling overwhelming and uninteresting projects, big and small, you'll find yourself applying this tactic to the rest of your life, and you won't continue to come home to stacks of unpaid bills and dishes in the sink.

"Better three hours too soon than a minute too late."

—William Shakespeare

Show Up on Time for Meetings and Be Prepared

If you want to get on the wrong side of your coworkers, make a habit of showing up late and unprepared for meetings. Most people believe they're already wasting precious minutes by being stuck in a meeting, and if you wander in late with nothing to add, you can be sure you'll be getting the stink eye.

On the other hand, if you take all of your meetings seriously and show up to each on time and with ideas that you researched in advance, not only will you impress your coworkers (who, if they didn't come prepared might feel they've gotten off the hook), you'll also win points with your boss. Though your boss and colleagues might not want to use the ideas you present, you'll at least prove to them that you're a confident, creative thinker, that you're dedicated to your work, and that you're a team player. These are the kinds of strong qualities supervisors look for when they're considering who to promote and who deserves a raise.

> *"We cannot live only for ourselves. A thousand*
> *fibers connect us with our fellow men."*
>
> —Herman Melville

Volunteer

When you volunteer, whether on a regular basis or only for an occasional activity, you bring happiness to others, and in turn, you bring happiness to yourself. Though sending checks to charities is a great thing to do, as it helps them continue to fund their social programs, getting out there and physically and mentally getting involved will give you a greater sense of joy. You'll get to see, firsthand, the impact of your contribution.

There are many different ways to volunteer. You could volunteer in your local community by helping to clean it up, by visiting seniors, by starting a food or clothing drive, by being a foster parent for an animal, by teaching people how to read, by reading to the blind . . . the list is pretty much endless. The urge to volunteer only strikes some people around the holidays. While helping out at a soup kitchen at Thanksgiving is good, keep in mind that these organizations need volunteers year round and consider volunteering once a month or periodically throughout the year.

If you want to volunteer but aren't sure what opportunities there are within your community, visit *http://Serve.gov* and find out.

"The woman just ahead of you at the supermarket checkout has all the delectable groceries you didn't even know they carried."

—Mignon McLaughlin

Eat Before You Go Grocery Shopping

Don't shop hungry. If you do, you're much more likely to make impulse purchases, buying items that aren't healthy for you just because they sound good at the moment. Those muffins do look delicious, don't they? And what about those chips? Frozen pizza seems like a good idea for dinner tonight . . . and so on. These items then loom at you from the fridge and the pantry, begging you to eat them.

This lack of willpower isn't entirely your fault. According to a 2009 study, it might be hard-wired into our brains. The study revealed that when we're hungrier, food looks more attractive (even foods we might not otherwise eat), so unless you think you can beat science, eat before you go grocery shopping, even if it's just a small snack. You can also use this tactic before going out to dinner if you're starving. Eat something small before you go, and you won't be tempted to order the biggest dish on the menu.

"I was asked to memorize what I did not understand and my memory being so good, it refused to be insulted in that manner."

—Aleister Crowley

Memorize Your Grocery List

Did you know you can enhance your memory through mind games? Here are some tips for improving your memory:

1. **Turn things you have to remember into memory challenges**. For example, before you go to the grocery store, make a list of what you need. Memorize it as best you can, then put that list in your pocket or purse. Don't look at the list again until after you've shopped and think you've gotten everything on it. At first, you might miss quite a few items, but with practice you'll be able to improve.

2. **Use acronyms and acrostics**. Acronyms, such as ROYG-BIV, and acrostics, such as Every Good Boy Deserves Favor, can help you remember items that need to be sequenced in a specific order.

3. **Divide data into chunks**. Breaking large bits of information—such as number sequences—into smaller bits will make them easier for you to recall later.

4. **Connect words with images**. This works very well with names of people. When you need to remember the name of someone you just met or the names of presidents try to associate each person's name with a specific image. By memorizing these together, you'll probably find that bringing the image up in your mind will help jog your memory into remembering the name you need.

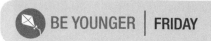
"As for butter versus margarine,
I trust cows more than chemists."

—Joan Gussow

If It Came from a Plant, Eat It / If It Was Made in a Plant, Don't

Want to know an easy way to stay healthy? Don't eat manmade (processed) foods. This rule is one of the sixty-four that Michael Pollan recommends in *Food Rules: An Eater's Manual.* Although cutting back on your saturated fat intake, maintaining a low-cholesterol diet, and keeping an eye on your calories are impor-tant to your health, eating foods that weren't made in a plant is a great way to start taking control of your diet, your health, and your longevity.

By manmade foods, I don't mean cheese, butter, etc. I'm refer-ring to processed foods that contain ingredients like corn syrup solids, artificial flavor, hydrolyzed soy protein, monoglycerides, and so on. These products are made in a factory by humans and machines, and since they're all relatively new in terms of humans consuming them, the court is still out on their long-term effects on your body, which doesn't necessarily know how to process them. It's best not to take that chance. Instead, shop the perimeters of your supermarket to get your fresh produce, meat, and dairy and avoid the aisles full of processed food. Or buy your food fresh from the farmer's market.

"Men are those creatures with two legs and eight hands."

—Jayne Mansfield

Find the P-Spot

The male version of the G-spot is the P-spot, or prostate gland. The prostate is responsible for that pumping sensation men feel during ejaculation as the gland pushes the semen out of the head of the penis. To give a prostate massage, make sure that the man is already extremely turned on. Using a latex glove or other protective barrier, spread a liberal amount of lubrication onto his anus. Tease and massage the anus until it becomes relaxed and your partner lets you know he's ready for you to insert your middle finger. Enter him slowly and remind him to breathe deeply as you do, possibly massaging his penis at the same time with the other hand. Once your finger is fully inside and your palm is facing upward, lift your finger until you can feel a mass about the size of a walnut. By this time, your partner might have moved from apprehension back to arousal. Try tapping, rubbing, or tracing around the edges of the prostate until he reaches orgasm or is satisfied. Then, remove your finger slowly as he takes a few more deep breaths. It may take a couple of P-spot massages for your partner to fully succumb and enjoy the sensation, but once he does he'll probably ask you for more.

"People count the faults of those who keep them waiting."

—Proverb

Stop Being Late

If you're chronically late, it's time to change this bad habit. Not only is always running late stressful for you, it also makes you look unprofessional and makes the people who are waiting on you feel that you don't respect their time.

Start by addressing why you're often late. Perhaps you underestimate the time it takes to drive or take public transportation to a certain place. If this is the case, use a tool like Google Maps to determine how long the trip will probably take, and then add ten to twenty minutes to give yourself a cushion. If you find you're usually late because you spend too much time getting ready, try laying out your clothes the night before or determine how long your routine really takes you and set your alarm to wake up earlier. If you're the type who needs to do "one more thing" before you leave, talk yourself out of it by asking yourself how often doing that "one more thing" has made you late in the past. Then walk out of the door on time!

"The secret of success lies not in doing your own work, but in recognizing the right man to do it."

—Andrew Carnegie

Advance Your Career

When you're working on a big project, do you try to take it all on yourself or do you divide the tasks among your coworkers? If you're the type to put in long hours to complete a project that would be better served by multiple brains and hands, it's time to learn how to delegate if you want to be an effective manager. For instance, an editor of a magazine isn't expected to write, edit, and design the entire magazine herself. To put out a quality publication, she hires staff members or freelancers who are experienced in those areas and gives them job responsibilities or assignments. In this way, the editor isn't overworked, and the magazine benefits from these different minds.

Are there parts of the project you're overseeing that another colleague is more qualified to deal with? If so, assign it to that colleague. Not only will you be giving someone work and showing that person that you trust in his or her ability (which also makes your colleague look good to your boss), but you also are giving yourself more time to oversee the entire project instead of becoming lost in the details. As you learn to delegate effectively, it's likely that your boss (or client) will start to see you as an even bigger asset to the company and will enlist you to work on bigger and bigger projects.

"We can do no great things, only small things with great love."

—Mother Teresa

Build a House with Habitat for Humanity

Since 1976, Habitat for Humanity has been building affordable homes for low-income families. From its inception, the organization has built more than 350,000 homes and housed more than 1.75 million people in need. Habitat for Humanity affiliates are located all across the world, and there is probably a local chapter within your community.

There are many ways you can get involved with this nonprofit group. You can help to physically build a house for a family. You'll work hard, burn some serious calories, and know you have had a direct impact on a family's happiness. This is a great feeling. You can also volunteer in one of their home-improvement stores, which, like Goodwill, take donations of materials and resell them at a low cost to the public. The profits are reinvested in the charity's efforts. Another way to help is to be a part of the team that interviews potential Habitat families, determines who is eligible for a home, and works with them until that dream has been realized.

No matter what aspect of the charity you get involved with, just knowing you are helping to erect a stable roof over someone's head will put a smile on your face.

*"You've got bad eating habits if you use
a grocery cart in 7-Eleven."*

—Dennis Miller

Shop the Perimeters

Challenge yourself to avoid the middle aisles of the grocery store—where most of the processed food products are usually located. Instead, shop primarily on the perimeters of the store, where most of the whole foods are stocked. By staying away from the center, you limit yourself to purchasing fresh produce, meat, seafood, and dairy instead of frozen dinners, cookies, chips, and more. This will make it easier for you to avoid temptations and to purchase healthy snacks, like fruits and vegetables.

BEWARE OF POTENTIAL PITFALLS

When you're shopping the edges of the store, you still need to be wise about your food choices. In the refrigerated section you'll come across ready-to-bake cookies, rolls, and whipped cream. In the meat section, you'll need to make the choice to choose lean meats like turkey and chicken over fattier options. In the bakery, you'll need to choose whole-grain breads (freshly baked if possible) and avoid those with preservatives, high-fructose corn syrup, and other unhealthy ingredients. And, in the produce section, stay clear of high-calorie dressings and don't even think about picking up that caramel dipping sauce for apples. Want to make apples tastier without the added calories? Just sprinkle them with a little cinnamon.

---

*"It's not how much we give but how much
love we put into our giving."*

—Mother Teresa

Aspire for Excellence in Your Volunteer Work

There's no point in doing anything if you're only going to do it halfway. Whatever you do, wherever you work, whomever you love, put your heart and your soul into it. By investing your energy fully, you'll be more likely to excel and you'll get more satisfaction from the experience.

That same attitude should go toward your volunteer work as well. Whether you're spearheading a food, clothing, or toy drive or working a crisis hotline, put care and consideration into every interaction. When others can see that you're putting in your best effort and not just going through the motions, those who benefit from your volunteering efforts will appreciate your efforts all the more, your co-volunteers will look upon you with even greater favor, and you'll be happier with yourself.

"High-tech tomatoes. Mysterious milk. Supersquash. Are we supposed to eat this stuff? Or is it going to eat us?"

—Anita Manning

Eat Real Food

A major part of Michael Pollan's philosophy in *Food Rules: An Eater's Manual* is to eat real food. What does this mean? It means preparing your food from raw ingredients—which doesn't mean necessarily eating "raw" (uncooked) food, although you certainly can eat some foods uncooked. Pollan advocates using fresh fruits, vegetables, whole grains, proteins (poultry, meat, fish, seafood), etc. to build a meal from scratch, instead of relying on packaged foods that have been processed in a plant. "Raw" or "real" food is what your grandparents and great-grandparents would have considered simply "food."

Michael Pollan recommends not eating anything packaged if it has more than five ingredients. Of course, if those ingredients are all "whole foods"—for example, a trail mix of dried fruits and nuts, with no processed ingredients or additives—you probably don't need to worry about it, but once you see an ingredient that you wouldn't buy to make this product on your own—such as guar gum or monoglycerides—put it back on the shelf. Pollan calls products like these "edible, food-like substances."

It is, admittedly, harder to eat real food. For one thing, it requires you to cook (at least a little bit). But in most cases, it tastes better and it's better for you, because there are less free radicals in real food. For you packaged-food junkies, there are some products on the market that fit Pollan's guidelines, such as Lara bars. But you're going to have to search for them.

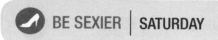

"Imperfection is beauty, madness is genius, and it's better to be absolutely ridiculous than absolutely boring."

—Marilyn Monroe

Leave the Lights On

You might be shy about your body, but don't worry, your partner doesn't see the "flaws" you do. Whether you feel you're too thin, too curvy, too heavy, too flat-chested, or too whatever, your partner is attracted to you; otherwise he wouldn't be having sex with you. Showing your insecurities in the bedroom can detract from his heat for you, so if you want to talk to your partner about your body issues (though, to be honest, it's probably better to talk to someone you're not having sex with about them), wait until a time when you're not about to have sex.

In the meantime, leave those lights on. Let your partner see your hot body as he kisses and caresses it. Allow yourself the pleasure of seeing your partner below you or on top of you as you make love. Enjoy looking at your partner as he goes down on you, and connect the intense pleasure you're feeling with the person you're looking at. Gazing into each other's eyes during sex and feeling close to your partner can generate the feel-good hormone oxytocin and increase your intimacy. So, unless you want to make love in the pitch black or wear a blindfold to heighten arousal, leave those lights on or those candles burning!

"To sit with a dog on a hillside on a glorious afternoon is to be back in Eden, where doing nothing was not boring —it was peace."

—Milan Kundera

Take Your Vacations and Long Weekend Breaks

Even if you can't get away for a long stretch at once, take time off. It can be a few days here and there, but even a little break can help you recharge and be more productive once you head back to work. These breaks will also reduce your stress levels and help you to be happier in your overall life because you won't feel like you're working yourself to the bone without a break.

Vacations don't have to be extravagant. Consider taking a camping trip somewhere nearby that you've never been before. If you pack in your food and use a gourmet camping cookbook like my favorite, *Camping Cuisine*, you'll be able to eat delicious, healthy meals and save money while you explore and enjoy the wilderness. If you can get away for an extended period, plan time for rest and relaxation so that you don't need a vacation from your vacation when you return home!

"To become an able and successful man in any profession, three things are necessary: nature, study, and practice."

—Henry Ward Beecher

Think of Two Reasons You Haven't Moved Forward in Your Career

At times, you need to evaluate where you've gone wrong so you can fix the problem and get back on track. If it's been some time since you've been promoted or received a raise or if your career hasn't developed in the way you want, take a hard look at what you're doing—or not doing—to prevent this from happening. The reason you haven't advanced may have nothing to do with you—for example, if the economy is in a slump—but if your actions or inactions have held you back, it's important to take the necessary steps to fix that so you can improve your earning potential and also provide yourself with greater job security.

Take a look at what the new hires are bringing to the table and ask yourself if you have, at the very least, the skills they're walking in with. If not, consider taking a course to update them. Whether you need to learn better time management skills, improve your technical know-how, or become more comfortable speaking in front of a crowd, you can take classes in these fields and become a greater asset to your company.

"I am still convinced that a good, simple, homemade cookie is preferable to all the store-bought cookies one can find."

—James Beard

Pack Food and Beverages for a Road Trip

When we eat healthier, we're often happier. And there's nothing more unhealthy than road-trip food. Day after day spent consuming fried foods high in saturated fat are a recipe for an in-the-car spat with your carpool friends or a tiff with your partner. To avoid the drama and spend your budget on your trip and not the food you're eating on your way there, prepare your own meals in advance.

Sandwiches and salads are good road-trip meals, and they're probably what you'd be eating anyway if you went through the drive-thru. If you want sandwiches that require items that need to be refrigerated, such as chicken salad or anything with mayo, don't make the sandwich until you're ready to eat it and keep the perishable items in a cooler. This way, you won't end up with a soggy meal. If you want to dine on salads, you can put together most ingredients before you leave and then add tomatoes and dressing when you're hungry. Snacks such as hummus, vegetables, fruit, and nuts also travel well.

You can also use these tactics to make up your lunches for the workweek. Instead of eating lunch out, take an hour every week to prepare your lunch meals in advance. Put the money you're saving into your savings account, and treat yourself to something you really want after a few weeks.

"To make a good salad is to be a brilliant diplomatist—the problem is entirely the same in both cases. To know exactly how much oil one must put with one's vinegar"

—Oscar Wilde

Use Flavored Vinegars and Oil in Your Salad

Instead of dumping dressing that is loaded with fat, sugar, and calories on what would otherwise be a healthy salad, avoid the high-calorie salad dressings (I'm looking at you, buttermilk ranch) and replace them with flavored oils and vinegars. There are a wide variety of fruit- or herb-infused olive oils and vinegars on the market, and when mixed together on their own or along with some Dijon mustard (if you want to enjoy a thicker dressing), you won't miss the creamy, fattening ones you used to eat and you'll actually be able to taste your salad. If you're the type who really pours on the dressing and leaves a leftover puddle in the dish when you're done with the salad, try putting the dressing in a spray bottle. This way, you can spritz some on in the beginning and add as you go without overdoing it early.

DECADENT OILS AND VINEGARS

The best way to dress your salad is with oil and vinegar, and here are some mouth-watering ones available on the market that add even more healthy goodness. Also, look out for the UK chain Vom Fass that is now opening shops in the States where they allow you to sample and bottle their wide range of healthy oils, vinegars, and more.

- Annie's Naturals Roasted Garlic Extra Virgin Olive Oil
- Boyajian Garlic Vinegar
- La Tourangelle Avocado Oil
- La Tourangelle Almond Oil
- Pristine Gourmet Blueberry Infused Wine Vinegar

"When we heal the earth, we heal ourselves."

—David Orr

Clean Up Your Environment

Perhaps you're eating organic so you don't ingest harmful chemicals. But what are you doing about the chemicals in your environment? You can purchase an electric or hybrid car to cut down on your fuel exhaust, but what about the pollutants that are lurking in your home? One thing you can do if you're a smoker is to stop smoking. According to a study done by Italy's National Cancer Institute, smoking cigarettes causes ten times more air pollution (indoors) than the pollution created by a diesel car. That's a lot of chemicals to put into the air in your home, not to mention your lungs.

Here are some other ways you can reduce your exposure to free radicals within your home, culled from *This Old House* magazine:

- Replace your vinyl shower curtain with a nylon or polyester one to avoid phthalates.
- Use organic dry-cleaning services or remove the plastic bags from your clothes before you go indoors to avoid breathing in perchlorethylene, a potential carcinogen.
- Stop using plastic containers that have BPA in them.
- Replace cracked cutting boards in which bacteria can thrive.
- Wash your hands before putting away the dishes.
- Avoid chemical-based cleansers and use a vinegar-and-water solution instead.
- Stop using mothballs.

"If organic farming is the natural way, shouldn't organic produce just be called 'produce' and make the pesticide-laden stuff take the burden of an adjective?"

—Ymber Delecto

Go Organic

Eating organic food can help you avoid a host of problems as you get older. Though once it was just deemed trendy to eat organic, today it's common knowledge that you should strive to eat organic as often as possible in order to avoid the chemicals and other substances that are in non-organic foods. With non-organic meats, eggs, and dairy products, the livestock can be injected with hormones or fed animal by-products. Non-organic vegetables can be sprayed with harmful chemicals. Many studies have found the chemical PDBE (most often used as a flame retardant) in non-organic ground beef, cheese, salmon, and butter.

It's best, if you can budget it, to eat products that are both organic and properly fed, free-range animals. Grass-fed beef, for example, is lower in overall fat and much lower in saturated fat and contains more heart-healthy omega-3 fatty acids than corn- or grain-fed beef.

"I want a bad boy in public, and a pussycat at home."

—Christina Aguilera

Change Locations

Having sex on the bed is fun, but don't be afraid to switch it up from time to time. Your house offers plenty of great places to have sex, and changing locations, even within your own home, can add some spice to your sex life. You'll find it hard to repress a smile the next time you're hosting a dinner party and you know what you and your significant other did right where the yams are resting. A few tried-and-true spots to get you started include the kitchen table, the counter, the laundry room (with one person on top of the washing machine during the spin cycle), the couch (either on it or over the back of it), the floor, and the shower.

If you've got guts and you're ready for glory, consider having public or semi-public sex. The adrenaline rush you'll get from potentially getting caught will add to the passion. Consider having sex in the woods, in the ocean or a lake, at a local park underneath a blanket, in the back of taxi cab (tip heavily if you do), or in the bathroom of a bar or restaurant. Let your imagination be your guide.

"He does not seem to me to be a free man who does not sometimes do nothing."

—Marcus Tullius Cicero

Take a Vacation Every Year

Vacation time is given for a reason: your employers, believe it or not, want you to take a vacation. Yes, you'll probably have to put in some extra hours to get everything in order before you take time off and again when you return to put everything *back* in order. But taking a vacation helps you to be more productive at your job in the long run. Like those little breaks I've suggested you take throughout the day, a vacation serves as a big break that can recharge you after a big project or get you ready to take one on, or simply provide relief from the daily grind.

Studies have revealed that many Americans fail to take all of their vacation time. Worse, studies also have shown that there is a correlation between not taking an annual vacation and suffering a fatal heart attack. Another problem for some people is that when they do take a vacation, they still check in with the office and clients through e-mail and phone calls.

Take your vacations. Your health and happiness depend on it. And to get the most out of your break and restore a healthy work-life balance in your life, put the cell phone and laptop down and really allow yourself time to relax and recuperate without distraction.

*"The most important persuasion tool you have in
your entire arsenal is integrity."*

—Zig Ziglar

Admit to Your Superiors You Screwed Up

No one likes to make mistakes, but when you've messed up at work, admit it to your boss. Though you might be afraid of taking the heat, accepting blame before your boss (or client) realizes what's happened makes you look trustworthy and confident. Explain why things went wrong and how you'll work to assure that it won't happen again in the future. Unless it's a major transgression, your superiors are more likely to remember that you had the guts to come forward about your mistake than they are to remember what you did wrong. And that can pay off for you in a big way in the long run.

WEEK FORTY-FIVE

"I never travel without my diary. One should always have something sensational to read on the train."

—Oscar Wilde

Pack Comforts from Home When You Travel

You've been looking forward to your long vacation for months, so you might be surprised to find yourself feeling homesick while you're out enjoying new customs and cuisines. Traveling the world, especially if you're doing it solo, can get lonely, and it's easy to start longing for the companionship you have back home. While we don't recommend you cut your trip short, there are some things you can do to get yourself through these rough moments.

One thing you can do is pack some personal products that remind you of your life back at home. These could be a pair of gloves or a scarf a loved one gave you, a small photo album of your friends and family, or your trusty umbrella. Another way to ward of homesickness is to stash away in your suitcase a few edible goodies that probably wouldn't be available somewhere else, such as your favorite tea or treat. These little reminders and comforts from your everyday life will help you move past the homesickness and help you to start enjoying your fun adventure again.

You can also try to make new friends while you're traveling. If you're staying in a hostel, this should be easy to do, as everyone is on the same general path and they're likely to be foreigners in the country as well. If you're in a country where you can speak the native language, try going to a bar, café, or sporting event and chatting up those around you. If you're friendly, you're likely to find someone who is interested in having a conversation, and this will give you a chance to get to know their country better and for them to learn more about yours.

*"The secret of staying young is to live honestly,
eat slowly, and lie about your age."*

—Lucille Ball

Eat Slower and Stop Before You Feel Full

Here's a trick you can use to feel full: eat slower. Sometimes, if you've waited too long between meals, you might inhale your food only to realize you didn't really taste anything and now feel a little sick. Humans are not dogs. We cannot enjoy or digest food as quickly as they can, and we shouldn't eat like they do. Turn off the television, sit down, and take the time to enjoy every bite of food you're going to eat. Put your fork, spoon, or chopsticks down between bites, and experience a full breath before you put another bite into your mouth.

It takes twenty minutes from the time your stomach is full for your brain to provide you with that information, so if you eat slower you'll have less of a chance of overeating and feeling uncomfortable. The Japanese from the area known as Okinawa have an average body mass index (BMI) of 21.5 (6.5 points *lower* than the American average BMI) and on average, they live longer than anyone else in the world. Their key to longevity might be tied to the way they eat, as they only eat until they are 80 percent full, which means they stop eating at the first feeling of fullness.

By extending your meals, you'll also extend the time that you spend with those you're eating a meal with, which means you'll enjoy more conversations and human interaction. It also means that your digestive system will be better equipped to process the food and to extract all of the nutrients it needs from them instead of getting overloaded.

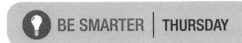
"The chemicals in the dishwashing process tend not to be too good for saucepans."

—Delia Smith

Avoid Toxic Chemicals

Toxic chemicals are bad for the environment and bad for your brain. Most of you are already familiar with the harm that lead can cause, but lead isn't the only harmful substance within your home. Dr. Martha Herbert, a pediatric neurologist at Massachusetts General Hospital, and Dr. Larry Silver, a psychiatric professor at Georgetown University Medical Center, separately reported there may be a connection between the toxic chemicals in our environment and autism.

In the past few years, the alarm has gone out regarding phthalates and bisphenol A (BPA). These fall into a group known as EDCs, or endocrine-disrupting chemicals. These products have been linked with hormonal disorders, such as cancer of the genitals and low sperm count, and scientists are now beginning to wonder if there is a connection between the increase in products made with these chemicals and the increase in autism.

The Best Ways to Avoid EDCs:
- Eat organic food.
- Don't heat food in plastic containers or store fatty foods in plastic containers or plastic wrap.
- Don't give young children plastic bottles, teethers, dinnerware, cups, glasses, or toys.
- If you eat fish from lakes, check to see if those lakes are contaminated.
- Avoid using pesticides in your home or yard.
- If you use sex toys, choose glass or silicone ones over plastic.
- Choose aluminum drinking bottles over plastic bottles.
- Avoid non-organic ground beef, butter, cheese, and farmed salmon.

"Today, sexual preference. Tomorrow, henna tattoos."

—From *Kissing Jessica Stein*

Don't Get Black or Blue Henna Tattoos

Stop getting dark henna tattoos. Sure, they seem harmless, and they're a fun thing to do if you're on vacation in a beachside community, but they can be harmful for your skin. While the dye made from the henna plant is safe to use on your hair and has been used to dye hair a reddish brown (henna's natural color), it has not been approved for use as a skin dye in the United States. Even so, getting a *mehendi* tattoo with the natural, reddish brown henna shouldn't give you any skin problems unless you're allergic to the henna plant or something in the pre-mixed henna paste. If your skin is sensitive, you might want to ask what is in the henna paste to make sure that it is pure and doesn't contain such ingredients as silver nitrate, chromium, or pyrogallol. If it's pure, it should be okay. People have been getting these natural, temporary tattoos since the Bronze Age without any real complications.

However, to create the black or darker henna dyes, the color can be derived not from henna but from indigo or contain p-phenylenediamine (PPD). PPD is sometimes used in hair dye, but it is not meant for the skin. Prolonged exposure—which you'll be getting if you get a black "henna" tattoo—can cause a severe allergic reaction in up to 15 percent of people. The result is intense scarring of the skin as well as a potential permanent sensitivity to PPD as well as to other dyes. PPD can also cause liver tumors, breathing problems, and other life-threatening complications.

So to be safe, make sure that any henna you put on your body is all natural!

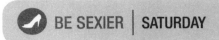

"Iteration, like friction, is likely to generate heat instead of progress."

—George Eliot

Use Lubricant

Take advantage of lubricant. It can make sex a lot easier and, depending on the act, a lot less painful. For example, if you're giving a guy a hand job, you *always* want to use some type of lube. If you're in a pinch, you can use spit or moisturizer, but real lube is preferred. This is because the head of the penis is very sensitive, and the friction of a hand job can make a guy go from *oooh* to *ouch* in a matter of seconds. By using lubrication, you allow your hand to slide easily so all he feels is pleasure.

Water-based lubricants are the most popular. They don't stain or irritate, and they're safe to use with condoms, dental dams, finger cots, and sex toys. They're available in the slicker, liquid form and in the longer-lasting jelly form, which works great for anal sex. Oil-based lubricants, such as olive oil, avocado oil, or safflower oil, can be used during sexual play—but only if you're having sex without sex toys or without latex products, as they can break down latex. These oils are great for the skin and have a wonderful silky feel that is more natural than what the water-based lubes offer. Silicone lubricants are also available, and these are very slippery and great for use in the water, where other lubricants won't do the job. However, they, like oil-based lubricants, shouldn't be used with condoms or sex toys.

"Take rest; a field that has rested gives a bountiful crop."

—Ovid

Take a Mental Health Day

If you're at the point where you're dreading going to work, you're dragging yourself through the days, you're getting irritable with your loved ones, and a vacation seems a million years away, it's time for a mental health day. If you've used up all of your vacation days at the beginning of the year, use a sick day. Just don't tell your boss we told you to do it.

Don't work on your day off. Don't run errands. Don't do anything that causes you stress. Spend the day on the couch napping and playing video games, if that makes you feel relaxed. Just do whatever you need to do to recharge your brain and your body so you can return to work and feel productive instead of burnt out.

"The tongue is the only tool that gets sharper with use."

—Washington Irving

Join Toastmasters to Improve Your Verbal Communication Skills

Many people feel uncomfortable doing anything that remotely feels like public speaking. If you're the type of person who shies away from speaking in front of your colleagues or from giving a speech to your peers, you might be holding yourself back from your full potential in the workplace and possibly also in your personal life. Toastmasters International has been training people to develop better public-speaking and leadership skills since 1924, and with thousands of Toastmasters clubs across the world, there's bound to be one in your area.

Through attending their meetings, you'll learn not only how to get up and speak in front of a group but also how to be a good leader. You won't be judged by an instructor, as there isn't one. Instead, you'll be evaluated by and receive comments from the other people in the group who are also learning how to speak and lead effectively. Along the way, you just might meet the person who provides you with the next job lead.

If you like the meetings, you might be able to volunteer with the organization as well, which will help you learn additional leadership skills, such as how to organize a meeting, how to run a contest, how to conduct a membership campaign, and more.

"Delay is hateful but it gives wisdom."

—Publilius Syrus, Roman author

Find Opportunities in Travel Delays

When your flight is delayed, or when your bus or train doesn't arrive on time, or when your significant other is late picking you up, it can be frustrating. But it doesn't have to be. Turn a negative into a positive and use this extra time to send a few e-mails, write postcards, call a friend, take some quiet time for yourself, read a book . . . the list could go on forever. Instead of seeing the time as wasted, reclaim it and relish the extra moments to do whatever you like. If you're traveling to a new place, this extra time could be a real blessing, as you'll have another chance to revisit the guidebook and you might read about a must-visit place you missed the first time around.

AVOIDING DELAYS

While it's best to use delays to your advantage, the best types of delays are often those that you can navigate around. Before leaving for your flight, check its status online. Before getting on the freeway, check the traffic and plan the best route. Before going to your doctor's office, call them and ask if they're running on time. Though some delays are unavoidable, making a few easy adjustments to your routine can add hours to your personal schedule.

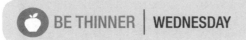

"Liberty exists in proportion to wholesome restraint."

—Daniel Webster

Just Say No at the Movies

Popcorn is harmless, right? Wrong. The popcorn you buy at the supermarket to pop in your microwave or to air-pop on your stove can be a great snack if you share it with a friend or stick to the ones that are already portioned at 100 calories a bag. On the other hand, movie popcorn is heavy on the fat, salt, and calories. A medium-sized bag will set you back somewhere between 590 calories and 1,200 calories and up to sixty grams of saturated fat, depending on how many cups are in a bag and what kind of oil the theatre uses. And the buttery topping you can add? That's another 200 calories for every tablespoon and a half.

Then there are the drinks. Soda is unhealthy for you, but if you get one of the super sizes available at the movies, you're consuming an incredible amount of sugar. If you must snack on something at the theatre and don't want to sneak in food or water, then go for the candy. Though it's certainly not healthy, if you share a box with someone, you'll probably consume around 200 to 300 calories. Of course, the best option is to eat before you go to the movies, to have plans to eat after, or to smuggle in healthy snacks.

"A laughing man is stronger than a suffering man."

—Gustave Flaubert

Watch a Funny Movie

Laughter really is good medicine. It's an instant stress reliever; it increases your happiness; and it can put those around you at ease. When you witness or use humor, you flex your creative muscles and help keep your mind active. But it also can do good things for your body. When you laugh, you boost your immune system by lowering serum cortical levels, which, in turn, increases the number of T lymphocytes, cells that kill intruders within the body. So do whatever it takes to keep laughing and keep living.

TOP-NOTCH COMEDIES

Not sure what to rent? Here's a shortlist of twenty-five comedies from the 2000s to check out:

- *Best in Show* (2000)
- *Meet the Parents* (2000)
- *O Brother, Where Art Thou?* (2000)
- *Scary Movie* (2000)
- *The Royal Tennenbaums* (2001)
- *Zoolander* (2001)
- *Barbershop* (2002)
- *Super Troopers* (2002)
- *Bad Santa* (2003)
- *Elf* (2003)
- *Old School* (2003)
- *Anchorman: The Legend of Ron Burgundy* (2004)
- *Harold and Kumar Go to White Castle* (2004)
- *Mean Girls* (2004)
- *Shaun of the Dead* (2004)
- *Sideways* (2004)
- *Wedding Crashers* (2005)
- *Borat* (2006)
- *Little Miss Sunshine* (2006)
- *Knocked Up* (2007)
- *Superbad* (2007)
- *Walk Hard: The Dewey Cox Story* (2007)
- *Baby Mama* (2008)
- *I Love You, Man* (2009)

> *"The merry year is born like the bright*
> *berry from the naked thorn."*

—Hartley Coleridge

Try Schizandra

This five-flavor fruit, also known as the "magnolia vine," is capable of stimulating all five taste buds and has been a long-time staple in Chinese medicine. The plant is high in antioxidants and has been found to be effective in helping the liver regenerate tissue that has been damaged by viral hepatitis. Herbalists believe that the berry aides the body by improving endurance, reducing sweating, aiding metabolism, regulating blood sugar levels, detoxifying the liver, and alleviating the stress response. Some also believe that it can improve concentration and improve vision and hearing.

You can take the berry as a supplement, or if you can find dried berries, you can make them into a tea. According to http://TeaBenefits.com, you can make the tea by placing two to four teaspoons of the berries into two cups of boiling water and allowing the mixture to boil for twelve minutes or until it has been reduced to one cup.

"People who make no noise are dangerous."

—Jean de La Fontaine, French poet

Make Noise

Get loud! When you're having sex, it's a major turn-on to hear your partner make noise, and doing so yourself can help you to let go of your nervousness and have fun. It can also help you to breathe, which can improve your orgasms, because your entire body is less tense. It's difficult to be tense when you're moaning!

By making noise when your partner is doing something that feels good, even saying "oh my god, that feels incredible," boosts your partner's ego and lets him know what works for you. For women, making noise is very important, because your signals of arousal can be harder to read than a man's. By moaning or verbally expressing how turned on you are, you can keep your partner in the loop.

By praising behavior that you appreciate, you're also more likely to get a repeat performance. However, the opposite is also true. If you fake an orgasm just because you want sex to be over, you can give your partner the impression that his movements work for you when they don't, and he'll probably try these again the next time you do it. So only moan when you're happy and feeling pleasured.

"For fast-acting relief, try slowing down."

—Lily Tomlin

Just Say No

It's okay to say no. It can be easy to get into a zone where you believe you can do everything everyone asks of you. But there are only twenty-four hours in a day, and you should spend eight of those sleeping. Stop the cycle before it starts by knowing your own limits and having the courage to say no. When you become too overburdened with activities and responsibilities, your own needs—exercise, relaxation, eating properly, etc.—can start to fall by the wayside and you start to neglect yourself, which only leads to more stress. If you've suffered through a few months or years of this, it's no wonder if you're feeling burnt out.

Not joining a committee or a group that your friend wants you to be part of or not signing up your children for another activity you have to take them to does not make you a bad person. It makes you someone who knows what she is capable of. It's better to do a few things well than to feel overwhelmed and get frazzled and snippy because you're trying to do too much. Start eliminating those things from your schedule that aren't essential or don't bring you pleasure. And if your kids are involved in too many activities, ask for their help in paring those back so they don't start to feel like they've taken on too much as well.

"The secret of my success is a two word answer: Know people."

—Harvey Firestone

Join a Networking Group

Have you ever heard the saying, It's not what you know, but who you know? When it comes to finding a job and moving up in the world, that statement holds a lot of truth. In fact, according to current statistics, more than 60 percent of people find their next job through a connection they already know.

But how do you network? An easy way to start is by joining a site that is centered around professionals who are open to networking, such as *www.LinkedIn.com*. The site allows you to search through your e-mail contacts and connect with others you know on the site. Each time you generate a strong new contact, look through that person's contacts and see if he or she knows anyone at a company you might want to work for and ask for an introduction. This method can be particularly effective when the company doesn't have a job opening in your area of expertise and when you still have a job somewhere else, because you can request a meeting to gain more information (also known as an informational interview) without the other person feeling pressured. If a position does come up in the future, reach out to your contact and let him or her know you're interested. Since you've already shown an interest in the company and have made a professional connection with someone in the company, your chances of getting the job or at least getting a sit-down interview have dramatically increased.

If you can, it pays to build your networks before you need a job. If it's too late for that, consider attending networking events, like pink-slip parties, and other events geared toward your field. Bring business cards, and stay positive about what you are doing to further your career and your life.

WEEK FORTY-SEVEN

"Beginning today, treat everyone you meet as if they were going to be dead by midnight. Extend to them all care, kindness, and understanding you can muster, and do it with no thought of any reward. Your life will never be the same again."

—Og Mandino

Help a Lost Traveler

If you've ever been lost, you know how upsetting it can be. After all, that's why they invented GPS, right? The problem is, if you're overseas, you have to rely on your skill in reading what you hope is a good map and your sense of direction. Depending on how good those two things are, you could end up at your destination on the first go or you might end up circling the Arc de Triomphe more times than you'd like to admit. Don't stress about it; it's happened to the best of us. It's in those times when you're ready to give up that you might want to ask a stranger—as clearly as you can in their language, unless you're fortunate enough to find someone who speaks English—how to get from where you are to where you're trying to go.

Do your best to return the favor. If someone stops you or you see travelers who look lost—map in hand, head looking in one direction and then another, then back at the map again—in your town or somewhere you're familiar with, offer to show them the way. If you can't go with them, make sure they understand the directions well enough so that they can make it without having to ask another person. You'll feel proud that you know an area well enough to guide them to their destination and happy that you could help out people who needed it.

"Hunger: One of the few cravings that cannot be appeased with another solution."

—Irwin Van Grove

Distinguish Between Hunger and Cravings

Most of the time when we're hungry, we're actually just dehydrated. In fact, one in three Americans mistake thirst for hunger, because it fools us by giving us the same symptoms, such as hunger pangs and irritability. So the next time you're feeling hungry, pour yourself a big glass of water. Ten minutes after drinking it, see if you still feel hungry. If you do, make yourself a healthy snack to hold you over until the next big or small meal.

If you feel that your momentary hunger is tied to a food craving, it's important to figure out what your body is really craving. Different cravings can correlate to your body's lack of certain vitamins and minerals, so instead of giving your body chocolate, give it what it really needs.

Here's a chart to help you match your craving with what your body needs.

CRAVING	BODY'S NEED
Chocolate	B vitamins
Salt	Less salt (Eating salt makes you want to eat more salt.)
Protein	Iron or other amino acids
Dairy	Less dairy (You might be allergic.)

"Life is short, but there is always time for courtesy."

—Ralph Waldo Emerson

Learn a Country's Etiquette Rules Before You Travel

Before you travel to a foreign country or a new part of the United States, take the time to learn the customs of that area. Each culture across the world and each community across America has its own way of life and its own rules of etiquette, and what may be acceptable in one place might be seen as offensive in another.

Traditional greetings are very important to learn before you travel. In some countries, businesspeople greet each other with a bow, whereas in others a handshake is preferred. If someone were to present a handshake instead of a bow, or vice-versa, in those countries, the receiving party might be confused or even offended. You'll also want to learn about the table manners of a culture. In France, it's important not to butter your bread and to keep your hands where they can be seen (but keep those elbows off the table). In Egypt, you shouldn't eat with your left hand. In South Korea, don't cross your chopsticks when you set them down or place them across the top of a bowl. In Italy, avoid eating food with your hands, even if you would normally do this back home.

Some customs might surprise you. For instance, in England, it's not standard for the British to tip bartenders when they get a beer! The more you know about how people in a country interact day-to-day, the easier it will be for you to feel like you fit in and enjoy yourself.

"The flax seed is a good fat. So are nuts. The omega-3 fatty acids, every cell in your body needs them."

—Dr. Cathleen London

Eat Flax

Vegetarians, don't be sad that you can't get the benefits of heart-healthy fish like salmon. You can still get plenty of omega-3 fatty acids in your diet if you dine on flax. Flax is high in alpha linoleic acid, a precursor to omega-3. and when it breaks down into this substance, the fatty acids act the same way they do in salmon—bolstering cell membranes, lowering blood cholesterol, stabilizing blood sugar levels, improving glucose absorption, and raising serotonin. They might even help your bone density. Flax can be found in some breads, but it's also available as an oil or as ground flaxseeds, which you can toss into your salad, granola, or oatmeal.

SEEDS OR OIL?

You want to add flax to your diet but aren't sure whether to buy the oil or the whole seeds. Either is great, but each has its own benefits. The oil offers a more potent dose of your omega-3s than the seeds, while the seeds are high in soluble fiber, contain the vitamins B1, B2, C, and E and the minerals iron and zinc, and they are also high in lignin, a possible cancer preventing compound.

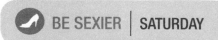
"Vibrators. I think they're great. They keep you out of stupid sex."

—Anne Heche

Try Sex Toys

Sex toys can be fun on your own or with your partner. There are a wide range of sex toys, but here's a basic rundown to get you started:

Dildos. These objects are shaped more or less like a phallus but vary in shape and size. Some are curved to stimulate the G-spot, while others are straight. Choose a nonporous dildo made from silicone, glass, or metal. They can be used for vaginal or anal masturbation.

Vibrators. Though sometimes similar in appearance to dildos, these electric or battery-powered devices are designed to stimulate the vulva, clitoris, or anus with their vibrations. Some are for external stimulation only, while others can be used for penetration as well. With higher-end vibrators, the user can adjust the speed and pulsating sensations.

Anal beads. These round, smooth beads are strung on a cord (nylon or silicone is preferable) and inserted into the anus prior to orgasm. During orgasm, they are pulled out to heighten the sensation.

Butt plugs. These objects are meant for insertion into the anus. They have a flared base, a thick middle, and a narrow top. These can stimulate the prostate gland in men.

Cock rings. These devices are made of leather, rubber, or metal and are placed around the base of the penis and testicles prior to erection. They prevent blood from flowing back out of the penis and create new sensations for the man during arousal and orgasm. Never keep one on longer than thirty minutes.

Handcuffs. Using handcuffs to restrain your partner from moving can be a fun way to tease him until he's so aroused he begs for an orgasm. If you don't have handcuffs, create a makeshift one out of a tie or a bed sheet.

"Happiness means quiet nerves."

—W. C. Fields

Take an Anti-Stress Vacation

Odd as it may sound on paper, vacations can be very stressful. Sometimes it's because you haven't picked a good travel partner. Other times, it's because you've planned way too much for your trip and you're determined to accomplish it all. Or maybe it's because you spent most or all of your vacation visiting relatives. By all means, try to see the sights, and definitely visit your family, but make sure you also schedule anti-stress vacations each year.

If you're traveling to a new destination, don't pack in quite so many sites and activities. With less in your schedule, you'll be able to relax and better enjoy those things you have planned. If you really like the place, you can always return and do the things you couldn't fit in this time.

If you haven't planned a trip yet, consider one in which you'll just be taking a load off. Head to a beach, go fishing, camp out in the wilderness, or do anything else where the main goal of the entire experience is relaxation. Make it a vacation just for you and your partner or for your immediate family to allow for maximum bonding.

*"No one has a greater asset for his business
than a man's pride in his work."*

—Mary Parker Follet

Think of Three Reasons You Should Be Promoted

You know you're good at your job. You hear it from your coworkers, you're praised by your boss, and your partner is impressed with your job successes. But it's been a long time since you've received a raise or a promotion. If you've been an A-level worker, then it's probably because you haven't asked for that raise or promotion. Before you step up to the plate, you have some work to do. You could present your boss with a giant list of all your successful projects and admirable qualities, but you'd be more likely to hold his or her attention if you present three clear, succinct reasons why you're a great candidate for a promotion or raise.

Generating these points will take some effort on your part, as you will need to review the work you've done and determine how you've benefited the company during the time you've been with them. You also may need to first write out a list of everything you've done in order to pull from what might feel like a motley collection of assignments those three things that really set you apart. If you're feeling modest, ask your friends and partners for help in coming up with these reasons. They're sure to be honest with you about what you do well. When you have these three reasons, write them down and write down what projects you've completed that best illustrate those points.

When the meeting finally arrives, let your boss know you enjoy the company and are willing to take on new responsibilities, but keep your request as to-the-point as you can. After all, you're both busy people!

"How far we travel in life matters far less than those we meet along the way."

—Anonymous

Make Friends with Fellow Travelers

The personal items you've brought from home have helped alleviate your homesickness. But traveling on your own can get lonely, and you can't talk to your personal products. Well, you can, but they're very bad conversationalists. Here's a better idea: if you're staying at a hostel, make friends with one or more of the people there. Ask them if they'd like to join you for dinner or a drink at one of the restaurants or bars in the neighborhood. As you talk with them over a pint, you might find that they'd also like to travel where you're heading, and perhaps the two or three of you could travel together. If not, then at the very least, you spent a few hours connecting with another human and you'll probably feel a lot less lonely.

If you're not staying in a hostel, there are other places you can make friends. Even if you're more of the introverted type who waits for people to come up to you, try to push yourself to introduce yourself to others on bus tours, bike tours, or anywhere you might come across others who are also traveling solo. As you branch out, you'll start to make friends—even lifelong ones!—and if you're traveling single, you could even meet your soul mate.

"Flattery is like chewing gum. Enjoy it, but don't swallow it."

—Hank Ketcham, creator of *Dennis the Menace*

Chew Gum

One way to avoid being tempted to eat something you know you shouldn't is to chew gum. Chewing gum will help you keep those cravings at bay by giving your mouth an activity and something flavorful to enjoy, and you'll be less likely to reach for something else, as your mouth is already busy. Just be sure to reach for gum that doesn't contain artificial sweeteners. It's better to have a little bit of sugar than added chemicals.

As an added bonus, a recent Mayo Clinic study found that chewing gum can boost metabolism by up to 20 percent and help you lose up to ten pounds a year. Other studies have found that chewing gum can also boost memory, prevent tooth decay, and relieve tension. What are you waiting for? Get chewing!

BETTER GUM = BETTER TEETH

If you're going to chew gum, it's best to avoid gum that has cane sugar and gum that has artificial sweeteners for your overall health and for the health of your teeth. So, what's left? Xylitol. This odd sounding ingredient is also known as birch sugar because it's derived from birch trees. It's been a popular sweetener in Finland for years and is lower in calories and has a much lower glycemic index than sugar, which means it can be used by diabetics in place of sugar. Plus, gum containing xylitol can actually help protect teeth from decay!

---

*"If we do not find anything very pleasant, at least
we shall find something new."*

—Voltaire

Taste New Foods and Beverages

As you're traveling, make an effort to enjoy local cuisines, whether you're driving through the Southern United States or are traveling abroad in Greece. Even though it may sometimes feel that every corner of the world has been taken over by a corporate food chain, the traditional cuisines of regions still remain and thrive. When you indulge in them, you can take this opportunity to converse with your server to learn more about the culture, the spices they use, and the history behind certain dishes.

If you're a picky eater, this is your chance to throw caution to the wind and take a chance to open up your palate to new flavors that you might fall in love with! If you do, you can find ways to incorporate these recipes when you return home.

"Algae? This is a color?"

—Albert Einstein

Consume Micro-Plants

When you want to turn back the clock, you might have to consume some "strange" foods to do it. One category of these unusual foods is micro-plants, or "green foods." These include blue-green algae, chlorella, spirulina, wheat grass, and barley grass—all of which are high in protein and contain many vitamins and minerals that are good for your body, such as vitamin C, vitamin E, B12, and magnesium. They are also good sources of chlorophyll and lycopene. Though more studies need to be done to prove its effectiveness in humans, chlorophyll may lower rates of colon cancer. Lycopene can have a protective effect against cancer, heart disease, diabetes, and osteoporosis. According to some scientific studies, these green foods, in general, may improve your body's ability to detoxify itself against heavy metals, toxins, and harmful bacteria.

Some of these plants may also be able to reduce wrinkles if they are applied to the skin. In particular, the brown algae *Padina pavonica* has been used to make various skin-care products that claim to reduce wrinkles up to 19 percent.

"The difference between pornography and erotica is lighting."

—Gloria Leonard

Flip on a Porno

You've probably watched porn on your own either on your television or via the Internet, but watching porn with your significant other can be a really hot experience. As you watch, you'll get to see firsthand what turns on your lover, and you can utilize these techniques later in the bedroom.

If you're not so sure about porn, keep in mind that there are many types of pornography available for your viewing pleasure, and if you open your mind just a little, you'll probably find something you enjoy. Though most pornography is still directed by men and for a male audience, it doesn't mean that women can't enjoy that type of porn as well, nor does it mean that's how all porn is. There is porn on the market directed by women and that focuses more on the woman's pleasure, porn that is known as "feminist porn," porn that features real couples having sex, and pretty much everything else you could possibly imagine. If you can think it, it's been done, and you can find it on the Internet or in the video store.

"Prince reeks of lavender. It turned me on, actually."

—Madonna

Set Out Lavender

Lavender, whose name comes from the Latin *lavare*, meaning "to wash," has been used in bathing since the Roman days. This member of the mint family—of which basil, mint, rosemary, and other popular aromatic herbs are also a part—has been shown to have calming and soothing effects on the body. And it's not just a placebo effect. Recently, a group of Australian researchers and another in Miami found that breathing in lavender can make you feel more relaxed, less anxious, and less depressed and can also induce sleepiness. So while it's not the best plant to breathe in before a big exam, setting out a bowl of freshly cut lavender afterward will help you wind down. If you're having a bout of insomnia, try placing a few sprigs near the bed or some drops of essential oil on the edge of your pillow. Lavender also has anti-inflammatory properties, and the essential oil extracted from lavender plants can soothe those suffering from skin ailments ranging from mild insect bites to psoriasis.

Dried lavender is carried by most nurseries as well as by many grocery stores and farmer's markets. But if you can't find dried lavender in your area, you can purchase essential lavender oil and use it within a diffuser pot, or you can buy some lavender lotion or even light some lavender candles. Though fresh is best, these substitutes can still have a positive effect on your mood.

"Everything comes to him who hustles while he waits."

—Thomas Edison

Choose a Date to Ask for a Promotion

Now that you've determined all the reasons you should be promoted, it's time to take the next step and schedule the date you'll ask for a promotion. Timing this right can be key to getting the green light. If you're in the middle of a big project, wait until you've completed it successfully. Make sure to plan your request for a day in which your boss isn't going to be busy with meetings or isn't about to take off for a major vacation. When you've figured out when a good time would be, schedule a meeting with your boss—instead of just knocking on her or his door—to ensure you have your boss's full attention.

When the meeting arrives, confidently convey to your boss why you deserve a promotion, and stress how much of an asset you are to the company. If, despite your preparation, the meeting doesn't go the way you had hoped, keep your cool, thank your boss for her or his time, and ask if you can schedule a follow-up meeting in three months to discuss the matter again. You might even want to ask what you can do in the meantime to help put you in a better position for the next talk.

If, in the end, it appears that you won't be able to move up in the company or that your company isn't considering any raises for the near future, you might want to start looking for a job at a company that will appreciate and be willing and able to compensate you for your hard work.

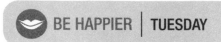

"The real voyage of discovery consists not in seeking new landscapes but in having new eyes."

—Marcel Proust

Take a Local Tour

If you're traveling to a new city for the first time, consider taking a guided tour. Whether on foot, bike, or bus, these tours give you a good overview of the city and its different areas. You'll learn some history, discover spots you want to return to, and find out places you want to avoid, whether a bad neighborhood or a tourist trap. Even for locals, these tours can be eye-opening and help you to have a deeper appreciation and understanding of where you live.

Guided tours are especially helpful if you're in a foreign country where you don't speak the language. The tours are often offered in multiple languages, which gives you the opportunity to meet fellow travelers and to get your bearings before you embark on your own. If you do the tour on foot or bike, you'll also get a little exercise while you're out there learning and making friends!

To find a good tour, call or e-mail the local tourism board, ask your hotel concierge in advance of your trip, or post on message boards for savvy travelers. After you have the names of a few companies, research them, and pick the one that works best for your trip.

"Everything in moderation—including moderation."

—Harvey Steiman

Follow the 90/10 Rule

When you're working on getting healthy, it's easy to see things as black or white. No more chips, ever again. Exercise six days a week, forever. And so on. This mentality becomes draining very quickly and makes it harder for you to maintain a positive outlook on achieving your goal. If you aim to eat healthy and to exercise most days of the week, then don't feel badly if you allow yourself to splurge on a treat or to relax in a nonphysical way during the other days. For instance, if you strive to eat lean protein, plenty of fresh produce, lean dairy, and whole grains 90 percent of the time, not eating as well the other 10 percent isn't going to derail your efforts.

"A hobby a day keeps the doldrums away."

—Phyllis McGinley

Choose Hobbies That Stimulate Your Brain

Hobbies are fun, but they also challenge your brain to learn new information. In his book *Making a Good Brain Great*, Dr. Daniel G. Amen recommends choosing an activity that requires you to continue to learn. He writes, "The best mental exercise is acquiring new knowledge and doing things you haven't done before . . . when the brain does something over and over, even a complicated task, it learns how to do it using less energy." That means, just as your body becomes more efficient and burns less calories as it gets used to an exercise, your brain works less hard after it's learned how to do an activity.

Let's say you're learning how to speak a language. At first, everything is difficult. There are thousands of words to memorize, verb tenses to learn, grammatical rules that need to be understood, colloquialisms that are necessary to understand. But as you spend months or years working with the language, things start to fall into place and comprehension becomes easier. Eventually, you notice you're fluent and can speak and write in the language without having to work to string words together. According to Amen's research, your brain works hardest when you're first struggling to learn something new, like a foreign language. Once you've learned the new language well, your brain doesn't work much harder than it would to speak in your native tongue. That's when it's time to learn a new hobby and continue to push yourself. If you make yourself a lifetime learner, you'll help keep your brain cells from deteriorating as you age.

"I send you a kaffis of mustard seed, that you may taste and acknowledge the bitterness of my victory."

—Alexander the Great

Harness Some Horseradish

Horseradish will give your sandwich that extra zing, and it can also help you look and feel younger. It's been said that horseradish is able to improve facial circulation and clear out your sinuses (though you probably already knew that). But it's also been used to treat urinary tract infections, and it may increase the liver's ability to process toxins and suppress the growth of cancer cells, because of the substances known as glucosinolates within it. Glucosinolates can also stimulate digestion of fatty foods, which helps improve your metabolism.

Glucosinolates are what give the horseradish its bite. They're also found in other tangy or bitter foods, such as kale, mustard, cabbage, broccoli, Brussels sprouts, and mustard. Another benefit of horseradish is that it might be useful, when mixed with other ingredients, in removing age spots. According to health and fitness expert Sharon Bell, if you mix together a teaspoon of horseradish, half a teaspoon of lemon juice, half a teaspoon of vinegar, and three drops of rosemary oil and rub this onto your age spots a few times a day, they should start to lighten.

"I've always felt that sexuality is a really slippery thing. In this day and age, it tends to get categorized and labeled, and I think labels are for food. Canned food."

—Michael Stipe

Be Open to Role Playing

Does the thought of your girlfriend in a nurse outfit—or your boyfriend pretending to be your boss turn you on? Role playing during sex, with or without costumes, can really spice up your love life, because by fantasizing with your partner you're allowing each other to explore possibly taboo scenarios and get those butterflies fluttering in your stomach again. Permitting each other to be open and vulnerable in this way can build deeper intimacy if both of you are nonjudgmental of the experience. It can also lead to the two of you coming up with new things to try within your relationship that hadn't crossed your minds before.

However, if your partner suggests trying out a fantasy that really makes you uncomfortable, you can politely tell him (or her) that you're not interested. If you can, come up with a less intense variation that you would be comfortable with and that still lets him enjoy part of his fantasy.

To get role-playing started, you can let it happen spontaneously by starting a story in your partner's ear as you're getting intimate, or you can plan it out by buying outfits in advance or by inviting your partner to a bar where you'll pretend to be a stranger he can hit on and try to take home.

"The best laid schemes of mice and men / Go often askew / And leave us nothing but grief and pain / For promised joy!"

—Robert Burns

Control What You Can, Accept What You Can't

Eventually, we all have to come to terms with the fact we can't plan for everything. Everyone has her or his own agenda, and the world is bound to throw a wrench into your plans from time to tome. You cannot control what others do, say, or feel. You cannot control what happens on a global scale from day to day. Accepting that can be scary, but it can also be a relief. Though it might seem paradoxical, if you live in earthquake country and live with the anxiety that the Big One might hit at any moment, learning to accept that it might happen and there's nothing you can do to prevent it will help you to prepare for that possibility as well as you can but then turn your attention to something more important—living your life.

Yet, you do have some control over some things in your life. You can choose how you react to others. You can pick your battles. You can volunteer and give back to your community. You can be kind and grateful, and when things go sideways, you can try your best to stay positive. Allow yourself to let go of the "what ifs," and work on being the best you that you can be.

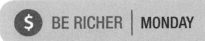

$ BE RICHER | MONDAY

"Footprints on the sands of time are not made by sitting down."

—Thomas Jefferson

Create a Time Line and Action List for Starting Your Own Company

You've decided to become an entrepreneur. Congratulations! Now comes the hard part—taking the concept from dream to reality. A good place to begin is setting up an action list and time line. Create a list of all the things you need to do to get the company off the ground and write down the date by which you will accomplish each one of these items. You can work backward from your ideal launch date, if that helps motivate you. Once you've done this, you just need to plug these dates into your calendar and start accomplishing them!

"The impersonal hand of government can never replace the helping hand of a neighbor."

—Hubert H. Humphrey

Spearhead a Donation Drive for a Charity

Charities need help year-round, so consider starting a gift, book, or donation drive through your work or within your social circle. Find a charity that moves you, and reach out to them to find out what they could use. Although November through December might be the "season of giving," due to Thanksgiving and Christmas, birthdays occur year-round if you're interested in serving a charity that benefits kids or the elderly, for example, and charities are always in need of help year-round. If your friends are cash-strapped or your work doesn't encourage or allow this type of activity, pool your friends together or ask your manager if you could schedule a volunteer day. Pitch it to your superiors as a team-building experience that could improve office camaraderie, and you'll probably get them to bite.

One charity you could get your family, friends, or work involved in is Operation Santa Claus, no matter what your religion. When a child in need writes a letter to Santa, participating post offices around the country save these letters for people such as yourself to read and then help fulfill that child's Christmas dream. Often, these letters are filled with requests for basic items to make their lives a bit more comfortable—like food, clothes, and blankets. Waking up on Christmas morning to find that Santa brought a gift they longed for will bring joy to children's hearts—and yours, knowing that, as one of Santa's anonymous helpers, you helped a child in need.

*"A man's health can be judged by which he
takes two at a time—pills or stairs."*

—Joan Welsh

Be Like Rocky and Do the Stairs

Every step counts. And the steps you take going up and down the stairs really count. Even after a minute of doing the stairs, you might feel the burn in your quadriceps, hamstrings, and calves, and you'll give your body a boost of energy and burn around eight calories each minute you keep at it. As you climb, do your best to keep your core tight, as this will take the pressure off of your knees and allow you to glide up and down the stairs with less pain in your joints.

If a public building in your city has a set of stairs—like the steps of city hall in downtown Philadelphia—take advantage of them. Start with one full set (up once, down once), if you can, and work your way up to more. Whatever you do, don't push yourself on your first attempt. I learned this lesson the hard way by doing three sets (one of which included running up and down the two hundred stairs) the first time and couldn't walk properly for days afterward. Like everything, start slowly.

If a regular exercise routine of going up and down a certain set of stairs is not an option for you, take the stairs instead of the escalator or elevator anytime you can or use the step climber machine at the gym. You can also take mini-breaks during the day at work to walk up and down the stairs (if the building has any) whenever you're feeling your energy start to sink.

"You sit at the board and suddenly your heart leaps. Your hand trembles to pick up the piece and move it. But what chess teaches you is that you must sit there calmly and think about whether it's really a good idea and whether there are other, better ideas."

—Stanley Kubrick

Learn to Play Games

One hobby that will keep your brain challenged is chess. That's because even after you've learned the moves and the rules, each game of chess is different and challenging in new ways. Every opponent you face will bring something new to the board, and you'll have to use your strategic skills to determine how to win. Doing so can help improve your brain function.

If chess isn't your cup of tea, there are other games that can improve your brain. Doing logic puzzles, playing a complex card game like bridge, or sitting down for a game of Scrabble can also force your brain to make connections that will pay off: you'll be more likely to solve problems creatively and therefore more likely to succeed. If you want a game you can play on the go, Nintendo came out with a series of portable games meant to stimulate your brain, and other companies followed suit. Since an idle brain loses cognitive power, according to Dr. Frank Lawlis in his book *The IQ Answer*, look for fun ways to stimulate your mind!

*"The sandwich is good . . . although I would rather
have alfalfa sprouts. We're negotiating."*

—Al Roker

Eat Broccoli Sprouts

When reaching for broccoli, choose broccoli sprouts over mature stalks. In 1992, Dr. Paul Talalay, a researcher at the Johns Hopkins school of Medicine, discovered that the sprouts of a broccoli plant—which resemble alfalfa sprouts instead of the broccoli that we're accustomed to and are found in the same section of your grocery—were between ten and a hundred times more powerful at neutralizing carcinogens within the body than were mature broccoli. He also found that the sprouts contained twenty to fifty times the amount of compounds that protect against cancer than mature broccoli does, because of the enzymes glucoraphanin and myrosinase that are released when you eat the sprouts.

Broccoli sprouts are also a good source of fiber, vitamin C, and vitamin E. They may lower blood cholesterol levels; reduce the risk of heart disease, macular degeneration, and stomach ulcers; and help lower cholesterol and high blood pressure.

If you cannot find broccoli sprouts in your grocer's produce section or at your local farmer's market, you can purchase the seeds and grow your own.

*"Sex is one of the nine reasons for reincarnation.
The other eight are unimportant."*

—Henry Miller

Read the Kama Sutra

The most popular sex book of all time is the Kama Sutra. This tome, written by Mallanga Vatsyayana in A.D. 350, offers quite a few sex positions for you to try, and many of the ones featured in this book are derived from those Vatsyayana wrote about. However, this ancient book is more than just a guide to sexual positions. It talks about love and many of the aspects of lovemaking, from courtship to foreplay and beyond. When Sir Richard Burton translated the Kama Sutra into English in the 1800s, it was the beginning of a new sexual revolution.

The Kama Sutra, while certainly the most famous sex book, isn't the only classic sex manual out there. Plenty of poets from the Roman era were busy crafting naughty verses, and there are other ancient sex manuals known as "pillow books," Which were guides, sometimes illustrated, about sex and how to please your partner that were not so different from the guides we have today. The Anaga-Ranga, written in the sixteenth century in India, featured information on seduction techniques, Kegel exercises, sexual spells, and positions, while the Secrets of the Jade Bed Chamber was an ancient Chinese manual that also included techniques for courting, improving potency, sexual positions, and help for troubled relationships.

"Reason is our soul's left hand, faith her right,
by these we reach divinity."

—John Donne

Take Part in Ritual

Sometimes, it helps to communicate with a higher power to achieve peace in your life. Studies show that participating in a religious or spiritual practice can help you lead a purposeful, self-actualized, meaningful, and happy life. Participation in such experiences also allows you to be a part of a community, and having that can help you to feel stronger in unsure times. To find a church, synagogue, mosque, or other group or spiritual center that works for you, ask your friends of similar faith if they attend a service or event on a regular basis and where they go. If you go and it's not your thing, that's okay. You can keep trying until you find something that fits.

Even if you're not the spiritual or religious type and don't believe in a higher power, you can still take advantage of the calming aspects of ritual. Find something that helps to put you at peace—walking in nature, reading a book, watching the sunset—and turn that into ritual by making it something you prepare for and do each week. When you're stressed, remembering this ritual and knowing it is coming up will help you to unwind when you can't see the light at the end of the tunnel.

"Pray as if everything depended upon God and act as if everything depended upon you."

—St. Augustine

Schedule Thirty Minutes a Day to Work on Your Dream

Throughout the year, you've been working to improve your life in many different ways. You've become happier, healthier, and richer. As you move into the next year and the years beyond, it's important to keep the skills you've learned but also to look at the bigger picture. Now that you've got the basics down, is there a dream that you've been wanting to turn into a reality? It's time to stop incubating it and to give it the freedom to soar.

You've learned how to manage your time well, so take a look at your calendar and figure out how to fit in thirty minutes of each day to work on your dream, even if that means not watching one of your TV shows. Then, buy a blank journal or notebook, perhaps one you feel a "connection" with, and write down all the steps you can think of that you have to go through to complete your dream. Do you need to go back to school? Do you need to raise funding? Do you need to write a business plan? Do you need to take a hiatus from your job and write eight hours a day? Whatever you think achieving your dream might take, write it down. Once that's in place, start figuring out the order in which those steps need to happen and how you can make them happen. Start recording your daily progress in your journal.

As you start to write and make a list of things that have to be accomplished, you'll start to understand your dream more thoroughly and it won't seem quite so daunting.

"Never doubt that a small group of thoughtful, committed citizens can change the world. Indeed, it is the only thing that ever has."

—Margaret Mead

Give a Party for Charity

The next time you want to throw a dinner or cocktail party, consider throwing one for charity. Start by finding a charity you feel strongly about through *www.CharityWatch.org* or *www.CharityNavigator .org* and determine what they need. Charities look for all sorts of different donations. There are animal shelters that want blankets for their cages so the dogs and cats are more comfortable. There are cancer charities that look for hand-knitted chemo caps. There are children's charities that accept unused video games for ill children to occupy themselves with while in the hospital.

Whatever cause you choose, ask each guest to bring a small physical or monetary donation in place of a host/hostess gift. Your friends and you will feel good when you know you're having fun and helping out others while doing it. The next day, be sure to send out thank-you letters to everyone who was involved, and if you get a response from the charity, let them know as well. Your friends might even like the idea so much that they'll choose to throw a charity bash of their own.

"The nice thing about doing a crossword puzzle is, you know there is a solution."

—Stephen Sondheim

Park as Far Away as You Can

Here's an easy addition to your fitness routine: park as far away as you can. Whether you're going to the grocery store or to a concert, parking your car as far as you can from the place you're going allows you to get in at least a few hundred extra steps a day and gets you closer to your goal of 10,000 steps a day. While the walk won't take you that much longer, you'll feel better for doing it. You'll also save on the gas you'd spend circling for a spot and reduce your chance of getting a door ding, since there probably won't be as many cars in the area you've picked.

TAKE IT A STEP (OR TWO) FURTHER

Start considering walking to other places you usually drive to. Is the coffee shop you frequent within a mile or so from your house or office? Can you walk to pick your kids up from school and spend time together as a family walking back home? By lessening the amount that you drive and increasing the amount that you walk, you're not only doing your health a favor but you're doing the environment one too.

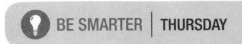

"If I could not walk far and fast, I think I should just explode and perish."

—Charles Dickens

Puzzle Your Mind

A recent study conducted by researchers at the Albert Einstein College of Medicine may have proven that challenging word games, such as crossword puzzles, anagrams, and logic puzzles, may not only be fun, they may also be good for your brain. Though a quarter of the study's participants did eventually develop dementia, it took longer for it to manifest in those who were engaged more often in activities that stimulated the mind.

But working out your brain isn't just something older adults need to think about. That's because, while your brain isn't a muscle, you've got to exercise it if you want to keep it in peak condition. By strengthening your mind when you're young, you can build up a "cognitive reserve" against future memory problems. And by challenging your brain to think in different ways than you're accustomed, you can help yourself find new solutions to life- or work-related problems while you learn new words and phrases.

Don't stress yourself when you're starting out, though, as you don't want to get frustrated and quit. After all, these are supposed to be games. Start with puzzles at your skill level, and when those start to get too easy, move up to the next to continue stretching your mind.

"You needn't tell me that a man who doesn't love oysters and asparagus and good wines has got a soul, or a stomach either. He's simply got the instinct for being unhappy highly developed."

—Hector Hugh Munro

Dine on Asparagus

Asparagus is a vegetable worth falling in love with. The high levels of vitamin C, vitamin K, and folate help the body ward off heart disease and aid bone health, while the vitamin A works to improve your vision. In addition, the green spear contains inulin, an indigestible carbohydrate that acts as fiber and increases the healthy bacteria in your intestine. The low-calorie veggie can also directly help with slowing down the aging process. It contains high levels of glutathione, an antioxidant that protects the skin from sun damage, encourages healthy cell development, and protects and repairs DNA.

The one time you might, however, want to avoid asparagus is if you're on a date or over at your significant other's house for the first time. That's because for some people, asparagus can give their urine a very intense, unpleasant odor. This doesn't mean your body is having a bad reaction to asparagus; it just means that your body has the enzyme to break down mercaptan, a sulfur compound found in the vegetable.

"Anything worth doing is worth doing slowly."

—Mae West

Give Tantric Sex a Try

Tantra isn't just about sex. Before you jump into intercourse, you begin your journey into tantric sex by doing a *lingam* (penis) or a *yoni* (vagina) massage. While these massages are forms of manual stimulation, the feeling your partner gets will be much different, as the purpose is not orgasm but for your partner to relax and surrender to intimate physical pleasure. Both of these massages begin with your partner lying down on the bed and breathing deeply.

The Lingam massage: Place some oil on his penis and testicles and begin to massage these areas slowly. Gently take hold of the penis with one hand, squeeze lightly, move your hand up and down, then slide it off and repeat the same movement with your other hand. Place one hand at the base of the penis and use the other to massage the shaft, finishing by cupping the glans. Then begin to massage the prostate through the perineum (you'll feel a small, pea-sized spot when you're on it) as you continue to massage the penis with the other hand.

The Yoni massage: After you have aroused your partner, place oil on top of her vulva Massage the vulva all the way to her pubic bone, then begin to stroke the clitoris using circular motions. When she is ready, slip your middle finger inside her vagina and find the G-spot. Experiment with using pressure, speed, and various strokes, making sure she is breathing deeply the whole time.

Following these two massages, consider having intercourse, but keep the same relaxed breath and attention to your partner's body that you had during these two massages. Men may find that they have an orgasm but don't ejaculate, allowing them to have multiple orgasms.

"Journalism is popular, but it is popular mainly as fiction. Life is one world, and life seen in the newspapers is another."

—G. K. Chesterton

Take a News Break

Want to completely stress yourself out? Watch the daily news. Read newsy websites throughout the day. Listen to the news on your way home from work. Soon enough, you'll start to believe that murderers and con men lurk around every corner and that a devastating natural disaster could strike at any moment. Today's news is structured so it is sensational and tries to capture its audience much in the same way a summer blockbuster does. Long gone are the days when we just got the facts, because the news manufacturers no longer believe people would tune into this sort of report.

It's important to learn about current events, but it's also important to occasionally back away from the twenty-four-hour news cycle and to look at what is positive and joyous in your own life. If you must tune into the news daily, look for stories about hope and success rather than death and heartbreak. Or consider selecting one source that is less sensational in its delivery of the news. By keeping in mind that today's news is based primarily around building an audience through shock value and by trimming down your addiction to the news, you can start to feel less anxious that something bad is about to happen to you.

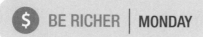
*"It matters not what a person is born,
but who they choose to be."*

—J. K. Rowling

Support Your Partner's Dream

Working on your dream is important to achieving your ultimate potential, but it's also important to support the dreams of your partner and your children. Offer words of encouragement and suggestions to help them move forward. If they're having a difficult time getting a foothold, sit down with them and help them put together a game plan just like you've done for your own dreams. By being a positive, supportive force in their lives, you'll end up in a happier relationship and family because you'll be surrounded by those with upward momentum. In the long run, allowing your heart and your dreams to guide you can lead you to a richer life not only in spirit but also in income.

"Animals are such agreeable friends—they ask no questions, they pass no criticisms."

—George Eliot

Adopt an Animal from a Shelter

Bringing a pet into your life might save the animal's life and will most likely make you happier. That's because if you treat an animal well, they'll shower you with love in the form of attention, cute looks, kisses, head butts, wagging tails, and more, and it's hard to feel down when you have a pet that is always happy to see you. In addition, they can relieve tension after a long day. Think about how hard it would be to feel stressed out when you're playing fetch with a dog! But those aren't the only benefits. Having a pet that enjoys going outdoors gives you the chance to exercise by taking it on walks and playing with it in the park, where you might make friends with another animal lover.

If you're considering getting a pet for your health or just because you want a fun companion, please do an animal a favor and adopt a homeless pet from a shelter instead of going to a breeder or a pet shop. Every year, shelters kill between 5 and 9 million dogs and cats that ended up homeless; you can be a force in changing that statistic. Animal shelters are filled with puppies and kittens, older pets, purebreds, mutts, and everything in between, so you'll be able to find the right pet for your family.

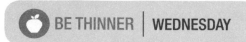

"Golf seems to be an arduous way to go for a walk.
I prefer to take the dogs out."

—Princess Anne

Make Your Pet's Exercise a Regular Part of Your Routine

If you have a pet, it's important to make sure you keep your pet healthy. And pets stay healthy just like you do: with the right balance of diet and exercise. Cats are more difficult to exercise with, but I know people who chase their cat around the house, play wrestle with it, and play fetch on a regular basis. It all depends on the cat. If you have a dog, though, it's easy. Play fetch with sticks, balls, or other toys. Make it part of your daily routine to take the dog for a walk after you get home from work. You'll reduce your stress level and burn calories doing it! On weekends, take Fido to a dog park or somewhere it can socialize with other dogs. By keeping your pets active, you'll help them to live longer and you'll find you get trimmer too.

WHY EXERCISE IS IMPORTANT FOR PETS

Exercising with pets isn't just a bonding activity that keeps them from becoming overweight. It has other benefits too. It can improve their overall health, as well as improve their circulation, bone density, and the efficiency of their lungs and heart. Also, it can help pets get out their extra energy or reduce their boredom so they're less likely to chew on the furniture. Just remember, especially in the summer, to carry an extra bottle of water with you for your animal so it stays hydrated too!

"Every wall is a door"

—Ralph Waldo Emerson

Keep an Eye Out for Opening Doors

A wise person once said when one door closes, another opens. It's true. Even though, when a relationship ends or your career evaporates, it may *feel* like all doors are closed to you, they're not. As painful as it might be, you have just been given the keys to the crossroads. The direction you choose to head is up to you. Why not follow in the words of the late mythologist Joseph Campbell and "follow your bliss"?

If you're having trouble getting on a positive track, take out a piece of paper or open to a page in your journal and write what door closed on the top of the page. Then, start making a list of what opportunities you have now that you didn't have before or, at least, that you were not taking advantage of. Consider going back to school. Starting your own business. Pursuing a hobby or interest in greater depth. Finding a partner who is a better match. Rediscovering who you are at your core. Traveling or moving to another country.

Like the death card in the tarot deck, closed doors bring change. And sometimes change is exactly what you need.

"If you want to get a sensual thunderbolt, then you have to be cocked, locked, and ready to rock, doc. I find that whole milk and lots of vitamin D help."

—Ted Nugent

Take an Extra Dose of Vitamin D

Vitamin D works hard to make you look and feel younger. This water-soluble powerhouse helps build stronger bones and teeth, which enables you to be more active and to have a confident smile. Vitamin D can also have an impact on your weight. When taken in conjunction with calcium, it works to prevent you from gaining weight and can possibly even help you lose a quarter of a pound. It's not much, but when you're trying to get thinner, every little bit counts.

As you age, a supplement of vitamin D can help protect your brain's cognitive abilities and it can reduce the chance you'll be diagnosed with heart disease and colon cancer. Then there's the impressive study conducted by scientists at King's College in London, who found that higher levels of vitamin D can make your cells age more slowly. To enjoy vitamin D in your diet, healthy sources include milk, fortified cereal, eggs, salmon, and mackerel.

"Yield to temptation. It may not pass your way again."

—Robert Heinlein

Seek Out New Sensations

Never stop exploring. Whether you try new positions, new techniques, new places to have sex, or new partners to have sex with, it's important that you (and, if applicable, your significant other) keep the sexual fires burning throughout your relationship. Sex helps keep you happy, helps you reduce and manage stress, and helps you stay connected with the person you love, so keep it up.

If you're ever feeling in a rut and you've exhausted these ideas, look for more. There are many resources on the Internet— sites such as *www.Nerve.com* and others—that are jammed with ideas on how to make your sex life a positive, fulfilling one. In the meantime, here are a few more fun ideas:

- Learn how to have a multiple orgasm.
- Try cybersex.
- Write your lover an erotic letter.
- Shave your partner's pubic hair.
- Discretely send lingerie to your partner's office.
- Use a French tickler.
- Get a genital piercing.
- Do couples yoga.

"Part of being a winner is knowing when enough is enough. Sometimes you have to give up the fight and move on to something that's more productive."

—Donald Trump

Move On

You've learned a lot during the last year. You've learned about changes you can make in your life to lead a happier, healthier, and perhaps even longer life. You've worked on integrating some of these ideas into your own life. One of the most important lessons I hope you've learned is to accept yourself. Accept what you're willing to change, what you're not willing to change, and what you can and cannot change within your world.

Allow yourself to build strong social connections and to give yourself and others the benefit of the doubt. You'll find that this will help alleviate the stress in your life and will help you to see the positive events that you experience each day. Find ways to center yourself when troubling events happen, and focus on the present to stop time and soak in a blissful moment. When life does throw you a curveball, meditate on what you can learn from that experience and how it can help you in the future. All moments pass, even the bad ones. Remember: this too will pass.

Now, look up and gaze into your future and imagine all of the gifts it will bring.

INDEX

ABOUT THE AUTHORS

Rebecca Swanner (Los Angeles, CA) is a freelance writer. She has served as an editor for numerous publications—including *Penthouse*. Her work has appeared in *Men's Journal*, *Inked*, *Alternative Press*, *US Weekly*, *Stuff*, *Blender*, *Geek Monthly*, and *Metromix*.

Eve Adamson (Iowa City, IA) is a stress management consultant and freelance writer. She is the author of *365 Ways to Reduce Stress*.

Carolyn Dean, MD (City Island, NY) is a medical and naturopathic doctor and herbalist with expertise in acupuncture and homeopathy. She is a coauthor of *365 Ways to Boost Your Brain Power and 365 Ways to Look—and Feel—Younger*.

Rachel Laferriere, MS, RD (Providence, RI) is a Licensed Dietitian/Nutritionist and Certified Nutrition Support Clinician. She is the author of *365 Ways to Boost Your Metabolism*.

Meera Lester (San Jose, CA) is an internationally published author who has written more than two dozen books including *365 Ways to Be Happy and 365 Ways to Live the Law of Attraction*. She is also the coauthor of *365 Ways to Look—and Feel—Younger*.

Getting Where Women Really Belong

- Trying to lose the losers you've been dating?
- Striving to find the time to be a doting mother, dedicated employee, and still be a hot piece of you-know-what in the bedroom?
- Been in a comfortable relationship that's becoming, well, too comfortable?

Don't despair! Visit the Jane on Top blog—your new source for information (and commiseration) on all things relationships, sex, and the juggling act that is being a modern gal.

Sign up for our newsletter at
www.adamsmedia.com/blog/relationships
and download a **Month-ful of Happiness!**
That's 30 days of free tips guaranteed to lift your mood!